£27.50

WITHDRAWN FROM
THE LIBRARY
UNIVERSITY OF
WINCHESTER

Tractarian Semantics

PHILOSOPHICAL THEORY

SERIES EDITORS
John McDowell, Philip Pettit and Crispin Wright

For Truth in Semantics
Anthony Appiah

Tractarian Semantics
Finding Sense in Wittgenstein's Tractatus
Peter Carruthers

The Dynamics of Belief: A Normative Logic
Peter Forrest

Abstract Objects
Bob Hale

Fact and Meaning
Jane Heal

Conditionals
Frank Jackson

Sense and Certainty
The Dissolution of Scepticism
Marie McGinn

Reality and Representation
David Papineau

Facts and the Function of Truth
Huw Price

Moral Dilemmas
Walter Sinnott-Armstrong

TRACTARIAN SEMANTICS

Finding Sense in Wittgenstein's Tractatus

Peter Carruthers

Basil Blackwell

© Peter Carruthers 1989

First published 1989

Basil Blackwell Ltd
108 Cowley Road, Oxford, OX4 1JF, UK

Basil Blackwell Inc.
3 Cambridge Center
Cambridge, MA 02142, USA

All rights reserved. Except for the quotation of short passages for the purposes of criticism and review, no part of this publication may be reproduced, stored in a retrieval system, or transmitted, in any form or by any means, electronic, mechanical, photocopying, recording or otherwise, without the prior permission of the publisher.

Except in the United States of America, this book is sold subject to the condition that it shall not, by way of trade or otherwise, be lent, re-sold, hired out, or otherwise circulated without the publisher's prior consent in any form of binding or cover other than that in which it is published and without a similar condition including this condition being imposed on the subsequent purchaser.

British Library Cataloguing in Publication Data

Carruthers, Peter
Tractarian semantics: finding sense in Wittgenstein's
Tractatus. – (Philosophical theory).
1. Philosophical logic. Wittgenstein, Ludwig, 1899–
1951. Tractatus logico-philosophicus
I. Title II. Series
160

ISBN 0–631–16956–3

Library of Congress Cataloging in Publication Data

Carruthers, Peter. 1952–
Tractarian semantics: finding sense in Wittgenstein's Tractatus/
Peter Carruthers.
p. cm. — (Philosophical theory)
Bibliography: p.
Includes indexes.
ISBN 0–631–16956–3
1. Wittgenstein, Ludwig, 1889–1951. Tractatus logico
–philosophicus. 2. Logic, Symbolic and mathematical. 3. Languages–
–Philosophy. I. Title. II. Series.
B3376.W563T73226 1989
192—dc 19

88–35711
CIP

Typeset in 11 on 13pt Baskerville by Vera-Reyes Inc.
Printed in Great Britain by The Camelot Press Ltd., Southampton

Contents

Abbreviations

MT	Carruthers *The Metaphysics of the Tractatus* (forthcoming). References by chapter number.
FA	Frege *The Foundations of Arithmetic* (1968). References by section number.
BLA	Frege *The Basic Laws of Arithmetic* (1952) and (1964). References by section number.
NB	Wittgenstein *Notebooks 1914–16* (1961b). References by page number.
PTLP	Wittgenstein *Prototractatus* (1971). References by section number.
TLP	Wittgenstein *Tractatus Logico-Philosophicus* (1922) and (1961a). References by section number.
PR	Wittgenstein *Philosophical Remarks* (1975). References by section number.
PI	Wittgenstein *Philosophical Investigations* (1953). References by section number.

KING ALFRED'S COLLEGE
WINCHESTER
149.94
CAR
00051588

for Susan

— sense and sensibility —

Preface

This is the first of two books to be devoted to *Tractatus Logico-Philosophicus (TLP)*. It deals with the principal semantic doctrines of the early Wittgenstein, whereas the sequel will consider his treatment of metaphysics and its relation to his views on logic. I begin with some remarks about the motivation of the project.

WHY BE AN INTERPRETER?

Why ought we to be interested in the classical texts of our subject? Why should we, as philosophers, give up our time to the pursuit of accurate interpretations of our predecessors? To these questions some would answer that their role is that of an historian, charting a moment in the history of ideas; or that they take an interest in interpretation for its own sake, showing the respect due to past philosophers by understanding them in their own terms. Others would reply that they use classic texts purely for inspiration, taking little interest in issues of interpretation as such, so long as they can get ideas from the text which they find useful for their own purposes. My own motivation is different. I believe that close textual study can subserve our search for truth.

What I want as a philosopher is to know the truth (or at least to achieve reasonable beliefs) on a wide range of subjects. Engagement with the thoughts of other philosophers is one way of pursuing this aim. Perhaps in many cases it is the best way. This is especially likely to be so in connection with those writers, such as Wittgenstein, the interest of whose work has survived the test of scrutiny and debate by successive generations of thinkers. For this gives us reason to believe that their problems will be deep ones, and their arguments powerful. So if our concern is to know the truth on some matter which has been addressed by one of the great philosophers of the past, we can often do no better than begin by trying to understand and assess their treatment of the issue.[1]

Looked at in this way, interpretation becomes a self-directed rather than an other-directed activity. For the interest in the thoughts and arguments of the other is instrumental rather than intrinsic, subservient to the desire to discover the truth for oneself. But this does not mean that we may simply plunder the text for our own purposes: abstracting from it doctrines and arguments which we find congenial, and allowing thoughts to be sparked off in us by our reading without concern for whether or not those thoughts are genuinely the author's. For if the tradition is reliable, giving us reason to believe in the greatness of the text, then the author's own position will be more interesting than anything we are likely to glean from it on a cursory reading. In my view this is the main reason why we ought, as philosophers, to concern ourselves with the minutiae of textual interpretation: if the text is rich and many-faceted, as major texts in philosophy so often are, then the author's actual doctrines are likely to differ from, and be more powerful than, any which may be inspired by our initial reading of it.

My idea of philosophical interpretation is thus something of a compromise: positioned midway between those who pursue it as a means to historical or biographical understanding, and those who are unconcerned as to whether or not their reading of the text is actually correct, so long as it is interesting and defensible in its own right. My response to the first group is that my primary concern is to know the truth on the matters dealt with in the classical texts of our subject, not with who said what or when or why. My reply to the second group is that if we have reason to believe in the greatness of some piece of philosophical writing – as plainly we have in the case of *TLP* – then the correct interpretation of it (if it differs from the current one) is likely to prove more interesting and powerful still. But I make no claim to exclusiveness in these remarks. I merely mean to state my own attitude as an interpreter, not to reject the other approaches as illegitimate.

AIMS AND SCOPE

The aims of the present work are two-fold: to argue firstly, that there is a plausible set of semantic doctrines implicit in *TLP* which can be held separate from Wittgenstein's more dubious metaphysical views and associated programme of analysis; and to argue secondly, that these doctrines are actually correct, deserving at the very least to be treated as a semantic paradigm, providing the same sort of focus for contemporary debate as does the Fregean paradigm.

The more I have made use of *TLP* as a foil in my thinking about the nature of language, thought, reality and the relations between them, the more I have come to feel that it contains a defensible set of ideas on these matters which are independent of Wittgenstein's programme for the analysis of ordinary language; and these have not been sufficiently appreciated. Indeed I think it can be said that hardly anyone working in the philosophy of language reads *TLP* at all seriously now. In this respect the contrast with Frege is striking. For there exists a cluster of ideas in contemporary work in semantics which can appropriately be labelled 'Fregean', and both opponents and defenders of these ideas read Frege's writings with great attention. Yet there appear to be no standpoints within the current debate which can bear the title 'Tractarian', and consequently *TLP* is read by hardly anyone except Wittgenstein scholars. I believe that this state of affairs is unjust. When properly interpreted, *TLP* can be seen to contain a set of doctrines which, where they differ from Frege's, are in almost every respect a decisive advance. This is what I shall argue.

Perhaps the best way of summarising how my reading of *TLP* differs from that of most previous commentators, is to say that I regard it as having been much more heavily influenced by Frege than by Russell.[2] In particular, I believe that it employs a distinction which is closely related to the one Frege drew between sense and reference, applying to almost all types of expression including proper names. But there is disagreement, both over the nature and semantic significance of the distinction, as well as with Frege's view that senses have necessary existence. It is in these differences that the Tractarian paradigm has, I shall argue, the decisive advantage. It is also the case that Wittgenstein wholeheartedly accepts Frege's belief in the objectivity of logic, meaning and truth. But he thinks that this belief has consequences for metaphysics which Frege himself never considered; in particular, leading to the demand for a programme of analysis which will terminate in a class of logically independent elementary propositions involving reference to necessarily existing individuals. This latter set of ideas will be explored in the sequel to the present work, *MT*.

The scope of my investigations here, will be confined to Wittgenstein's views on the nature and content of propositions, the nature of private thinking, and the semantics of proper names and predicative expressions. I shall have little to say about his views on logic. For while some of these are surely semantic in nature, they are in fact either truistic (as is his proposed non-referential semantics for the logical connectives[3]), demonstrably inadequate (as is his treatment of the predicate calculus[4]) or of merely historical interest (as are his reasons for wanting to employ only a single logical connective[5]). And as for what is still controversial in his views on logic – namely the commitment to the objectivity of logical relations and principles – this will be best discussed in the sequel, since it is intimately connected with his views on metaphysics, and since it is in fact independent of the set of doctrines which I propose to defend here as a semantic paradigm.

STYLISTIC NOTES

Since the present work is concerned not only with interpretation but also truth, both textual discussion and substantive philosophical argument will be found in the chapters which follow. Some chapters are primarily interpretative (this is particularly true of the early ones, which lay the foundation for what follows), whereas some just argue for the correctness of some aspect of the Tractarian paradigm. But the majority contain a mixture of interpretation and independent argument. This is partly because questions of interpretation and assessment cannot in fact be held apart from one another, as I argue in chapter 1.

There are two sorts of understanding available to an interpreter in philosophy: that which arises from seeing the reasons the author has for their views, and that which derives from noticing connections between those views and antecedently understood philosophical standpoints. The former is clearly the more fundamental of the two. It is thus accorded pride of place in the main body of my text, philosophical comparisons being confined to notes. Also confined to notes are my points of agreement and disagreement with other commentators, in order to leave the main text as uncluttered as possible. References to Wittgenstein's own writings, however, are included in brackets, so as to prevent the numbers of notes from spiralling out of all control.

No one can read *TLP* without being struck by its extraordinary resonance and beauty. But my own view is that art and philosophy ought not to be mixed. This is the one respect in which I am profoundly out of sympathy with my subject. Since my concern is with 'the truth and nothing but the truth' I try to write as clearly and plainly as I can, making explicit the reasoning behind my views. Fine language can serve only as a distraction, and oracular statement as a shield behind which confusion can shelter.

Throughout this work I opt to use the colloquial plural pronouns 'they' and 'their' in impersonal contexts, in place of the pernicious masculine singular required by strict grammar.

ACKNOWLEDGEMENTS

My greatest debts are to Michael Dummett, without whose pioneering work on Frege this book would not have been possible, and to Roger White, who first initiated me into the mysteries of *TLP*. I also owe a great deal to Crispin Wright for his advice and encouragement over many years.

I am grateful to the following for their helpful comments on earlier drafts: David Bell, Gregory Currie, Laurence Goldstein, Jane Heal, Hide Ishiguro, Susan Levi, Christopher McKnight, Howard Mounce and Tim Williamson. Thanks also go to the following for their comments on specific chapters or groups of chapters: Anthony Grayling, A. D. Smith and Rachel Vaughan.

Some of the ideas published here are based upon previous papers of mine, in particular my (1983a), (1983b), (1984b) and (1984c). Although this material has been substantially revised and corrected, I am grateful to the Editors of the *Philosophical Quarterly*, *Theoria* and *Mind* for permission to make use of it.

I am grateful to Wittgenstein's trustees for permission to quote from posthumously published sources, and to Routledge for permission to quote from *TLP* and *PTLP*.

Peter Carruthers

1

Principles of Interpretation

Although this work is generally truth-oriented, the foundations of the enterprise are interpretative. The task of this chapter is to discuss the main principles to be employed, both in this book and in its sequel *MT*.

1.1 FIDELITY TO THE TEXT

The most obvious and important principle to be used in seeking an accurate interpretation of *TLP*, or indeed of any piece of philosophical writing, is that of fidelity to the text itself. In general we should refuse to accept an interpretation which conflicts with a claim made in, or with some clear implication of, the text under study. (However this rule is not absolute, as we shall see in the next section.) Here our task is one of careful reading and weighing of words; and, in the case of *TLP*, of choosing between alternative translations. It also means, especially in the case of *TLP*, paying close attention to the textual context of the passage being considered, since this can often throw valuable light upon its significance.

It might be suggested that an additional way of remaining faithful to the text of *TLP* is to respect its numbering system. For Wittgenstein himself tells us, in a footnote to the very first remark of the book, that the decimal expansions of a given number should be regarded as comments upon the remark which bears that number. If taken at face value, this may place fairly severe constraints upon an interpreter. But in fact Wittgenstein's explanation is only partially accurate. Often, it is true, 'long-numbered' remarks share their subject matter with the 'short-numbered' remarks which precede them – but not always. For sometimes they have to be seen as building up to, and sharing their subject matter with, the 'short-numbered' remarks which come *after* them. The numbering system is much more intuitive – and the structure of *TLP* much closer to that of a piece of music, with its crescendos and diminuendos and themes and variations – than Wittgenstein's official explanation would allow.[1] Nevertheless it remains true that the relationships between the numbers of different remarks can be an important ingredient in their interpretation, even if this constraint is a great deal weaker than we might have been led to expect.

Of course the role of an interpreter in philosophy cannot be confined merely to establishing what it is that the author does and does not claim to be the case. For the goal of interpretation, no matter how narrowly conceived of, must be to achieve an *understanding* of the author's thoughts. And understanding, in philosophy, means knowing what reasons the writer has for making their claims. So at the very least, interpretation must involve stringing together claims made in the text (perhaps in quite disparate parts of it) into plausible arguments, and also inserting premises which have obviously been suppressed. This is the main reason why *TLP* is so difficult to understand, since it contains little that gives even the appearance of explicit argumentation, and since it would seem that the vast majority of its premises – if premises there are – are suppressed. The would-be interpreter of *TLP* is thus constantly thrown back on invention in attempting to make sense of its various explicit doctrines. We are left with no alternative but to construct arguments on Wittgenstein's behalf, if we are to stand any chance of understanding him. But note that many would wish to draw a sharp distinction here between actual interpretation on the one hand, and understanding on the other; allowing perhaps that invention may have a role to play in connection with the latter, but insisting on strict fidelity to the text in connection with the former. I disagree, for reasons which will become apparent shortly.

What has now emerged is that there are at least two distinct reasons why this book (and its sequel) will be filled with arguments. Firstly because, as was explained in the preface, my overall goal is truth. The doctrines of *TLP* must therefore be assessed, which means arguing for and against them. And now secondly, because my subsidiary goal is to achieve an understanding of *TLP*; which means seeing what arguments Wittgenstein had (or might have had) for his views. But as we shall see in the next section, there is yet a third role for argument to play, this time an interpretative one.

1.2 THE PRINCIPLE OF CHARITY

Suppose that we have reason to believe in the greatness of a particular text, for which we can provide two competing interpretations. One appears to be consistent with most, but not all, of the author's claims, yet involves attributing to the author a set of doctrines which are both powerful and interesting. The other is consistent with all of the author's claims, but ascribes a set of doctrines which are weak and anodyne by comparison. We may then reasonably prefer the former interpretation, either writing off the conflicting statements as some sort of slip or aberration, or perhaps rendering those statements consistent with it by interpreting some of the terms involved in a non-standard manner. This will be especially plausible if we can provide some independent explanation of how the author could have come to have made such an error, or to have selected those terms in order to express what they wish to say.

This is an instance of what I call 'The Principle of Charity of Interpretation', which enjoins us to maximize the *interest* of the text under study.[2] Its application will often pull against the principle of Textual Fidelity, which tells us to select the interpretation which most naturally fits the details of the text. When they do conflict, some sort of balance must be struck. It will be a matter of weighing up our respect for the intelligence of the author and our reasons for supposing the text to contain a powerful set of doctrines on the one hand, against the plausibility of supposing such a writer to have expressed their views so unfelicitously on the other. Indeed the task of interpretation is best seen as a search for a kind of reflective equilibrium, moving backwards and forwards between detailed study of the text and independent assessment of the power and plausibility of the doctrines which can – again with more or less plausibility – be read into it.

In connection with many texts, where the author is explicit in stating their position, and is careful to detail their arguments, the principles of Charity and of Fidelity may rarely come into disagreement. But with a text such as *TLP*, on the other hand, the role of

Charity becomes maximal. For *TLP* is extremely sparing in explanations of its own doctrines, and rarely takes the trouble to spell out supporting arguments. This leaves room for many alternative readings. We therefore have no option but actively to seek, and attribute to Wittgenstein, those views which have the greatest philosophical interest, and in support of which the strongest arguments can be given.

This is not to say that in interpreting *TLP* there is no place for close study of the details of the text. On the contrary, this is a necessary prerequisite to thinking up interpretations, and can sometimes be used decisively to refute a suggested reading. But the value of such textual study is strictly limited, since there are just too many variables to control. For example, one critical factor will be the extent to which we take Wittgenstein's use of his terminology to be consistent. In some instances it is clearly not (on pain of attributing to him inconsistency in his beliefs[3]), and the possibility of further divergences leaves open an indefinite range of possible interpretations. So the ultimate proof of an interpretation, of any text of *TLP*'s obscurity and manifest genius, must lie in its explanatory power: both in throwing light on some of the darker sayings, and more importantly in providing arguments which enable us to make sense of – to see the point and power of – some of the doctrines. Though given the open-ended nature of philosophy and philosophical argument, it is no doubt inappropriate to speak of 'proof' here. In so far as an interpretation is governed by the principle of Charity, it will be subject to the same constant revisability as any other piece of philosophy.

It is an interesting question – and one not entirely without philosophical significance – why Wittgenstein should have come to express his thoughts in the form which he did. No doubt his reasons were partly aesthetic.[4] (He is said to have responded to Russell's admonition to provide more arguments, by remarking that they spoiled the beauty of his conclusions, like dirtying a flower with muddy hands.[5]) And there is no question but that the result was a piece of writing of extraordinary resonance and elegance. I am also sure that he had great difficulty in organizing and expressing his thoughts at all. For when we read his own early notebooks we do not find a man articulating clear positions and presenting very explicit arguments, which are later to be honed down for purely aesthetic effect. On the contrary, we find obscurity and confusion and constant struggle. But perhaps the most interesting reason behind the form of *TLP* may be found in the remark in its preface, that the book would only be understood by someone who had had similar thoughts (a remark echoed in the preface to *PI*, where Wittgenstein says that he should not want his writing to save anyone the trouble of thinking). I suspect that it was always Wittgenstein's aim in writing to produce a book to think with, which would stimulate readers to thoughts of their own. His idea was to force readers, through the application of the principle of Charity, to struggle towards a correct perception of the issues for themselves.

1.3 PRE-TRACTARIAN WRITINGS

Besides the principles of Textual Fidelity and of Charity, are we also constrained to be faithful to the pre-*TLP* writings, namely *NB* and *PTLP*? In the case of the former, clearly not; though it can be an extremely valuable source. For its contents were written between two and six years earlier, during which time Wittgenstein may have changed his mind. So we cannot simply assume that any doctrine or argument enunciated in *NB* will (in the absence of textual evidence to the contrary) survive into *TLP*. And even where a remark from the early writings is reproduced verbatim in *TLP*, we cannot always take for granted that it will have retained its earlier significance. It may have been employed because of its phrasing or the image used, but turned to quite another purpose. For a self-conscious stylist like Wittgenstein, the process of compiling a text from remarks in earlier notebooks would almost certainly not have been simply a matter of selecting those with which (as originally intended) he still agreed.

Having sounded this cautionary note, however, I believe the writings in *NB* can be useful aids to the interpretation of *TLP*. At the very least they can give an indication of the issues with which Wittgenstein was wrestling in the years leading up to the composition of the latter work. We should expect that, even if these issues do not survive into *TLP* in quite their original form, they would at least have descendants which do. Moreover they can often suggest ways of reading some of the more obscure remarks in *TLP*, and can provide arguments which might explain why the latter contains some of the theses which it does. But note that I only say 'suggest'. The main burden of proof still falls on fidelity to the text of *TLP*, together with the principle of Charity.

The case of *PTLP* is rather different, in that it may have been composed immediately prior to *TLP* itself, during the same two month leave from the army in the summer of 1918.[6] However the evidence which it provides is by no means unambiguous. For there may be any number of possible explanations of the differences which exist between the two texts, ranging from the entirely trivial, through the stylistic, to substantial changes of mind. Nevertheless, if handled carefully, *PTLP* can be a valuable aid to the interpreter.

1.4 POST-TRACTARIAN SOURCES

There are four different types of post-*TLP* source which might be thought to bear on the interpretation of that text. These are: (a) Wittgenstein's remarks in letters to Russell and others in the years immediately following the completion of TLP; (b) Wittgenstein's reported comments on *TLP*, amongst those recorded by Waismann between 1929 and 1932 and in published lecture-notes;[7] (c) written references to *TLP* in *PR*, *PI* and elsewhere; and (d) comments on doctrines which at least bear a family resemblance to those of *TLP*, but where the latter work is not explicitly mentioned. (Many of the remarks in the early part of *PI* – on names, simples and analysis – fall into this last category.)

Material falling under (a) should obviously be given very considerable weight, since it is so close in time to the composition of the text itself. However we must remember that these letters did not purport to give a polished exposition of Wittgenstein's ideas, and were apparently written with much impatience. Material under (d), on the other hand, should be given no independent weight by the would-be interpreter of *TLP*, for there is nothing to indicate that their target is (the later Wittgenstein's view of) *TLP* itself, rather than Russell, or Frege, or just a general tendency of thought which he felt to be widespread.[8]

But what of material under (b) and (c)? How much weight should be given to the later Wittgenstein's explicit pronouncements on the doctrines of *TLP*? In my view, very little; but this will require some defence. Notice to begin with that there is a gap of eleven years between the completion of *TLP* in 1918, and the first of the conversations recorded by Waismann, and the first of the later writings, in 1929. During this time he did virtually no philosophy, and by all accounts found thinking about his own work extremely slow and painful.[9] Note also that, so far as we can gather, *TLP* was written with extraordinary compression and intensity during a two month period of leave in the summer of 1918.[10] He had been at the Italian front, and was due to return there, so he must have felt that he had to work with desperate urgency.[11] This was not a frame of mind in which to distinguish carefully between ideas, and in which to set out and assess the strengths of competing arguments – even had he normally been disposed to such modes of working. Small wonder, then, if after a gap of eleven years he were to find it impossible to think himself back into the full richness and complexity of his finished text.

Moreover, Wittgenstein's return to philosophy in 1929 was apparently occasioned by contacts with philosophers working in areas which were new for him – Brouwer on Intuitionism, and the Vienna Circle on Phenomenalism – and he immediately began to turn his thinking in new directions.[12] This, coupled with the restless and forward-looking nature of his intellect,[13] suggests that he would have viewed his earlier writing very much through the medium of his new interests, rather than from the standpoint of dispassionate memory and self-interpretation.

Consider also the style in which *TLP* itself is written. It is impossible to believe that it represents the obscure, if highly polished, tip of an iceberg of clearly articulated ideas and arguments, which Wittgenstein chose to present in that form for purely aesthetic or pedagogical reasons (especially when we consider the almost equally opaque writing in *NB*, which was intended purely for his own use). *TLP* is undoubtedly a work of genius. But like so many works of genius, it gives every appearance of having been produced intuitively, with the author himself perhaps having only a tenuous grasp on the nature of his own product, even at the time of writing. It is sometimes said of works of literature that their authors are the last people to understand them, or to be trusted to interpret them. I suspect that this may be more true of *TLP* than of any other work in philosophy.

Putting these points together suggests that would-be interpreters of *TLP* should approach comments made by the later Wittgenstein with extreme caution. A similar conclusion can also be reached from a different direction. For on general methodological grounds, if we wish to understand and assess the contrasts between Wittgenstein's early and late philosophies, then we certainly ought not to assume at the outset that he later both understood and had the measure of all aspects of his earlier way of thinking. On the contrary, we ought at least to hold open the possibility that the later philosophy might have passed the earlier uncomprehendingly by, and perhaps also that the quality of Wittgenstein's thought might have gone steadily downhill (as Russell believed). Our preferred interpretation of the early writings should therefore be established before we begin to consider the later work.

1.5 FREGE AND RUSSELL

The last – but not the least – of aids to the interpreter is Wittgenstein's acknowledgement of the influence of 'the great works of Frege' and 'the writings of my friend Mr Bertrand Russell' in the preface to *TLP*. We may presume that he took many of his problems and ideas from them. It is also reasonable to assume, at least as a working hypothesis, that the different tones in which the acknowledgements were expressed reflect the degree of significance of their influence.[14] We may therefore take the work of Frege, and to a lesser extent that of Russell, as providing the background against which the doctrines of *TLP* can be set. But obviously we need to be cautious. Ideas taken over from them may have been put to quite a new use, his readings of other philosophers having been more inspirational than interpretative. And he may, for the same reason, have badly misunderstood their views.

SUMMARY

Our interpretation of *TLP* will be founded on a balanced application of the twin principles of Textual Fidelity and Charity. We shall also make considerable, if cautious, use of *NB*, *PTLP* and letters written soon after 1918, as well as the known views of Frege and Russell. But we shall ignore almost wholly the evidence of Wittgenstein's later writings and reported remarks.

2

Background: Frege and Russell

My task in this chapter is to explain the main outlines of the semantic theories of Frege and Russell, in so far as they may be presumed to constitute the background for Wittgenstein's own investigations.

2.1 PRELIMINARIES

Frege and Russell are the only known influences on the philosophy of *TLP*. Each is acknowledged in the preface, and is mentioned many times in the body of the text. The only other philosophers mentioned in *TLP* are Moore (once), Whitehead (twice) – each in conjunction with Russell – Kant (once) and Hertz (twice).[1] Indeed, Frege and Russell are the only significant philosophers whose writings we know Wittgenstein to have studied with any seriousness. (There is evidence that he once read – and hated – Moore's (1903).[2] There is anecdotal evidence that he had read Schopenhauer as a boy.[3] And there is some reason to think that he may have been influenced by the form, if not the detailed content, of Hertz's (1899).[4])

As for what exactly of Frege and Russell Wittgenstein would have read, I think it is reasonable to assume an acquaintance with all their major publications prior to the outbreak of the war in 1914.[5] We also know that he saw at least a part of Russell's manuscript 'Theory of Knowledge' (now published in Russell, (1984)[6]), and that he wrote to Keynes in 1915 asking to be sent a copy of Russell's (1914), though we do not know whether or not Keynes ever complied .[7] Clearly, however, our account of Frege's and Russell's views should not commit the anachronism of relying upon their later writings, particularly Russell's 1918 'Lectures on Logical Atomism' and Frege's 1918 papers 'Thoughts' and 'Negation'.

Since it will be one of the main themes of this book that the semantic doctrines of *TLP* are much more influenced by Frege than by Russell, I shall begin by explaining Frege's semantic theories, contrasting them with those Russell where appropriate. It should be said that my reading of Frege is substantially the same as – indeed derived from – that of Michael Dummett, though it differs slightly in emphasis.[8] I regard Dummett's interpretation of Frege as controversial only in the sense that it has been controverted.[9]

2.2 SENSE AND REFERENCE

A central idea of Frege's middle-period writings is the distinction he draws between sense (Sinn) and reference (Bedeutung), which is applied to almost all expressions of natural language including sentences. The sense of a sign is that which competent speakers will grasp in virtue of their understanding of it (and the sense of a complete sentence is the content of the thought which it expresses for those who understand it); whereas the reference of a sign is that item in the world (in the case of a sentence, a truth-value) which we speak about when we use it. Reference is the object of, sense the content of, our thought and speech.

The relations between sense and reference are as follows: the truth-value of a sentence is held to depend upon the reference of the component expressions of that sentence, and the reference of those expressions, in turn, to depend upon their sense. There is thus a non-symmetric dependence of truth-value upon reference, and of reference upon sense, which can be expressed (with slightly misleading temporal and causal connotations) by saying that sense determines reference and reference determines truth-value. The idea is that it is in virtue of the fact that an expression has the sense which it does that it refers to the item in the world which it does; and that it is in virtue of having the reference which it does that sentences containing it have the truth-values which they do.

In drawing this distinction, Frege should be seen as arguing that there can be no such thing as bare knowledge of reference. His idea is that we cannot simply devise a theory which assigns referents to the various component expressions of the language, and hence which assigns truth-conditions to the completed sentences of the language, and leave it at that. For this is not something that any speaker could be said to know, or at least not directly. Yet precisely what we want from a theory of meaning is an account of what it is for a speaker to understand their language, and understanding is surely a cognitive state of some sort. So with each expression there must be associated an immediate object of knowledge, which will constitute the speaker's mode of thinking about the referent. This will be the sense of that expression.

Note also that a purely referential theory would leave us puzzling over the question how it is possible for a sentence – most obviously a statement of identity – to convey information. Indeed this is Frege's most explicit argument for introducing the notion of sense, his claim being that it is needed to account for the cognitive significance of the different expressions of a language – for example, how a statement of identity can be informative, or how we can believe one of two logically equivalent sentences without believing the other.[10] Thus not only should a speaker be credited with the knowledge that a particular individual is the referent (the bearer) of a proper name, but they should also be credited with some means of identifying, or 'picking out', that individual.[11] And not only should they be credited with a knowledge of the extension, say, of a predicate, but must also be credited with a grasp of some rule for determining that extension.[12] The mode of determining the reference of an expression which a speaker employs, in Frege's terminology, is the sense which that speaker attaches to it.

These reasons for the introduction of a notion of sense impose upon it very tight identity-conditions. If knowledge of sense is to constitute each speaker's mode of thinking about the referents of the expressions of their language, and if we are to use the notion of sense in explaining cognitive significance, then we shall have to equate sameness of sense with sameness of information-content. We must say that two sentences will possess the very same sense for a given speaker if, and only if, were they to believe the one to be true, they could not learn anything new on being told of the truth of the other. (Note the modality of this criterion. The idea is that sentences are identical in sense for a given speaker just in case that person *cannot* take differing cognitive attitudes towards them, no matter what else they happen to believe. For example, they cannot believe the one while doubting the truth of the other.) And two sub-sentential expressions will possess the same sense for a speaker if, and only if, all sentences which differ only in that the one expression has been substituted for the other will possess the same information-content. Frege explicitly commits himself to such criteria of identity of sense at a number of points in his writings.[13]

The idea of sense thus far introduced is not especially social, or intersubjective, in character. (However, Frege would want to insist, at a minimum, that senses are at least possibly intersubjective – that they are, as it were, within the public domain. For as we shall see, he maintains that senses are objective in their existence.) Rather, it provides us with a theory of speakers' understanding, of the knowledge which individual speakers have of their own idiolects. Nothing has as yet been said about what is required for there to be communication through the use of language, beyond the claim that speakers must at least be in possession of some means – not necessarily the same for each speaker – of determining the referents of all the component expressions involved. But in fact Frege supposes that we may speak simply of *the* sense of such-and-such an expression. He supposes, that is, that the idiolects of particular speakers will generally coincide, and that such speakers will only understand one another, in general, in virtue of knowing the senses of the expressions of their common language.[14]

This is the second major role for the notion of sense: to underpin a theory of communication. Frege's view is that understanding the statements of another requires you to grasp the thoughts expressed. You yourself must (at least on this occasion – you may know the speaker's idiolect to be non-standard) associate with the sentences which you hear the very same modes of determination of reference as the speaker does. Your way of taking each sentence must thus be such that, were the speaker to employ another sentence, to be understood in the way in which you understand their spoken sentence, then those two sentences would have the same information-content for the speaker (e.g. it would be impossible for them to believe the one while doubting the other). Let us coin the phrase 'cognitive content' to refer to the mode of thinking associated with an expression in the idiolect of a particular speaker. And let us employ the phrase 'semantic content' to refer to that of which mutual knowledge is required for linguistic communication (or what comes to the same thing: to refer to that which an expression contributes to what is communicated by the literal assertion of sentences containing it).[15] Then Frege's thesis is that cognitive content and semantic content are one and the same. On the other hand the *TLP* view (to anticipate) is that cognitive content (what may be informative to the individual) and semantic content (what is literally communicated) are distinct from one another.

In Russell's writings from this period no trace of a sense/reference distinction appears. In its place we have a doctrine of direct acquaintance: that any proposition which I understand must be wholly made up of constituents with which I am acquainted.[16] In understanding a sentence, my cognitive relation to what that sentence is about is to be direct, and unmediated by any mode of presentation or mode of thinking. There are said to be two sorts of thing with which we are acquainted: individual sense-data (and perhaps myself) on the one hand, and simple universals on the other.[17] This then commits Russell to an ambitious programme of analysis of the sentences of ordinary language, in that all meaningful sentences must be shown to concern, ultimately, only sense-data and simple universals. We shall return to this idea in a later section.

It might be felt that Russell does in fact employ an analogue of the sense/reference distinction, in the contrast he draws between meaning and denotation with respect to certain sorts of complex expression, particularly definite descriptions.[18] But this contrast is really quite different, since it does not satisfy the principle of semantic ordering essential to the sense/reference distinction. As we saw above, the role of an expression's sense is to determine its reference, which in turn contributes to determining the truth-values of sentences containing it. Russell's meaning, on the other hand, does not determine a truth-value via determining a denotation. On the contrary, as we shall see in more detail later, the meaning of a description only fixes a denotation via the determination of a truth-value. (This is part of what Russell has in mind in insisting that definite descriptions are not logical units.)

2.3 THOUGHTS AND THINKING

Frege calls the sense of a complete sentence 'a thought' (Gedanke). In thinking, he says, a subject comes to grasp a thought. And a case of successful communication consists in two subjects coming to grasp (and knowing that they come to grasp) the very same thought. So far, perhaps, this is anodyne. But Frege also claims that thoughts are objective. He says they have an existence which is independent of the human mind and of the psychological processes which take place in acts of thinking. Indeed they have an existence which is at least omnitemporal, and perhaps necessary: they exist at all times in the actual world, and perhaps at all times in all possible worlds.[19] His theory therefore is that in thinking one comes to stand in a cognitive relation ('grasping') to an objective, mind-independent, entity: a thought. He never says what the grasping-relation is supposed to consist in, though there is more than a suggestion in his writing that it is somehow linguistically mediated.[20] But it is at least clear that it must be a real, as opposed to an intentional, relation. (That is, that one does not grasp a thought by virtue of mentally representing it.) For as we in effect saw in the previous section, it is the notion of sense itself which is to explain intentionality: it is by virtue of expressing different senses that different terms can be about the very same thing, and yet figure in different beliefs and different statements.

Such a theory of thinking faces very severe difficulties, as we shall have occasion to see in later chapters. But as we shall also see, Frege believed that it was forced upon him by his commitment to the objectivity of logic and of truth. He felt that the only alternative to his doctrine of the mind-independence of thoughts would be some version of psychologism: the doctrine that thinking reduces to private psychological processes, and that the laws of logic are merely the principles governing the (for the most part) actual operation of such processes. This was his lifelong enemy, to be overcome at all costs.

Although Frege certainly did hold the theory of thinking sketched above, it might be doubted whether Wittgenstein would have been aware of the fact. For it is most clearly articulated in the late paper 'Thoughts', whose publication in 1918 was too late to have influenced the author of *TLP*. Now one sort of reply to this would be to point out that most of the ideas presented in 'Thoughts' were by no means new. They had been fully worked out in a draft paper entitled 'Logic', probably composed in 1897, but never published in Frege's life-time.[21] So it is possible that Frege gave Wittgenstein a copy of this paper, or explained his theory of thinking to him in the course of their conversations together. However, this must remain entirely conjectural, since the details of their correspondence have been lost, and since we do not even know what general topics were covered in their discussions.

A better reply is that the doctrine of the omnitemporal existence of thoughts is very close to the surface of the tirade against psychologism which forms the bulk of the introduction to *BLA*, even if it is not explicitly enunciated there. For example he says that what is true or false (i.e. a thought) is something objective and independent of the judging subject. He then goes on to speak of there being a domain of objective entities, which although genuinely existing are not actual, in the sense that they do not affect our sense-organs (nor, presumably, have any other causal impact upon the world). Then a little later he says that the metaphor of 'grasping' is well suited to elucidate judgement, in that what we grasp with the mind in judging or knowing (i.e. a thought) exists independently of the human mind. Moreover, at number of points he employs his doctrine of the omnitemporality of truth in such a way as to suggest that what is true (a thought) must be omnitemporal also. It would have taken no great interpretative skills on the part of the young Wittgenstein to have extracted from *BLA* the theory of thinking sketched above.

Russell's theory is very different (although as we shall see, it does have an element in common with Frege). It is that judgement (as well as other psychological attitudes such as wondering and supposing) is a relation between a thinker and the elements of the world which make up what Russell calls 'a proposition', the relation somehow being mediated by the thinker's acquaintance with those elements. Thus if Mary judges that Jack loves Jill, then there is a direct cognitive relation obtaining between Mary, Jack, Jill and the relation of loving.[22] (Or there would be on the supposition that 'Jack loves Jill' were a simple sentence . In fact Mary's judgement will be analysed in such a way that the objects of the judgement are all either sense-data or simple universals.) The judgement is not mediated by any mode of presentation of, or any mode of thinking about, its objects. Here the differences with Frege are just what one might expect, given the manner in which Russell tries to do without a sense/reference distinction.

The one point of contact is that Russell too holds that thinking must always involve a direct cognitive relation to an abstract, presumably omnitemporal, entity, namely a universal. For all propositions must contain at least one universal, and the thinking of that proposition must then, on Russell's view, presuppose acquaintance with that universal. But here, unlike the case of Frege, the abstract entity is itself the object of the judgement; whereas for Frege it constitutes its content. Russell has little more to say than Frege about what a cognitive relation to an abstract omnitemporal entity might be supposed to consist in. But he does appear to have attempted a marriage of Platonic ontology with empiricist epistemology. For he says that we become acquainted with simple universals by abstraction, when we notice that a number of sensible objects have a feature in common.[23]

2.4 THE IDEA OF ANALYSIS

Both Frege and Russell have a programme of analysis of ordinary language. Indeed both are concerned to construct an ideal, or logically perfect, language, and see this as being the key to progress in philosophy. They are also in considerable agreement as to what the construction of such a language might be expected to achieve. It is to display the structures of propositions in such a way that their consequences can be worked out in a wholly rigorous manner; it is to represent in a syntactically distinct way notations which are semantically very different from one another, emphasizing the gulf, in particular, between concepts of first order (such as those expressed by 'is red' and 'loves') and concepts of second order (such as those expressed by 'all' and 'some'); and most importantly, it is to provide a mode of representing both the contents and proofs of mathematical propositions, so that it can be demonstrated that they reduce ultimately to the truths of logic. (In this last *desideratum* their motives are partly epistemological: to explain how we can have knowledge of the truths of mathematics.)[24]

It is worth noting that Frege has some difficulty in providing space for an adequate account of the role of analysis.[25] For recall that he lays down very tight criteria for identity between thoughts. In order for two sentences to express the same sense, it must be the case that no one could believe the one while doubting the other, for example. It follows from this that the *analysans* and *analysandum* in any proposed analysis of a sentence cannot share the same sense unless the differences between them are entirely trivial and uninformative. So an analysis, if it is enlightening, cannot be regarded as elucidating the content of the analysed sentence. It must rather be thought of as a reconstruction. The role of analysis is then not to throw light upon the contents of our sentences, but rather to replace them with a distinct, but logically equivalent, set of contents. Although different, these are to be preferred to the originals because they are better suited to the pursuit of truth.

Frege also has other reasons for accepting a reconstructive account of analytical activity. In particular, he thinks that natural languages have features which prevent the laws of logic applying to them, thus rendering them unsuitable for use in science. (Here 'science' just means, I think, any systematic enquiry after truth.) The defects in question are that natural languages may contain names which fail to refer to anything, and predicates which are vague.[26] In both cases Frege thinks we need to engage in reconstruction.

One major difference between Frege and Russell is over the idea of what a complete analysis would look like. In Frege's case this just means that a notation has been provided which is logically unexceptionable, and whose syntax perspicuously displays the important semantic distinctions between types of expression. But Russell demands in addition that analysis should break up the contents of our thoughts into what he believes must be their simplest elements. A completely analysed language would contain, as primitives, only names referring to sense-data and predicative expressions which refer to universals abstractable out of acquaintance with those sense-data. Frege, on the other hand, is quite happy to retain without further analysis terms referring to physical objects, as well as concepts which apply to such objects.

Russell's motives in this are epistemological. He thinks that all our knowledge of the physical world must be founded on knowledge of truths which are intuitively certain, which means truths about our own sense-data, or involving simple relations between universals. These basic truths, in turn, can only be certain if they are wholly concerned with things with which we are immediately acquainted. The process of analysing what we know, or at least have reason to believe, must then consist in showing how the content of such knowledge is related to the objects of our acquaintance.

2.5 NAMES AND DESCRIPTIONS

In one respect both Frege and Russell are agreed about the semantics of singular sentences. They both hold that the contribution made by a singular referring expression to the truth-value of sentences in which it occurs (sometimes spoken of nowadays as the 'semantic role' of the expression)[27] is exhausted by the object to which it refers. Singular sentences express truths or falsehoods about the bearer of the referring expression, in such a way that if the expression were to lack a bearer, then the sentence would be neither true nor false. But from this point onwards their views diverge radically.

Frege is extremely liberal over what he will allow to be genuine referring expressions. He counts as belonging to this category not only all ordinary proper names and demonstratives, but also all definite descriptions of the form 'The such-and-such'. (Indeed he even classifies sentences themselves as a species of complex name, which refer either to the True or the False.) And although the contribution made by a referring expression to the truth-value of sentences in which it occurs is exhausted by its referent, its contribution to the thought expressed is not. On the contrary, he holds that each referring expression will have a sense, in virtue of which it has the reference which it does, and which must be known by anyone who is to understand sentences containing it. In the case of expressions which fail to refer, his view is that they will characteristically still have a sense. So he holds that there are sentences in natural language which express a complete thought but lack a truth-value. This is one of the defects of natural language which it is the business of analysis (philosophical reconstruction) to eradicate.

As to what the sense of an ordinary proper name might look like, Frege is often credited with a version of description-theory. On this account, each proper name will be correlated, by convention, with a particular definite description (or perhaps a cluster of such descriptions), in such a way that an understanding of sentences in which the name occurs requires knowledge of the appropriate description. But in fact Frege nowhere commits himself to this theory. True enough, whenever he gives examples of senses of proper names he uses definite descriptions, but this may simply be for ease of exposition. It would certainly be consistent with what he says to suppose that the sense of a name can at least be partly constituted by a recognitional capacity. Since this is so, and since such a reading would make his theory much more plausible, Charity requires that we should interpret him thus.

Russell, on the other hand, is extremely sparing as to what he will allow to be a genuine singular referring expression. In his view this category includes only the demonstratives 'this' and 'that' (when used to refer to sense-data), and perhaps 'I'. (He has doubts as to whether we really have acquaintance with ourselves.)[28] All ordinary proper names and demonstratives are to be analysed as expressing definite descriptions, which are supposedly added in thought by the person using that expression on a particular occasion(not necessarily the same description each time).[29] And definite descriptions themselves are analysed in accordance with his famous Theory of Definite Descriptions. On this view, expressions of the form 'The such-and-such' do not really have any meaning on their own, but only in the context of a sentence which will typically have the form 'The such-and-such is so-and-so'. If we represent this as 'The F is G', then Russell's theory is that such sentences may be analysed as saying: 'There is one and only one F and that thing is G'.

It is an immediate advantage of the theory that sentences containing bearerless proper names or uninstantiated (or multiply instantiated) definite descriptions come out false, rather than neither true nor false. If 'Vulcan is hot' may be analysed as saying something like 'The planet closer to the sun than Mercury is hot', and this in turn is analysed in accordance with Russell's Theory of Definite Descriptions, then naturally it may be accorded the truth-value False when it is discovered that there is no such planet. For it is then false that there is one and only one planet closer to the sun than Mercury. This saves natural language from conflict with the principles of logic (particularly Excluded Third), and means that no reconstruction is necessary.

Russell does allow that definite descriptions may be said to 'denote' the unique thing which instantiates them (if there is such a thing). But it is now easy to see why this is quite unlike according them reference. For it is not facts about the denotation, in the first instance, which render sentences containing the description true or false. Rather what makes them so is whether or not there exists a unique object satisfying a certain description, which also satisfies a certain other description (that is, whether there is a unique F which is also G). A definite description comes to have denotation, if it does, in virtue of the partial truth of such an existence claim (that is, in virtue of there being a unique F). So it is not that the meaning of a definite description determines a denotation, which in turn determines a truth-value; it is rather that the meaning of the description determines a truth-value, in virtue of which it may then have a particular denotation.

SUMMARY

In the semantic background to *TLP* a number of issues are in play: whether there is a distinction between sense and reference(between modes of thinking and thing thought about); whether thinking consists in a relation to an abstract entity; what an analysis of ordinary language should look like; and the proper semantics for names and definite descriptions.

3

Sinn and Bedeutung

The terms which Frege uses to express his contrast between sense reference are 'Sinn' and 'Bedeutung' respectively. It is well known that these terms occur frequently in *TLP*, for example in the claims that names have Bedeutung(3.203), and that only propositions have Sinn(3.3). But to what extent does the *TLP* use of the terminology coincide with Frege's?

3.1 PRELIMINARIES

Our terminological and exegetical task belongs within a wider debate over the nature of the semantics of *TLP*, which will occupy us throughout many of the succeeding chapters. The main issue is whether or not there is a sense/reference distinction at work in *TLP*; and if so, to what categories of expression it applies.

Some have naively assumed that Wittgenstein's use of the terms 'Sinn' and 'Bedeutung' is essentially similar to Frege's, with the former to be translated as 'sense' (as indeed it is in both English versions of *TLP*) and the latter '(Russellian) meaning'.[1] They have then seen him as accepting Frege's view that sentences have sense (whilst rejecting the idea that they refer to the truth-values), but as rejecting the Fregean doctrine that names have sense as well as reference, adopting in its place something like Russell's view, that to understand a name is to have direct knowledge of, or to be directly acquainted with, its bearer.

Although in my view this reading of the *TLP* terminology is determinately incorrect, that it finds a place within Wittgenstein's thinking for a notion similar to Fregean sense is at least something to recommend it. For the notion of understanding is not treated disparagingly by Wittgenstein, but seems, on the contrary, to be central to his concerns. Thus although the world 'verstehen' does not occur very often in his presentation, a large part of the point of the Picture Theory, for example, is to provide an account of our capacity to understand new sentences. (See 4.02–4.0311.) Yet the notion of sense is, as we saw in the last chapter, intended to be the correlate of understanding: the sense of a sentence is what will be grasped, or immediately known, by anyone who understands it, in virtue of which it has the truth-conditions that does. Indeed it is hard to see how Wittgenstein could attempt an account of the notion of understanding *without* employing something like the notion of sense. For we know that he was devastatingly critical of Russell's attempt to characterize judgement (and hence also understanding) in terms of a direct cognitive relation to the objects with which the judgement deals.[2] And it is by no means clear how there can be room for any other alternative.

Others have attempted a purely referential reading of *TLP*, seeing Wittgenstein as rejecting the notion of sense altogether, as belonging to the province of psychology rather than of logic.[3] On this view, both the notions of Bedeutung and of Sinn operate at the same semantic level: the level of reference, of what we talk about; 'Bedeutung' being translated as something like 'reference', and 'Sinn' by 'truth-condition' (rather than, as in Frege, a mode of thinking of a truth-condition).

Although the claim of pure referentiality is mistaken, this view too has something to recommend it. For as I shall argue later in this chapter, its reading of the 'Sinn/Bedeutung' *terminology* is largely correct. Moreover it can point to the *TLP* insistence that all logically equivalent sentences should be counted as expressing the very same proposition, which is a thoroughly un-Fregean conception (4.461–4.465, 5.141). For it is crucial to Frege's idea of sense, remember, that there may be logically equivalent expressions with different senses, since sense is to explain cognitive content. Nevertheless I shall argue in chapter 4 that Wittgenstein does employ a notion of sense, although his doctrines concerning it are substantially different from Frege's.

3.2 SENTENCES AND NAMES

The one aspect of *TLP*'s use of the 'Sinn/Bedeutung' terminology which is uncontroversial is that it is intended to emphasize the distinction between sentences on the one hand and names on the other. For as 3.3 insists, only propositions may be said to have Sinn. (Whether we also take Wittgenstein to maintain that only names may strictly be said to have Bedeutung, will depend upon whether or not we think his use of the term is univocal throughout *TLP*. This will be discussed shortly). The point of so emphasizing the distinction is to facilitate a rejection of Frege's middle-period doctrine that sentences are a kind of complex name (like a definite description), referring to either the True of the False (which are treated as abstract objects).

Note that besides insisting that only propositions have Sinn, 3.3 also contains the claim that a name only has Bedeutung in the context of a proposition, which is an echo of Frege's famous Context Principle, annunciated in *FA*, but no longer mentioned in his middle and late writings. At least part of the significance of that principle had been to emphasize the primacy of the sentence within language – surely rightly, since it is only by means of a sentence that you can (non-parasitically) say anything; a sentence being the smallest linguistic unit with which you can, in general, effect an assertion. It is this primacy which is then lost in Frege's later doctrine that sentences are complex names. For in the presence of such a doctrine there is nothing to distinguish sentences, as against other sorts of name, as having an especially central position within language. Indeed the account of assertion to which Frege is then committed is that in asserting a sentence one is putting it forward as a name of the True. He is then obliged to regard it as merely a contingent psychological matter that we do not have, for example, a linguistic activity of Carruthersizing: of putting forward a name as a name of Carruthers, in such a way that 'That only British philosopher to have been born in Manila' might constitute a complete linguistic act, on a par with 'Carruthers is wise'.

In reserving the term 'Sinn' as an attribute of sentences, Wittgenstein is meaning to reinstate the early Fregean doctrine of the centrality of the sentence within language. One consequence for semantics is immediate, and is emphasized at 3.31–3.314. It is that any sub-sentential expression ought properly to be presented by means of a propositional variable – so that 'runs' would be presented by 'x runs', and 'Mary' would be presented by 'Mary Øs' – since such expressions are, essentially, incomplete sentences.[4] And it follows that to explain the meaning of such an expression must at the same time be to fix how it will contribute to the Sinn of any proposition in which it might occur. For with the centrality of the sentence duly emphasized, what it is for a word to have meaning is just that it be capable of fitting together with other words to form a significant sentence. (See 3.263.)

Although this aspect of Wittgenstein's use of the 'Sinn/Bedeutung' terminology is perfectly genuine, it is at least partly independent of the issues which concern us – namely, to what extent this usage resembles Frege's, and the question whether there is a notion of sense at work in *TLP*. For example, it could consistently be claimed that Wittgenstein does indeed find room for a notion of sense which applies to all types of expression including sentences, but that he chooses not to express this notion using the term 'Sinn'; reserving the latter to mark, among other things, the centrality of the sentence within language. Indeed, a claim of precisely this sort will be defended in the next chapter.

3.3 SINN

It is obviously misleading to translate the *TLP* use of 'Sinn' as 'sense'. For when the notion of the Sinn of a picture is first introduced at 2.221 it is said to be *what* a picture represents, rather than (as we might have expected given Frege's famous metaphor of Sinn as the 'mode of presentation' of Bedeutung)[5] the *way* in which it represents what it does. Even more clearly, at 3.13 we are told that a proposition – that is to say, a sentence standing in its projective relation to reality (3.12) – does not actually contain its Sinn, does not contain *what* is projected. This makes it obvious that for Wittgenstein the Sinn of a sentence is much more like its truth-condition – something belonging, as it were, to the level of reference – than its Fregean sense. (The contrast may have been obscured, in the minds of some, by Frege's statement at *BLA* 32 that the sense of a sentence may be identified with the thought that its truth-conditions are fulfilled. But it is clear that for Frege there may be many such thoughts – many sentences with different senses – determining one and the same truth-condition.[6] Notice, however, that Frege's notion of a truth-condition differs from Wittgenstein's in that it is characterized extensionally. For Frege, but not, as we shall see, for Wittgenstein, sentences that differ only through substitution of coextensive predicates may be said to have the same truth-conditions.)

I believe that the above usage is consistent throughout *TLP*, with the exception of a few merely colloquial phrases such as 'in the ordinary sense' (4.011, 6.422) and 'in certain sense' (4.014, 4.122, 4.52). For even in those passages where the term 'Sinn' occurs in such a way that it might very naturally be interpreted to mean something like Fregean sense, the surrounding remarks make clear that this is not what Wittgenstein has in mind. Thus at 4.02, for example, he speaks of 'understanding the Sinn of a propositional sign', which would, on the face of it, suggest a Fregean reading. But then in the very next remark he says that to understand a proposition is to know the situation which it represents, which suggests that what is known in understanding (the Sinn) is the situation represented (i.e. the truth-condition). This impression is then confirmed in the next remark (4.022), where he explicitly equates the Sinn of a proposition with how things stand in the world if it is true. Similarly, at 4.03 Wittgenstein talks about a proposition using old expressions to communicate a new Sinn, but then in the very next sentence goes on to speak of the proposition communicating a situation to us (rather than a Fregean thought). So it is clear that by the Sinn of the proposition he means the situation communicated.

Although I remarked earlier that Sinn, for Wittgenstein, belongs at the level of reference – the level of what we talk about – there is a clear respect in which this is misleading. For the situation represented by a proposition (the Sinn) may not actually exist in the world, because the proposition may be false. But still the remark has a point, since 4.1211 implies that the Sinn of a proposition 'Fb' will contain the object b itself. So it is the referents of those component expressions in a sentence which have reference, and not their Fregean senses (supposing that they have such senses) which figure in its Sinn. In the respect 'Sinn' is like Russell's 'proposition', in that the Sinn of a sentence will contain the actual entities with which that sentence deals, and substitution of co-referring terms within a sentence will leave it with the very same Sinn. But the Sinn will also involve a representation of those entities being related to one another in a certain way, and whether or not this is true (whether the represented situation exists or fails to exist) will depend upon the state of the world. Then since a Sinn consists of merely possible arrangements of actually existing things it is, as it were, partly of this world and partly not.

From the remarks which occur between 4.02 and 4.031 (some of which have already been mentioned above) it is a clear that Wittgenstein takes the Sinn of a proposition to be the object of both linguistic understanding and of communication. What is communicated by a proposition is its Sinn, and what you know when you understand a proposition is its Sinn. Now recall from the last chapter the notion of semantic content, which was whatever you must know about a sentence in order to understand it and communicate with it. (This was one of the functions to be performed by Frege's notion of sense.) The *TLP* use of 'Sinn' can then be seen to embody a theory of semantic content. The idea is that it is sufficient for the understanding of a sentence that you know the situation it represents (rather than requiring, as Frege would have it, knowledge of the particular manner in which the situation is represented). We shall return to this in more detail later.

3.4 BEDEUTUNG

Let us begin our discussion of the *TLP* use of 'Bedeutung' by considering the famous 3.203, where we are told that a name bedeutet an object, the object being the name's Bedeutung. We might try using as our translation here 'refer' and 'referent' respectively, so that these remarks would tell us that a name refers to an object, the object being its referent.[7] This would certainly have the ring of truth about it, if not of truism. But there are at least two difficulties with the suggestion.

The first problem is that such a reading of 'Bedeutung' cannot be maintained throughout the whole of *TLP*. For there are many passages where Wittgenstein speaks of the Bedeutung of expressions where he is either explicit that they do not refer, or where a good interpretative case be made for saying that he thinks they do not. To take just some of the most obvious examples: At 5.02 we are told that both the argument 'P' in '−P', and the affix 'c' in '$+_c$', enable us to recognise the Bedeutungen of '−P' and '$+_c$' respectively.[8] Yet it is extremely doubtful, to say the least, whether Wittgenstein would regard either a sentence or the plus-sign as having reference. Then at 5.451 we are told that piecemeal definition would leave it in doubt whether the Bedeutung of '–' was the same in both '–P' and '–(P v Q)'. Yet Wittgenstein is of course explicit that the logical connectives do not refer (5.4). Again, at 6.232 he speaks of both

'1 + 1' and '2' having the same Bedeutung. Yet it is surely part of the import of 6.02–6.03 and 6.2–6.241 that Frege is wrong to believe numbers to be objects, and in thinking that numerals serve to refer to them. (Quite what is the positive import of these passages is another and more difficult question, to which I shall return briefly in *MT* chapter 2.) It may also be worth noticing 3.314–3.315, where Wittgenstein is apparently prepared to speak of any expression whatever ('any part of a proposition which characterizes its Sinn' – 3.31) as having Bedeutung. If we take this literally, and read 'Bedeutung' as 'reference', then it would conflict with many of his explicit doctrines.

Of course this argument is by no means conclusive. It is possible that the *TLP* use 'Bedeutung' is not consistent, and that in the passages mentioned above it may be translated simply as 'meaning' (which is, after all, the normal German sense of the term). But the argument does at least create a *presumption* against taking the word to mean 'reference' at 3.203. For in the absence of considerations to the contrary it is surely reasonable to assume that the terminology of *TLP* – or indeed any text – is univocal. Claims of ambiguous usage need to be argued for on the basis either of Textual Fidelity or of Charity.

The second (and, together with the first, conclusive) reason against taking 'Bedeutung' to mean 'reference' in 3.203, is that this would give us a reading of those remarks which clearly fails to encapsulate Wittgenstein's views on the semantics of names. (Indeed as we have already noted, thus interpreted it becomes entirely truistic.) For example, just a few remarks later at 3.24 he says that a proposition which mentions a complex will not be nonsensical (unsinnig) if the complex does not exist, but simply false. The implication is that a proposition mentioning a Simple which failed to exist (*per impossibile*, in the light of the supposed necessary existence of Simples – see 2.022–2.0272) would, in contrast, be nonsensical. That is to say (since in *TLP* usage, a name is a name of a Simple – see 3.2–3.26): that a sentence containing a bearerless name will lack Sinn.[9] So, as we have already seen above in our brief discussion of the *TLP* notion of Sinn, Wittgenstein's idea would seem to be that the Bedeutung of a name (a simple object) will itself figure in the Sinn of sentences in which it occurs, in such a way that in the absence of the object there would be no Sinn. All this would be missed by our wholly anodyne reading of 3.203.

A quite different suggestion might be to translate the occurrence of 'Bedeutung' in 3.203 as 'Russellian meaning'. This would at least have the advantage that the Bedeutung of a name would itself then constitute its semantic content; that is to say: its contribution to the semantic content (Sinn) of sentences in which it occurs. But it is still subject to the first set of objections raised against the previous suggestion. For a Russellian meaning is always an item in the real world, with which we are supposed to be directly acquainted. Yet Wittgenstein speaks of 'Bedeutung' in connection with expressions such as the negation-sign, where it is quite clear that he does not think of them as standing for items in reality.

Once again this point is not by itself conclusive. But it does mean that it is incumbent upon a defender of the suggestion to do each of two things. Firstly, they must show that Wittgenstein does indeed accept the Russellian doctrine of direct acquaintance with the objects of our thoughts. And secondly, that he chose to express this, for that class of expressions for which he accepted the doctrine, by using the word 'Bedeutung'; while yet continuing to use that term in the ordinary sense of 'meaning' in connection with all other expressions.

We shall consider the supposed Russellianism of *TLP* in chapters 4, 9, and 15, where it will be wholly rejected. So in my view the first *desideratum* cannot be met. But even if it could, if there is an alternative way of taking the term 'Bedeutung' at 3.203 which both leaves open the possibility of Russellianism and makes possible a consistent reading of it throughout *TLP*, then it is hard to see how the second could be. If there are two interpretations of a term, one of which enables it to be taken univocally throughout a text and the other of which does not, but where both are equally compatible with the substantive doctrines which our best interpretation otherwise ascribes to the text, then surely the former of the two is to be preferred. In my view there is indeed such a reading of 'Bedeutung' available, as I shall now try to show.

The suggestion is simple: that we take 'Bedeutung' throughout *TLP* to mean 'semantic content'.[10] The Bedeutung of a sub-sentential expression would be its contribution to the semantic content of sentences in which it occurs; which in turn would be the Sinn of those sentences (the truth-condition, or situation represented). Then 3.203 would tell us that the semantic content of a name is the object to which it refers, which of course entails the claim that the object itself figures in the Sinn of the sentences containing the name. But it would be left open whether or not a doctrine of direct acquaintance with such objects is being endorsed. Moreover, there would be no objection to speaking of the negation-sign, for example, as having Bedeutung. For on any account of the matter such a sign will make a contribution to the semantic content of sentences. (The crucial point being that the semantic content – the Bedeutung – of a sign *need* not be a item in the real world.) Even sentences themselves may be said to have Bedeutung on this reading, as Wittgenstein appears to do at 5.02. For the semantic content of a sentence is its Sinn. Indeed, Sinn is a kind of Bedeutung: it is the distinctive kind of semantic content that sentences have.

Since this suggestion has all of the advantages, and none of the disadvantages, of the others, I propose to adopt it; subject of course to future correction in the light of our later discussions. The one minor awkwardness involved is that the noun 'semantic content', unlike 'Bedeutung', has no associated verb. Here I propose that we might co-opt the verb 'to signify' (German 'bezeichnen'), since Wittgenstein does in any case appear to use this as an equivalent of 'bedeuten'. (A sign may either bedeuten or bezeichnen its Bedeutung – see 3.203, 3.317, 3.322, 3.3411, and many others.) I therefore propose to read 3.203 as saying that a name signifies an object, the object being its semantic content.

3.5 T←F CONDITIONS

Although I regard our proposals for reading the *TLP* terminology of 'Sinn' and 'Bedeutung' as well established, what does require some explanation is that 'Sinn' should have been chosen to express Wittgenstein's theory of the semantic content of sentences. For such a use of the term is no more natural in German than would be the corresponding use of 'sense' in English, and it flies in the face of an already established Fregean terminology. What, for example, would have been wrong with 'truth-conditions' ('Wahrheitsbedingungen') itself, which Wittgenstein does in any case use occasionally in talking about the truth-functions?

The crucial clue is to be found at 3.144, which says that names are like points whereas propositions, like arrows, have Sinn. On the face of it this remark is puzzling. A first thought might be that the intended contrast is between expressions which can, and those which cannot, be used to *say* anything. But this would render the metaphor very lame. For of course a point can 'say something' just as well as an arrow can. (A point marked on the stage can say to an actor 'Stand here', just as an arrow on a road-sign can say 'Go this way'.) In fact the only relevant differences are that a point is one-dimensional whereas an arrow is both two-dimensional and has direction.

The first aspect of the metaphor we can grasp immediately if we recall the *TLP* doctrine of the bi-polarity of the proposition, according to which any genuine proposition will be associated with two poles: true and false. (A genuine proposition is both capable of being true and capable of being false – see 4.2, 4.461–4.5.) So in the sense in which a name points in just one direction – towards the object which is its bearer – a proposition points in two directions at once: to the circumstances under which it is true, and to the circumstances under which it is false. This is sufficient to give us a difference in dimensionality between the semantics of names and propositions. But what of the aspect of directionality? Why should Wittgenstein not have said that names are like points whereas propositions are like *lines*?

This can be explained by referring to Wittgenstein's belief in the priority of truth over falsity, which I shall discuss in some detail in *MT* chapter 11. On this view a proposition is not, as it were, neutral between the two sets of circumstances. Rather it directs us *from* the one set (the circumstances under which it would be false) *towards* the other (the circumstances under which it would be true). Hence the semantic content (Sinn) of a sentence may itself be characterized as having a direction. For in understanding it you must of course grasp which of the two sets of circumstances you are being directed towards.

Within the framework of the doctrines of *TLP*, the Sinn of an elementary proposition is a directed pair of possible situations. The possible situation which the proposition directs us towards is called a 'state of affairs' ('Sachverhalt'). If that state of affairs exists then the proposition is true, if it does not then the proposition is false (2, 2.12–2.15, 2.201–2.221). All other propositions are truth-functions of elementary propositions (4.4, 5). The Sinn of such a truth-function is a directed division within the set of possible assignments of truth-values to the component elementary propositions, between those in which the truth-function is true and those in which it is false (4.3–4.52). These two ideas together, when combined with the characteristic metaphysical theses of *TLP*, yield the wider conception of the Sinn of a proposition as directed division within the set of all possible worlds.[11] Then if we represent the set of such worlds by a box, we can picture the Sinn of a proposition thus:

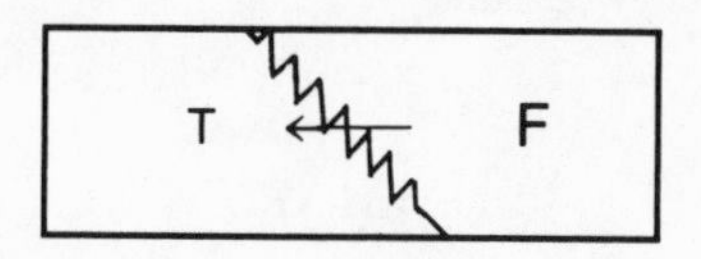

This explains the metaphor of the arrow: the semantic content of a proposition is essentially directional.

But why should the directional character of semantic content make the term 'Sinn' appropriate to designate it? The answer is simple: it can literally *mean* 'direction'. Consider first the English cognate 'sense'. Its use to mean 'direction' is not very common in ordinary discourse (though I have seen a novelist write of 'travelling beside a river, but in the opposite sense'; and in a piece with which Wittgenstein would almost certainly have been familiar, Russell characterizes directional relations – such as being larger than – by saying that they have sense).[12] But it is quite frequent in science, where one may speak, for example, of the sense of a force. A similar use of 'Sinn' is equally common in scientific German, and would have been extremely familiar to Wittgenstein through his background in mechanics.

So my suggestion is that Wittgenstein selected the word 'Sinn' to refer to the semantic content of a sentence characterized in terms of truth and falsity conditions because of his belief in the essential directedness of such content.[13] It is not easy to find a simple translation which reflects these features. The best that I can propose would be 'T←F conditions'. This is barbaric, but does at least capture everything required. But because of the barbarity, I shall in future either leave 'Sinn' untranslated, or will use 'semantic content of a sentence' or 'truth-conditions' according to the needs of the context.

Note finally that in terms of the idea that the semantic content of a sentence is a directed division within the set of all possible worlds it is easy to make sense of Wittgenstein's remark at 4.0621, that 'P' and '–P' have *opposite* Sinn. For to these two propositions correspond one and the same division within that set; the only difference lying in the direction in which they point (namely, towards opposite sides of it). Similarly with the remark that negation reverses the Sinn of a proposition (5.2341): for attaching the negation-sign to a proposition leaves the associated division within the set of worlds unaffected; what changes is which of the two sets the proposition points as towards.

SUMMARY

The *TLP* use of the terms 'Sinn' and 'Bedeutung' may be said both to mark the primacy of the complete sentence within semantics, and to embody a substantial theory of semantic content. 'Bedeutung' may reasonably be translated as 'semantic content' throughout, leaving it open that the Bedeutungen of some expressions are not items in the real world. Sinn, which is the kind of semantic content possessed by sentences, is to be understood as a directed division within a set of truth and falsity conditions.

4

In Search of Sense

The interpretation of the *TLP* terminology of 'Sinn' and 'Bedeutung' provided in chapter 3 leaves open that Wittgenstein might in addition have employed a notion which is more closely analgous to Fregean sense. In the present chapter I shall argue that this possibility is in fact realized.

4.1 SYMBOL AND SENSE

At 3.31 Wittgenstein explicitly introduces the notion of a symbol, saying that by a symbol he means any part of a proposition which characterizes its Sinn. He also there treats 'symbol' as the equivalent of 'expression' ('Ausdruck'), an equivalence which I believe is maintained throughout *TLP*. I shall argue that a symbol, or expression, is a sign together with its Fregean sense (though without Frege's commitment to the mind-independent existence of senses).

There are at least two possible ways of reading 3.31, depending upon how the verb 'to characterize' is understood. On the one hand it may mean that a symbol is any part of a proposition which *determines* a contribution to the semantic content (Sinn) of the whole. A symbol would then be any part of a proposition which contributes to the latter's truth-condition by determining a semantic content (Bedeutung) for itself. This would certainly echo one aspect of Frege's notion of sense, since the sense of a sign is supposed to contribute towards determining the truth-conditions of sentences in which it occurs, via the determination of a Bedeutung (referent). Yet on the other hand 'characterize' may only mean 'contribute to' rather than 'determine a contribution to'. That is, 3.31 may merely tell us that a symbol is any part of a proposition which has associated with it something which contributes to the semantic content of the whole. This would leave us with something closer to a Russellian, rather than a Fregean, conception, suggesting an interpretation of 'symbol' to mean 'sign which has reference (Russellian meaning)'.

Against the second of these interpretations we might point to 3.32, which tells us that a sign is what can be perceived of a symbol. Then if a symbol has both a perceptible and an imperceptible aspect, we might be tempted to argue that the latter would have to be something like a Fregean sense, an abstract mode of thinking of a Bedeutung.[1] But in fact it can be replied that the imperceptible aspect could just as well be the (bare) fact of the sign's having Bedeutung. What we really need is some evidence that Wittgenstein is prepared to think in terms of a symbol *determining* its semantic content, with perhaps a number of different symbols being able to determine one and the same such content.

At 3.317, in discussing the stipulation of values for a propositional variable (e.g. the stipulation that 'the chair' may occur as an argument in 'x is red', whereas '7' may not), Wittgenstein insists that the stipulation should only be concerned with symbols, not with their Bedeutungen. He then glosses this by emphasizing, in italics, that the stipulation should merely be a description of symbols, and should state nothing about what is signified. So a Bedeutung (semantic content) is *what is signified* by a symbol. Then at 3.321 he says that a sign will, if it signifies in two different ways, do so in virtue of being part of two different symbols. So a sign will come to signify in the way in which it does (and hence have the semantic content that it has) in virtue of being (part of) the symbol that it is. That is to say, part of what it is to be a symbol is to be a way of signifying (and hence of determining) a semantic content. And differences of symbol may result from differences in their way of signifying.

The notion of a symbol thus meshes with one aspect of the Fregean conception of sense, namely that senses are ways of determining Bedeutungen. (Though as we argued in the last chapter, for Wittgenstein not all Bedeutungen need be elements of the real world.) But equally important for Frege is the idea that the same Bedeutung may be determined by a number of different senses. In this respect, too, Wittgenstein seems thouroughly Fregean. For at 3.3411 he implies that one and the same object may be signified by a number of different symbols. So if differences in symbol mean differences in the way of signifying (3.321), then we are being told that there can be a number of different names with the same Bedeutung, where those names signify that object in different ways. So names with the same Bedeutung can have different Fregean senses.

This is of course an extremely controversial reading of *TLP*, and there are many objections to it which need to be overcome before it can be regarded as properly established. To this task we shall return in chapter 12. But it is worth replying at this point to an objection against the argument just presented. This is that 3.321 does not actually say that differences in symbol are always due to differences in the mode of signifying. It says only that if one sign expresses two symbols, then this must be because it symbolizes in different ways. But since a symbol is a sign plus a way of signifying (3.32), Wittgenstein may also wish to say that two different signs with the same way of signifying would also be two different symbols. So when he implies at 3.3411 that one and the same object may be signified by a number of different symbols he may only mean that it can be signified by a number of different signs. And of course this is true, on any account of the matter.

There are two points to be made in reply. The first is that this suggested reading renders 3.3411 wholly trivial. For no one has ever supposed that any particular syntactic composition is essential to a name. What may *have* supposed (notably Frege) is that names have associated with them a mode of determining their bearers (a sense) which forms part of their semantic content. On my reading, 3.3411 would be denying just this combination of views, as we shall see in more detail in chapter 12. Wittgenstein would be conceding that names do have senses (modes of determining reference) but would be denying that these senses are part of their semantic content – he would be denying that in order to understand an utterance involving a proper name you have to know the speaker's mode of determining the referent of that name. My reading is therefore favoured by Charity, since it at least makes 3.3411 look interesting.

The second point is that just two remarks after 3.3411, at 3.3421, Wittgenstein seems to be making a cognate point; but he there talks about different modes of signifying, rather than differences of sign. While 3.3411 tells us that all kinds of composition are inessential to a name, 3.3421 says that although different modes of signifying are unimportant, it can still be philosophically illuminating to realize that they are possible. We get the smoothest reading here if we assume that the earlier remark, too, is talking about different modes of signifying – thus implying that there can be names which signify the very same object in different ways.

We are beginning to build up a tentative case that Wittgenstein uses the term 'symbol' to mean something like 'sign together with its sense'. But he also says – and this is the bit that Frege would not have endorsed – that these different ways of signifying (different symbols) belong to the realm of what is inessential in language. From the point of view of what is essential, he believes, all names signifying the same object are the very same name. (Just what this point of view may be we shall discuss in chapters 5 and 12.) Indeed this is how the idea of there being different symbols with the same Bedeutung gets introduced again and again throughout *TLP*: it comes in under the guise of the distinction between what is essential and what is inessential in language.

Thus at 3.344 he tells us that what signifies (i.e. what *really* signifies, what is essential) in a symbol is what is common to all the symbols that the rules of 'logical syntax' allow us to substitute for it. He then illustrates with the interdefinability of the logical connectives. So he is saying for instance that in 'P v Q' and '–(–P & –Q)' we have different symbols – those sentences determine their truth-conditions in different ways – but that, because they have the same truth-condition (Sinn), they may be regarded as the same from the point of view of what is essential. Similarly at 4.465, with reference to the relationship between 'P' and 'P & (Q v –Q)' Wittgenstein remarks that it is impossible to alter what is essential to a symbol without altering its Sinn. So again he is implying that these two sentences signify their truth-condition in different ways (they are different symbols). But he is insisting that because their truth-condition is the same, the differences in 'way' belong to the realm of the inessential in language.

There is a possible objection to my interpretation of the above passages which parallels the earlier objection to my reading of 3.3411. It is that Wittgenstein may mean by distinct (but essentially the same, because having the same semantic content) symbols here, only differences in the *signs* involved and not their way of signifying. My view is that Wittgenstein is speaking of signs with different (if inessentially different) ways of signifying the very same Sinn or Bedeutung. But the objection is that he could equally well be taken as speaking only of differences of sign.

My only reply is to fall back on the principle of Charity. For on this reading the essential/inessential contrast becomes utterly trivial. Wittgenstein would merely be noting – what surely no one would ever have wished to deny – that the use of any particular sign to say something is always inessential to the thing said. And it would then be unintelligible that he should have given this idea such prominence. On my reading, on the other hand, he has a substantial point to make, involving an important criticism of Frege's theory of communication, as we shall see in the next chapter. But for the present all that matters is that Wittgenstein appears to agree that a sign can be used with different ways of signifying.

4.2 AN AMBIGUITY IN 'SYMBOL'

Before continuing any further we need to notice an ambiquity in Wittgenstein's use of 'symbol', which threatens the clarity of the account presented so far. For at 3.322 – immediately after we have been told at 3.321 that different symbols may involve different ways of signifying – we are told that the use of the same sign to signify two different objects can never indicate a common characteristic of the two, if we use that sign with different *modes of signification* (italics in original; I take it that Wittgenstein uses them to signal that he has shifted to quite a different sense of the phrase. See also the italics in 3.323). There is simply no way of making this intelligible if we interpret different modes of signification, and different symbols, to mean merely differences in Fregean sense. For the statement implies that the use of the same sign to signify two different objects *can* signify a common characteristic of the two, if used with *the same* mode of signification. And it is of course impossible, on the Fregean account, for one sign to signify two different objects without being used in two different senses.

What Wittgenstein has in mind is made clear in the next section (3.323), where we are told that in the sentence 'Green is green' (where the first word is a proper name and the last an adjective) the words do not merely have different Bedeutungen, but are *different symbols* (italics in original). I take him to mean that the name and the adjective do not merely contribute to the truth-condition of the sentence in different ways (by having different senses and different Bedeutungen), but that they contribute in different *kinds* of way, the signifying relation being of quite a different sort. Similarly in the immediately preceeding remark in the section, he is saying of the three different uses of the word 'is' – as copula, as identity-sign, and as an expression for existence – that they are three different *kinds* of use. It is not merely that the word has three different senses. Rather it has three different *kinds* of sense, which would be represented in a conceptual notation (Begriffsschrift) by signs as different from one another as a quantifier is from a proper name. (See 3.325.)

So although in general Wittgenstein understands different symbols to be signs with different ways of signifying (with different Fregean senses), in the passages immediately following 3.322 he understands them to be signs with different *kinds* of sense (belonging to different logical categories). This usage continues as far as 3.326, where we are told that in order to recognize a symbol by a sign we must observe how it is used in signifying. This would be barely intelligible if we took it to mean that in order to discover the sense of a sign you must observe how it contributes to the truth-conditions of sentences in which it occurs. For unless you already understand the sign (know its sense) you will be in no position to know those truth-conditions. By 'recognise a symbol' here, he must mean 'recognise the *kind* of sense'. And this is confirmed in the next remark (3.327), where he says that a sign only determines its logical form (i.e. the logical category to which it belongs) when taken together with its 'logico-syntactical employment'. What is at issue in these remarks is the methodology to be employed in constructing a conceptual notation.

The use of 'symbol' to mean 'kind of sense' does not last very long however. By 3.341 and 3.3411 we are back with its original meaning once again, and we remain there throughout the remainer of *TLP*. These are the passages where Wittgenstein talks of a single object being signified by a number of different symbols. Since it is surely unintelligible that a single entity might be signified by a number of signs belonging to different logical categories, he must here have in mind only signs with different Fregean senses.

4.3 PROPOSITIONS AND SENSE

I have been arguing that the *TLP* notion of a symbol (or an expression) embodies something very close, at least, to Frege's notion of sense. Now 3.31 tells us that a proposition (Satz) is itself an expression. So if my interpretation were correct we would expect Wittgenstein to be using 'proposition' to mean 'sentence together with its sense'. And indeed, at 3.12 a proposition is defined as a propositional sign in its projective relation to the world. Similarly, 3.11 implies that a proposition is a sentence used as a projection of a possible situation. These remarks are strongly reminiscent of Frege, since the idea of a 'projection' for a sentence appears to be the exact mirror-image of Frege's famous metaphor of sense as the *mode of presentation* of Bedeutung.[2] Indeed, you could say that the metaphor of projection combines not only the Fregean idea of a mode of presentation – with different projections of the very same Bedeutung being possible – but also the Fregean thesis that sense *determines* Bedeutung.

However, it can be objected that this reading is by no means forced upon us. For notice firstly that the notion of a method of projection might be taken to be the analogue, in the case of sentences, of the notion of a pictorial relationship for pictures. As 2.1514 tells us, this consists in the correlations between the elements of the picture (the names in a sentence) with the objects in the state of affairs pictured (the bearers of the names). This interpretation combined with a Russellian view of Tractarian names would leave us with an entirely un-Fregean conception of a proposition. A proposition would be 'projected' onto reality by virtue of the correlations between the names in the sentence and the objects in the state of affairs represented, these correlations being mediated by the speaker's immediate acquaintance with those objects. There is nothing in this that is in any way similar to Fregean sense.

There are two replies to this objection, though neither of them can be properly substantiated here. The first is that nothing has yet shown that Tractarian names do not have senses. Certainly 3.3 does not show this, if 'Sinn' means something like 'truth-condition'. Nor does 3.203, if 'Bedeutung' means 'semantic content'. Moreover we have the contrary evidence of 3.3411, as we saw above. These issues will be pursued in more detail in chapter 12. For the moment we may merely note that there is nothing to show that the 'correlations' spoken of at 2.1514 must be immediate, rather than holding by virtue of the names expressing Fregean senses.

The second reply to the objection is this: although it is true that the pictorial relationship consists only of the correlations between elements of the picture and things in the world, this is only one half of Wittgenstein's account of how a picture comes to depict what it does, the other half being the notion of *form*. (See 2.15–2.17.) The interpretation of this notion, too, is controversial. But I shall argue in chapters 11 and 15 that it is, roughly, the conventions enabling us to map any given arrangement of picture elements onto a determinate arrangement of their referents.[3] This certainly ought to belong within the notion of the 'method of projection' for a picture. And whatever we might say about the name/bearer relation, such conventions must surely involve something similar to the idea of Fregean sense.

Thus far the suggested Fregean reading of 'proposition' is only partly established, waiting on the arguments of later chapters. But we can here adduce some further evidence in its favour. For as we noted above, at 3.31 we are told that a proposition is a kind of expression; and we have already argued that an expression (symbol) is a sign together with its mode of determining a semantic content. Moreover, just as symbols in general have essential and inessential aspects – the particular mode of determining a Bedeutung belonging to the inessential – so too does a proposition (3.34). This idea is developed in more detail at 3.341, where we are told that what is essential in a proposition is what all propositions which can express the same Sinn have in common. This of course implies that there can be a number of different propositions with the very same truth-condition. And as I argued above in connection with symbols in general, what is meant by difference of proposition here should not be thought of as a difference only at the level of signs. On the contrary, it may result from differing modes with which the truth-condition is determined. This is confirmed a few remarks later at 3.3421, which speaks of the unimportance of different modes of signifying, rather than the unimportance of differences of sign.

One further argument for our interpretation is as follows. If, as we have been maintaining, 'proposition' in *TLP* means 'sentence with its sense',[4] then it will of course follow that there can be logically equivalent sentences which express distinct propositions. For there can be different modes of determining the very same truth-conditions. It will also follow that tautologies and contradictions are propositions, since they are sentences with a determinate mode of determining a truth-condition (though they turn out not to have a directed truth-condition, or Sinn) and since they can certainly have cognitive content. And just as we might have expected, at 4.461 we find Wittgenstein saying that propositions show what they say, tautologies and contradictions showing that they say nothing; which implies that tautologies and contradictions are themselves propositions. Similarly, 6.1 says that the propositions (plural) of logic are tautologies. (See also 6.11–6.1222 and 6.126.) Nor can we take 'Satz' in these remarks to mean merely 'sentence', since it can only be a symbol (a sign in use) rather than the sign itself which shows what it represents, and since what makes something a logical Satz is that it can be recognized to be true from the *symbol* alone (6.113).

4.4 PROBLEMS WITH 'PROPOSITION'

I believe that the above quasi-Fregean use of 'proposition' is maintained throughout most of *TLP*. However, just as in our earlier discussion of 'symbol', there are some exceptions and difficulties which need to be noted before our account can be allowed to stand. One clear case is 5.541, where Wittgenstein says (expounding Russell) that it might be felt that the sentence 'A believes that P' ascribes a relation between A and the proposition P. Here 'proposition' must be understood as Russell understands it, as an entity which itself contains the objects of thought. For otherwise the remark would embody the most fundamental misunderstanding of Russell, who certainly did not hold that belief is a relation between a thinker and a sentence, nor a relation between a thinker and a sentence with sense. But there is no problem for us here: it is entirely natural that Wittgenstein should have used 'proposition' in a Russellian way when discusssing Russell.[5]

A second class of cases are some remarks among the 5s, where 'proposition' gets used to mean a sentence individuated by its Sinn (truth-condition), rather than a sentence individuated at least partly by its Fregean sense. Such a use implies that all sentences with the same truth-conditions are the same proposition, and that sentences which lack directed truth-conditions (Sinn) are not propositions at all. Thus 5.141 tells us that all logically equivalent sentences (all sentences with the same truth-conditions) are one and the same proposition; 5 and 5.3 say that all propositions *are* truth-functions of elementary propositions (rather than, as we might have expected given a Fregean reading of 'proposition', that all propositions are *logically equivalent to* truth-functions of elementary ones); and 5.513 asserts that every proposition has only one negative.

If taken on their own, these passages need cause us no special difficulty. For it is easy to see how Wittgenstein could have slipped naturally into such a use, since he is dealing throughout the 5s with the question of the general propositional form; that is to say: with the essence of the proposition. For as we have already noted, he believes that what is essential to a proposition is its truth–condition, differences in symbol (sense) being relegated to the realm of the inessential in language. So what could be more natural, in this context, than that he should say that logically equivalent sentences are all ('essentially') the very same proposition?

However, these remarks in the 5s cannot be wholly isolated from the remainder of *TLP*. For as Goldstein argues in his (1986), Wittgenstein makes various claims about the essential properties of propositions which he then later denies with respect to the propositions of logic; in which case it seems to follow that tautologies and contradictions are not propositions at all.[6] For example, propositions are claimed to have Sinn (3.144, 4.064), to be pictures of reality (4.01, 4.021) and to say that things stand in a certain way (4.022, 4.5). In contrast, tautologies and contradictions are claimed to lack Sinn (4.461), to fail to be pictures of reality (4.462) and to say nothing (4.461).

These facts, too, could possibly be accommodated without materially altering our conception of what 'proposition' in *TLP* literally means. For all that is necessary to render the above passages consistent with our quasi-Fregean reading, is to say that in the remarks where propositions are claimed have Sinn etc., the discussion is implicitly restricted to contingent propositions alone. Indeed this is not wholly implausible, since it is clear that Wittgenstein's strategy is to concentrate first upon characterizing the nature of contingent propositions (from 2.1 through to about 4.4), and then only later (4.46s, 6.1s and 6.2s) to show how very different the propositions of logic and mathematics are from these.

What emerges out of the above discussion is that we face a three-way choice. Firstly, we might maintain that 'proposition' throughout *TLP* means a sentence individuated by its Sinn, writing off all textual contra-indications as slips and aberrations.[7] But this would involve attributing implausibly many errors to Wittgenstein, especially as the passages in which the ideas of 'proposition' and 'symbol' are first introduced (3.1–3.4) are those which formed the basis for the quasi-Fregean reading outlined earlier. Secondly, we could claim that the *TLP* notion of a proposition is ambiguous, in some passages meaning a sentence individuated by its Sinn, and in others meaning a sentence together with its Fregean sense. This is a possible interpretation, but requires us to say that this crucial piece of *TLP* terminology shifts its significance backwards and forwards throughout the course of Wittgenstein's discussion without any signalling or acknowledgement. Finally, we could read 'proposition' in our quasi-Fregean manner throughout (with the exception of the Russellian use at 5.541); supposing that in some places the topic of discussion is restricted by the context to contingent propositions only, and that in other places Wittgenstein's mode of writing is elliptical (e.g. using 'same proposition' at 5.141 when he really means 'same in respect of what really matters about propositions'). Since this last suggestion gives us by far the smoothest, most natural, reading of the *TLP* terminology, I propose that we should adopt it.

SUMMARY

Let me now summarize the interpretation of *TLP* terminology presented so far (remembering that it is partly provisional, waiting on later arguments):

1 'Sinn' means the truth-condition of a sentence, equivalent to a directed division within the set of all possible worlds.
2 'Bedeutung' means the semantic content of a sign, this being the contribution which the sign makes to the semantic content (Sinn) of sentences in which it occurs.
3 'Symbol' generally means a sign together with its way of signifying its Bedeutung (i.e. together with its Fregean sense).
4 'Proposition' generally means a kind of symbol. It is a sentence together with a way of signifying a truth-condition.

Although these interpretations present the semantics of *TLP* as Fregean in spirit, it is worth remarking three major differences from Frege, which will occupy us through many of the chapters which follow. Firstly, differences between symbols with the same Bedeutung are said to be inessential. This doctrine, together with its consequences, will be discussed in chapters 5, 6, and 7, and again in chapters 12 and 13. Secondly, there is no place in the semantics of *TLP* for senses which are not the senses of some sign or other, as the very use of the terms 'symbol' and 'proposition' indicates; whereas for Frege on the other hand, senses have necessary existence, independent of the existence of any language. We shall return to this in chapters 8 and 9. Then finally: for Wittgenstein, unlike Frege, not all Bedeutungen are items in the real world. We shall consider this idea in connection with predicative expressions in chapters 15 and 16.

5

Essential Sense

As we argued at the outset, the proof of an interpretation lies in its fecundity, enabling us to make sense of the text under study. The task of the present chapter is to explain why Wittgenstein might have held both that language can contain a variety of signs with different senses but the same Bedeutung, and yet these differences are in some way inessential.

5.1 CONDITIONS FOR COMMUNICATION

One clue to the significance of this combination of views is provided by 4.024, which tells us that to understand a proposition means to know what is the case if it is true. We might initially be tempted to interpret this as a remark about idiolectic understanding, emphasizing once again that a speaker's understanding of a sentence is directed towards truth and away from falsehood. But the remarks which follow suggest, on the contrary, that what is at issue is understanding the statements of another. Thus 4.025 is about translating from one language to another, 4.026 speaks of using propositions to make ourselves understood (i.e. to another person), and 4.027 and 4.03 speak of the use of propositions to communicate. This suggests that 4.024 should be read as saying that to understand – to know the semantic content of – the statements of another, is to associate the very same truth-conditions with those statements as they do (i.e. not necessarily the same cognitive content). This reading is then confirmed by 4.03, which says that a proposition must use old expressions to communicate a new Sinn, suggesting that what is communicated is not, as Frege would have it, the thought expressed (the cognitive content), but rather the truth-condition.

In order to see what is going on here, we need to recall the main features of Frege's theory of sense, which can be summarized in the form of four separate theses:

1 Sense is the immediate object of idiolectic linguistic understanding – it is the way in which individual speakers understand the signs that they use.
2 Sense determines Bedeutung – it is in virtue of the manner in which a speaker understands it, that a sign comes to make its contribution to the truth-conditions of sentences.
3 Sense is cognitive content – its identity-condition is sameness of information content, and two sentences express the same sense for a given speaker if and only if the person cannot believe the one while doubting the other.
4 Sense is semantic content – knowledge of it is required for understanding the speaker's native language, and mutual knowledge of it is that in virtue of which speakers can communicate with one another.

I submit that Wittgenstein is accepting the first three features of Frege's theory, but rejecting the fourth.

In the last chapter we saw that there is a textual basis for attributing theses 1 and 2 to Wittgenstein, his notion of a symbol (and of a proposition) involving the idea of there being a manner in which speakers project their signs onto the world. We can thus see him as claiming that any sign must have associated with it a mode of projection (a sense) in the idiolect of each individual speaker. Now I know of no passage where he explicitly lays down identity-conditions for symbols, but the images used – of a 'method of projection' (3.11) and of a 'way of signifying' (3.321) – strongly echo those of Frege himself. So it is not unreasonable to take Wittgenstein as being committed to thesis 3 as well. But as we have also seen, he relegates differences in modes of signifying to the realm of the inessential in language (so long as the Bedeutungen signified are the same). This can easily be understood if we assume that he takes commuication to be of the essence of language. For then we can see his remarks on communication as denying that in order to understand the statements of another you have to know the particular mode of projection employed. On the contrary, knowledge of the truth-conditions will suffice.

I thus interpret the *TLP* contrast between what is essential

(Bedeutung) and what inessential (differences of symbol) in language, to be denying that mutual knowledge of modes of determination of Bedeutung is required for communication (which would have required mutual knowledge of cognitive content, in virtue of the identity conditions for sense). So differences in symbol (in the mode of projection employed) are inessential from the point of the view of successful communication. What is essential is not the thought expressed (not the sense which the sign expresses in the speaker's idiolect), but rather the truth-condition represented. Wittgenstein's thesis is that, at least in the case of non-atomic (compound or general) sentences, two speakers may be said to understand one another in the use of such a sentence if and only if they know each other's use of it to be at least logically (analytically) equivalent [1].

The position could be expressed somewhat loosely (as Wittgenstein does at 5.141) in the claim that all logically equivalent sentences express the same proposition (say the same thing)[2]. Alternatively it could be expressed by saying that the semantic content of a sentence is a division within the set of all possible worlds, between those in which the sentence is true and those in which it is false – all sentences which effect the same division having the same semantic content. But note that speakers would not be supposed somehow to have a direct cognitive grasp on a set of possible worlds. On the contrary, their grasp would be effected, in each case, by the sense which they attach to the sentence. It is simply that two speakers may be said to attach the same semantic content to a sentence so long as it would, in their respective idiolects (cognitive content) be true in just the same possible worlds; and they may be said to understand one another provided they know this to be the case.[3]

Although I have been explaining the essential/inessential contrast in connection with the requirements for successful communication, this is in fact only a more visible manifestation of something which is equally true at the level of the individual idiolect. For what matters to me about my own thoughts is not the particular way in which they represent what they do, but rather *what* they represent and whether what they represent is in fact the case. For example, I should not be greatly concerned to learn that, as a result of some mental defect, I am continually shifting the senses (cognitive contents) of the expressions of my idiolect, but in such a way as to preserve logical equivalence (i.e. in such a way as to preserve semantic content). So long as I can hold onto *what* my thoughts express, it is of small importance whether or not I am capable at later times of recovering the particular manner in which they express what they do.

We have thus, on the current interpretation of *TLP*, a disagreement between Frege and Wittgenstein concerning the essence of linguistic communication (whether the communication be with oneself over time or with another person). Frege believes it to require mutual knowledge of sense (of cognitive content), whereas Wittgenstein denies this, claiming that it requires only mutual knowledge of truth-conditions (Sinn). We must now consider which of them is right. I shall confine the discussion to the understanding of molecular and general sentences and of predicative expressions, holding over consideration of names to chapter 12.

5.2 THE POINT OF COMMUNICATION

The *TLP* account of communication is intuitively more plausible than the Fregean. Consider the following example. Suppose that I have been introduced to the sentential connective in 'P or Q' by means of its equivalence with '–(–P & –Q)', and that I always rely upon that defintion in particular cases. You, on the other hand, have been introduced to the connective in the usual way, perhaps by means of the standard truth-table. Now suppose that you say to me 'It will either rain today or tomorrow'. Do I understand you? Frege is committed to denying that I do, since the sentence will have different cognitive contents in our respective idiolects. (It is of course possible for someone to understand both 'P or Q' and '–(–P & –Q)', where both are understood in terms of the truth-table definitions of the connectives, without realizing that they are equivalent.) But at the very least, we lack any convincing reason for going along with Frege here. Intuitively it would seem that we do succeed in communicating.

However it is generally unsatisfactory in philosophy to remain at the level of intuitive plausibility.[4] For one thing, people's intuitions can conflict. For another, even if we manage to reach agreement we should only have learned something about ordinary English usage. What is really required is some account of the function and importance of the concept under investigation. For of course our classifications do not exist in a void, but are always connected with some interest which we have. So simply to describe our intuitive grasp of a concept can provide no insight into why it is that we employ that mode of classification rather than another. Moreover there is always the possibility that our actual concept may diverge, to greater or lesser extent, from the one which would be in accord with the point of our making such a classification in the first place. So the real question is not what our concept of communication actually is, but what it should be. Our most basic task is an instance of the doctrine I call 'conceptual pragmatism': it is to elucidate the purposes which lie behind the contrast between communicating and failing to communicate, so that we may see which concept would be most appropriate.

Thus when we say that knowledge of semantic content is what is required for mutual understanding through the use of language, just what purpose is it that is to be subserved? What purpose is it that communication itself subserves? Clearly, at least a partial answer is that it is communication which enables us to acquire new beliefs through the statements of other people. In normal circumstances a statement will provide its audience with some reason to believe what is asserted; and it is obvious that one can only safely make an addition to one's stock of beliefs if one knows *what* has been asserted. So from this perspective the notion of semantic content, and of mutual understanding, will be given to us as: whatever a person needs to know if they may be confident in relying on the statements of another person in making alterations to their own stock of beliefs. But this can only take us as far as: understanding requires mutual knowledge of *material* equivalence. If I could somehow know that sentences in my idiolect always have the same truth-values as they do in yours, then each of your statements would give me reason to add to my own stock of beliefs.

It might be said that the only way in which two speakers could know their idiolects to be such that their respective tokens of the same sentence types do always share the same truth-values, would be for them to know at least that they are logically equivalent. But this is not necessarily so. For example, suppose that we provide Mary, who is completely colour-blind, with a hand-held machine for detecting colour. It is sensitive to wavelengths of light between ultra-violet and infra-red, and vibrates in the hand with an intensity proportional to the wavelengths being received from the direction in which it is pointed.[5] We then teach Mary how to use the machine, providing what are in effect ostensive definitions for the use of the colour words. Then by 'is red' Mary will mean something like 'is an object which causes the machine to vibrate like *this*'.

It is clear that Mary and any normally sighted speaker would have every reason to suppose one another's understanding of sentences involving colour words to be materially equivalent (at least in transparent contexts).[6] Indeed they could use one another as reliable sources of new information: an assertion of Mary's that something is red would give other people reason to make an addition to their stock of colour beliefs, as expressed in their own idiolects. Yet I think we should be intuitively inclined to deny that Mary and the others would really succeed in understanding one another.[7] But this intuition will be of little importance unless it can be grounded in an account of the purpose of communication which goes beyond the acquisition of new beliefs.

There is in fact more to communication – even of that form of communication whose sole concern is truth – than the bare exchange of information. Factual communication is not simply a matter of swapping statements. We also challenge (demand evidence for, or provide arguments against) the statements of others, and attempt to justify our own. Since it is a matter of common experience that people often say what is false, we cannot reasonably add everything which they say to our own stock of beliefs. Indeed the point subserved by mutual understanding is surely the acquisition of *rationally grounded* beliefs. In which case communication will require a shared conception of what is to count as a rational ground. There will then have to be more to mutual understanding than merely knowing what alterations the statements of another give one (weak) reason to make within one's stock of beliefs. One must also have sufficient knowledge to mount a challenge to the statements of others, and to provide evidence which will be an attempted justification of one's own. This will require at least mutual knowledge of logical equivalence. For only thus will any challenge which I mount actually be a challenge to the statement as you understand it, and any evidence with which you respond be evidence for the statement as *I* understand it.[8]

Thus if, in our example above, I try to challenge Mary's statement that a certain object is green by saying 'How do you know, you have not even looked?', this simply is a not a challenge to the statement as she understands it. Not only that, but the question will be unintelligible to her, leaving her unable to see what possible bearing it might have on the statement which she made. Nor *will* she be able to see this in advance of knowing something of my method for determining the extension of 'green'. Moreover, if she does reply 'I have had my hand pointed at it all the time', then this is no justification for the statement as *I* understand it.

We have reached an account of the point of communication which supports the *TLP* position. Since our basic purpose is to acquire rationally grounded beliefs we require sufficient mutual knowledge to facilitate the giving and receiving of reasons. This in turn seems to require (at least in the case of non-atomic propositions and predicates) mutual knowledge of logical equivalence. Which is to say: the identity-condition for semantic content should (in these cases at least) be sameness of truth-condition, or of contribution to truth-condition.

5.3 THE ESSENCE OF LANGUAGE

There is an obvious rejoinder to the argument we have sketched on Wittgenstein's behalf. It is that there is a great deal more to language, and our use of language, than mere fact-stating and the attempt to acquire rationally grounded beliefs. We also: give and obey orders, tell stories, make jokes, solve problems in arithmetic, thank, curse, greet and pray – to name but a few of our linguistic activities.[9] Would not each of these have to be considered before we could pronounce upon what is essential for communication in general?

To this rejoinder Wittgenstein has a reply: it is that factual discourse (and only factual discourse) belongs to the very essence of language and linguistic representation.[10] The exact form of this reply, and the arguments supporting it, will be considered in detail in chapter 7. Here let us note only that the claim is at any rate plausible. For we can surely imagine a language in which people never give one another orders, nor tell stories, make jokes, curse, greet, or pray. But can we conceive of a language without a factual component? We might perhaps, at a stretch, be able to imagine a language with no assertoric mood, in which people never try to communicate their beliefs to one another. Perhaps they only ever issue orders. But for anyone who holds that thinking is essentially language-involving (as I shall argue in chapters 8 and 10 Wittgenstein does), it surely follows that such people must at least use language assertorically in the context of their own private thoughts. The idea of an agent who is intellingent enough to possess a language, but who never uses it to formulate hypotheses, or to represent to themselves some aspect of the real world, is surely unintelligible. For these activities belong to the very essence of rational agency. An organism which made use of public signs, but which was incapable of using those signs in the context of its own thinking, must surely fail to have the background of intentional structures necessary to count as a genuine language–user.[11]

5.4 INDIRECT DISCOURSE

We may confine ourselves now to questions concerning factual discourse. Having reason to move from material to logical equivalence, is there any reason for narrowing our concept of semantic content still further, insisting that communication requires, in addition, mutual knowledge of cognitive content? One argument sometimes suggested, and attributed to Frege, is that one needs such a concept of semantic content to serve as the reference of expressions within opaque contexts, such as reports of belief.[12]

The issue is complicated, because there are in fact two quite different perspectives that we can (and do) take towards descriptions of propositional attitudes. Sometimes our interest in the matter is belief-acquisitive, being closely analogous to the interest which we take in the statements of others. Being told what someone believes can give me reason to make an alteration within my own beliefs about the topic their belief concerns, just as can someone's outright assertion on the matter. If Mary is something of an amateur meteorologist, and you tell me 'Mary believes that it will rain either today or tomorrow', then you give me some reason to add such a belief to my own stock. From the standpoint of this perspective, it is of no importance whether or not the report of Mary's belief respects the exact cognitive content of her mental state. All that matters is that it should convey the correct truth-condition. For example, if you had chosen to describe Mary's belief by saying 'She believes that it isn't the case that it will neither rain today nor tomorrow' then you would not, in such a context, have said something false, despite the fact that Mary herself might have denied holding any such belief (that is, because she fails to notice the equivalence between the two). Indeed, as we shall see in chapter 13, it is reports of belief made from this perspective which are *de re*.

The other kind of interest which we take in descriptions of propositional attitudes is explanatory.[13] Often we wish to know what someone believes because we seek an explanation of some aspect of their behaviour. Here it will generally be crucial that the description should convey the precise cognitive content of the subject's belief, and not just its truth-condition. For this may make all the difference if their behaviour is to be rendered intelligible. For example, Mary may both be taking steps which presuppose precipitation in the near future, and yet reply in negative to the question 'Do you think that it is not the case that it will neither be wet today nor tomorrow?' This combination will be explicable only if we report the content of her belief by saying 'She believes that it will either be wet today or tomorrow'.

Now it is perfectly true that from the explanatory standpoint a description of a propositional attitude can be accurate, and be expressed in the form of a simple that-clause, only if the cognitive content which we attach to the sentence within the that-clause is the very same as the content of the subject's propositional attitude. But it does not follow that failure in this respect would mean that we should fail to understand the person if they were to assert that sentence directly. For it may be that one needs to know more to understand an opaque occurrence of a sentence than suffices for understanding its transparent use, just as one arguably needs to know more about the word 'black' to understand 'That was a black day for me' than one does to understand 'The dog is black'.[14] And indeed there is every reason to believe that this is the case, given that the function of communication, in transparent contexts, is to facilitate the acquisition of rationally grounded beliefs about the world.

What is true is that because of their shared background of linguistic practices and explanations, the idiolects of the speakers of a natural language will in many cases coincide. Where this can reasonably be assumed, it may then be exploited in describing the precise content of someone's belief. But it is not true that precise description can *only* be given in such a manner. To revert once again to our earlier example, if you wished to convey to a normal person the precise content of the belief which colour-blind Mary would express by saying 'That tulip is red', you obviously could not use the statement 'She believes that it is red'. But you could say something rather more complicated, like 'She has a belief concerning that tulip, where the content of the predication is given to her in virtue of her colour-detecting machine vibrating in her hand with its least intensity'.

I suggest that we in fact operate with the following convention governing ascriptions of belief made from the explanatory standpoint: in cases where we may reasonably assume that we attach shared senses to a sentence, placing that sentence within a clause of the form 'A believes that. . .' is to be understood to ascribe to the subject a belief with the cognitive content which that sentence has for us all. But there is nothing in this suggestion to force us to say that understanding, in general, requires mutual knowledge of cognitive content.

5.5 EASE OF PERSUASION

One further motive for adopting a narrower conception of semantic content would be this: only if we share mutual knowledge of cognitive content can I be confident that any evidence which I provide for the truth of my statement, or any challenge which I mount to the truth of yours, will immediately be recognized as evidence, or as a challenge. Thus suppose I object to your statement that P, by drawing your attention to the fact that not Q, where P implies Q. Only if we both attach the same cognitive content to the sentence 'P' can I be confident that you will immediately recognize, as I do – without the need for any sort of demonstration – that the truth of 'P' is inconsistent with the falsity of 'Q'. Only if this is so can I be confident that you will immediately see the relevance of what I at say, and recognize my challenge as such.

However, Wittgenstein could reply, and with justice, that we have here left the realm of the theory of meaning and have entered the province of psychology. The point of communication surely cannot lie in its guaranteeing me the ability to convince anyone of the truth of my (true) beliefs, if only because nothing *could* provide such a guarantee. Even mutual knowledge of cognitive content cannot guarantee that any challenge,or any proof, will immediately be recognized as such. For it my challenge takes several steps – with our mutual knowledge of cognitive content ensuring that you see the relevance of what I say at each step – you may still be unable to recognize the totality of what I say as a challenge to your belief. It is a familiar fact that one can be convinced by every step in a proof and yet fail to be convinced by the whole, precisely because one is unable to command a clear view of the whole.[15]

It is undoubtedly the case that mutual knowledge of cognitive content may ease the passage to conviction. But the point of making statements is to convey how things stand in the world, and to provide our beliefs about the world with a rational ground. Whereas what I should learn, when I come to know the cognitive content you attach to a sentence, would not be anything relevant to the acquisition of knowledge about the aspect of the world with which that sentence is concerned, but rather a truth about you. I should learn in what circumstances you might be surprised to be told of the truth of the sentence, in what circumstances you must see its truth straight away, and so on. Such knowledge surely plays no essential part in factual communication, unless of course (as in reports of belief from the explanatory standpoint) it is to be exploited to convey the precise cognitive content of someone's propositional attitude. Rather, what is important in factual communication is that it should be guaranteed that the evidence which I provide for the truth of my statement (as I understand it) should be evidence for the statement as you understand it, even if you cannot immediately see it as such. Just how easy it turns out to be to get you to see the relevance of what I am saying, is a comparatively trivial matter of psychology, having to do with convenience rather than with essentials.

SUMMARY

We have provided an interpretation of the *TLP* idea that differences in Bedeutung (and hence of Sinn) are differences in what is essential, whereas differences in symbol are inessential. It contains an important criticism of Frege's theory of sense. Wittgenstein is acknowledging that every speaker must employ some mode of projection of the Sinn of each sentence, but is denying that mutual knowledge of modes of projection is necessary for communication. All that really matters is mutual knowledge of truth-conditions (Sinn).

6

Sense and Nonsense

In this chapter we trace the connections between *TLP*'s account of semantic content and some of its other doctrines, particularly the showing/saying distinction, the idea that the propositions of logic and mathematics are senseless ('sinnlos'), and the consignment of the propositions of philosophy to the category of nonsense ('unsinnig').

6.1 SHOWING AND SAYING

Perhaps the most startling and paradoxical doctrine in *TLP* is the claim that all of its propositions (including, presumably, this very claim itself) are nonsensical – as are, indeed, all philosophical and metaphysical propositions (6.53–6.54). In Wittgenstein's view we cannot make assertions or entertain thoughts about logic or logical form, nor about the essence of reality. These things can, however, be shown or made manifest, in a number of different ways. Symbols (signs together with their mode of application) and internal relations between symbols can show us something, either about themselves or about the logical nature of reality (3.262, 4.1211, 4.125, 6.1–6.12); the existence of different ways of symbolizing the same Bedeutung can reveal something about the essence of the world (3.3421, 3.3441), and what the philosopher tries to say can sometimes be shown by the construction of a logically perpicuous notation (4.1272, 5.53–5.534). Rather more obscurely, a piece of nonsense can show something (though perhaps in quite a different sense of 'show'), since Wittgenstein thinks that the nonsensical propositions in a philosophical work can help us to see the world aright (6.54).

Undoubtedly the showing/saying doctrine has at least some of its historical roots in Frege, who frequently has to resort to metaphor in trying to express his views on logic, most famously in the metaphor of the 'incompleteness' of concepts and functions.[1] Frege often has to beg his readers to 'meet him half-way', claiming that he cannot give literal expression to his ideas.[2] Moreover his writings are riddled with sentences which are, by his own lights, nonsensical. For example, he says at one point that an object is anything which is not a function.[3] But what is he quantifying over here? The universal quantifier in this statement must be taken to range over both objects and functions, yet there is no provision for such a quantifier in his own semantic system. He allows for quantification over objects, and also for second-level quantification over functions (properties, relations, etc.); but there is no room for both kinds of quantification to take place at once.

Wittgenstein was also greatly influenced by Frege's idea of a conceptual notation ('Begriffsschrift'), in which logical structure would be reflected in surface syntax. (See 3.325.) For this holds out the possibility that what a philosopher attempts (but fails) to say, would be made manifest by the construction of some appropriate piece of conceptual notation. Thus what we attempt to express by saying 'Existence is not a property' – which is, for both Frege and Wittgenstein, strictly nonsensical – would be shown by the notation of the first-order predicate calculus, in which the sign for existence has not the slightest similarity to a predicate, and indeed in which there is no grammatically permissible way of formulating a sentence in which that sign takes a predicative role. When Wittgenstein says that the goal of philosophy is the logical clarification of thoughts, to be achieved by presenting clearly what can be said (4.112, 4.115), at least part of what he has in mind is the construction of a conceptual notation modelled on Frege's. Having created such a notation we should be able to 'pass over in silence' what previously had caused us puzzlement and confusion. (See 3.323–3.325, 4.003, 6.53–7.)

Nevertheless something, somewhere, has surely gone wrong with the showing/saying doctrine. We can allow that there are many things which can be shown rather than said; perhaps even that there are some things which can only be shown. (We shall consider a number of examples of alternative, and conceptual, notations, both in later chapters and in *MT*.) But it must be wholly unacceptable to claim that all of philosophy is nonsense. For either a nonsensical sentence can show us something or it cannot. If it cannot, then Wittgenstein's claim at 6.54 that anyone understanding

TLP would be led to see the world aright must be unfounded; indeed there can be no such subject as philosophy. But if, on the other hand, a piece of nonsense can show us something, then there must somehow be a distinction to be drawn between illuminating and unilluminating nonsense. There are two possible ways in which this might be attempted. Firstly, the distinction might be said to consist in the different causal properties of sentences, our psychology being such that some nonsense is capable of causing a sort of 'Gestalt switch' in us.[4] Yet it is surely clear that the actual effect of philosophical speech and writing is not of this purely causal, contentless, sort. Secondly, it might be said that illuminating nonsense gets us to see what the speaker means or intends but cannot say.[5] But this presupposes a distinction between thought and language which I shall argue in chapter 8 to be quite foreign to Wittgenstein.

Any release from these difficulties would be welcome. Somehow we must make room for the idea that the propositions of *TLP* – and philosophical propositions generally – have a kind of sense. For it is evident that they do. So our most urgent task must be to try to understand how Wittgenstein could have argued himself into such a position, in order that we may see how best to argue him out again.

6.2 SENSE WITHOUT SINN

At 4.461 Wittgenstein tells us that tautologies and contradictions lack Sinn and say nothing. But then in the very next remark (4.4611) he denies that they are nonsensical (unsinnig). The first part of this doctrine is easy to understand in the light of the discussion of previous chapters. For the idea of what it is for a proposition to say something is intimately connected with its having Sinn (4.022). A proposition with Sinn locates our world within a subset of the set of all possible worlds: directing us towards this subset and away from the remainder (4.463). And what the proposition says (its Sinn) may be equated with the directed division which it makes within the set of all possible worlds. But tautologies and contradictions effect no such division. A tautology, being true in all worlds, merely locates our world somewhere within the set of all possible worlds; which is to say nothing about what our world is in fact like. A contradiction, being true in no worlds, attempts to represent our world as falling outside the set of all possible worlds; which again says nothing about what our world is like. (See 4.461–4.463.) So neither sort of sentence has Sinn, nor tells us anything.

It might be said that all of this, so far, is merely a matter of moving around definitions, the terms 'saying' and 'Sinn' having been defined in such a way as to give the desired result. It might further be said (since tautologies can, manifestly, be informative and useful): so much the worse for the definitions. But this would be to miss the thrust of the essential/inessential contrast which we expounded in the last chapter. Wittgenstein will of course concede that there are many tautologies which we cannot immediately recognize as such, so that to be told of the truth of what is in fact a tautology may be informative (6.1262). He also concedes that they have a use, enabling us to pass validly between contingent propositions (6.1264, 6.211). But he would insist that this is merely an inessential matter of human psychology. (See 6.125–6.127.) All that matters in communication, and in the activities of saying and thinking generally, is the state of the world represented: the Sinn. And from the point of view of what matters, all propositions which effect the same division within the set of all possible worlds say the very same thing. So the definitions are by no means arbitrary, but reflect what is of fundamental importance in thinking and communicating.

Recall from the last chapter claim that all logically equivalent propositions are, essentially, the same proposition. Since it is obvious that simple tautologies and contradictions can tell me nothing about the world (as Wittgenstein remarks at 4.461, I learn nothing about the weather if I am told that it is either raining or not), and since all tautologies are logically equivalent to simple ones, it must follow that they all say nothing. For all are, essentially, the same proposition.

There is thus no particular difficulty in understanding why tautologies and contradictions should be characterized as saying nothing: this flows from Wittgenstein's conception of what is essential in communication. But what does he have in mind by denying that they are nonsensical (unsinnig)? This, too, is easy to understand: it is because they consist of perfectly legitimate symbols combined in perfectly legitimate ways (4.46, 4.4611). Thus a tautology of the form 'P v –P' consists of signs which have sense and Bedeutung: the sentences 'P' and '–P' will express propositions which signify (opposite) Sinn, and the sign 'v', too, will have both cognitive and semantic content. Moreover the signs themselves are combined quite legitimately: the rule of syntax for 'v' will tell us merely that it may be combined with any propositional sign on its left and any propositional sign on its right. So 'P v –P' is a proposition, being well-formed and expressing a sense. It is merely that the component symbols have been combined in such a way that the resulting sentence says nothing (lacks Sinn).

It might be objected against this account of Wittgenstein's views that he says at 4.466 that tautologies and contradictions are not really combinations of signs at all, thus suggesting something much more radical than that such sentences merely lack semantic content.[6] But in fact there are two things which he means by this, each consistent with our account. The first is that the semantic contents (Bedeutungen) of the signs employed in a tautology do not figure in the content of the end-product: the tautology itself. (Obviously they cannot do so, since tht end-product is wholly lacking in semantic content.) Although each of the signs in a tautology does have semantic content, they are combined in such a way that the resulting sentence is without such content. So a tautology is not a 'real combination of signs' in the sense that it does not serve to combine the Bedeutungen of its parts into a determinate whole.

The second thing he means is that it is no part of the essence, or purpose, of the signs involved in a tautology that they should yield a tautology when so combined. For at 4.4661, having conceded that the signs are after all combined with one another in tautologies and contradictions, he says that these combinations are not essential to the symbol. Now he cannot have meant by this that it is a contingent feature of the symbols involved that they can be combined into a tautology or a contradiction. For on the contrary, any signs with the semantic content of 'v' and '–' must be such that they will yield a sentence which is true come what may when combined in the form 'P v –P'. The idea must rather be that tautologies and contradictions are an unintended (but nevertheless inevitable) spin-off from the semantic contents assigned to their component parts. As Wittgenstein says at the end of 4.466, tautologies and contradictions are the limiting cases of the combination of signs. I take this to mean that although their existence is an inevitable consequence of the existence of a symbolic system, they form no part of our purpose in introducing such a system, and do not contribute to its content.

Not only have we uncovered the basis of the doctrine that tautologies, contradictions and propositions of mathematics lack Sinn, but we have also found hints towards the proper understanding of the doctrine that philosophical propositions are nonsensical. If the idea is that for a sentence to *fail* to be nonsensical is for it to consist of meaningful symbols combined in a legitimate manner, then presumably for a sentence to *be* nonsensical is for it either to contain a sign which lacks semantic content ('Snarks are dangerous'), or for it to consist of signs combined in ways to which no significance has been attached ('Lion tiger stag').

This suggestion may be partly confirmed by considering 3.24, where it is implied that a sentence containing a simple name would be nonsensical (unsinnig) if (*per impossibile*) the bearer of that name were to fail to exist. This is easily understood if we recall our suggestion in chapter 3 that the semantic content of a proper name is exhausted by its bearer. For then a name which lacks a bearer will lack semantic content, and all sentences containing it will lack semantic content as well. Yet it is entirely consistent with this that such sentences may nevertheless possess determinate senses (cognitive contents) in the idiolects of particular speakers, as we shall suggest in chapter 13. For to say that a sentence lacks semantic content by virtue of containing a word which lacks such content (to say that a sentence is unsinnig) is not at all to say that it might not express a determinate mode of thinking of the world within the idiolect of any given speaker.

6.3 PHILOSOPHY AS NONSENSE

We turn now to consider why philosophical propositions should be thought to fall into the category of nonsense (understood as above). Philosophy, on Wittgenstein's conception of it, is the attempt to study the essence of thought, the essence of reality, and the relationship between them.[7] Now at a number of points in *TLP* he apparently argues thus: Suppose we are attempting to describe logical form, either of language or the world.[8] Then either the sentences which we use in this attempt themselves possess logical form or they do not. If they do not, they will be nonsensical (like 'is bald is wise'). But if they do possess logical form, then they will presuppose a knowledge of precisely what they are trying to describe. (See 2.172–2.18.) For example, suppose we attempt to say that the sentence 'Fb' is about the object b. In fact this sentence is itself of the form 'Øb', and is about the object b. So we have presupposed a knowledge of what we were attempting to say. And how, on the other hand, could we say that 'Fb' is about the object b *without* talking about b?[9] (See 4.1211.)

There are a number of assumptions implicit in this argument. One is that there is something called 'logical form' which is common both to thought and to reality (2.18). Another seems to be that logical form is somehow all-of-a-piece, so that one could not use a proposition with one sort of form to describe another without taking for granted the logical form of the other. (Or perhaps the assumption is only the weaker claim, involved in the example from 4.1211 above, that in order to describe a given form one would have to employ that very form.)[10] But the most basic presupposition may be brought out by asking why we cannot rely upon an *im*plicit grasp of logical form in order to render out knowledge *ex*plicit. Since ordinary language disguises logical form, as Wittgenstein himself insists at 4.002, what could be wrong with using ordinary language – thus relying on our inchoate, implicit, grasp of logical form – in order to render those very same forms explicit and articulate? Part of Wittgenstein's reply is predictable: sentences used in the attempt to characterize logical form must either be necessarily true or necessarily false, and such sentences say nothing (lack Sinn).

Now so far this is only to place the propositions of philosophy in the same category as those of mathematics and logic. He could allow that such proposition have sense (cognitive content) and could allow that they can have an heuristic or inference-guiding use for us, but would deny that they have Sinn, or tell us anything about the world. Yet the position he actually adopts is much more radical: it is that the 'propositions' of philosophy are in fact nonsensical (which then of course makes it problematic how they can have any kind of elucidatory role). Why is this? Why are the propositions of philosophy treated differently from those of logic?

The answer to these questions is simple. It is that the symbols in a tautology are used in precisely the same sort of way as they are when they occur in a contingent proposition, the use of 'v' in 'P v – P' being no different from its use in 'P v Q'. But in philosophy, on the other hand, words have to be used quite differently. Words whose primary purpose in ordinary language consits in their contributions to the content of contingent propositions have to be turned in on themselves somehow, and used in quite new senses, to talk about essential features of propositions or of the world. And Wittgenstein's claim is that these (philosophical) senses can receive no coherent explanation.

The idea is easiest to explain in connection with the discussion of formal concepts in the 4.12s, though the point is really quite general. Wittgenstein believes that a word such as 'object', in its ordinary language use, functions as a kind of variable. In English we say 'There are two objects which . . .' where in logic we would write '∃x∃y . . .' (4.1272). But when we do philosophy we attempt to use the word as a predicate, as when we say that numbers are (or are not) objects. Yet such a predicate can, in the terms of Wittgenstein's semantic theory, be given neither sense nor Bedeutung. For recall that a symbol (sign together with its sense) is said to be any sign which contributes to the Sinn (truth-conditions) of sentences in which it occurs (3.31). And it might be felt that the peculiarity of a predicate like 'object', is that it can never occur in sentences which have Sinn, and so cannot count as a genuine symbol. For it might be said that all sentences predicating 'object' of something will either be necessarily true or necessarily false – if, that is, these sentences were really fit to be true or false at all. And we have seen how, in Wittgenstein's view, such sentences say nothing (lack Sinn).

In fact this exposition is slightly too simple, unless we help ourselves to the *TLP* doctrine that all (genuine) objects have necessary existence. For if Mary can count as an object, then 'Mary is an object' will be contingent because Mary's existence is contingent. Even so, the basic point can be allowed to stand. For anyone capable of understanding 'Mary is an object' must already know the various features of the use of the word 'Mary' by virtue of which the sentence is true. So the predicate 'is an object' can make no contribution to the semantic content of the sentence which has not already made by the name 'Mary' alone. Although that predicate might figure in contingent sentences, it can make no distinctive contribution to their semantic contents.

All of the terms which we characteristically use in doing philosophy, when not employed merely to mark a style of variable, suffer from the same defect. (Examples would be: 'Mary is an object', 'Being red is a concept', 'Seven is a number', 'It is necessary that $2 + 2 = 4$', 'It is impossible that $2 + 2 = 6$', and 'It is possible that

Mary has freckles'.) They are all such that either they can only ever occur in sentences which are necessary truths or necessary falsehoods, or they at any rate fail to contribute to the content of any contingent sentences in which they might occur. So there can be no fixing of Bedeutung for these terms, since to fix the semantic content of an expression is determine its contribution to the Sinn of sentences. Yet none of these terms can ever – in their philosophical use – make any such contribution. In which case it seems that their senses cannot even be coherently explained.

6.4 SENSE WITHOUT BEDEUTUNG

It might be objected against the argument I have been attributing to Wittgenstein that the doctrine of philosophy as nonsense does not strictly follow, even given his characterization of philosophy and of the use of terms in philosophy. For if I have been correct in arguing that the *TLP* notion of a symbol is that of a sign together with its cognitive content (sense), then there should be no reason in principle why some perfectly genuine symbols might not happen to lack Bedeutung – and this despite the fact that 3.31 appears to imply that only signs with Bedeutung are real symbols (we might regard this as merely a piece of stipulative definition). We could then concede that 'Seven is a number' lacks Sinn, and does so by virtue of containing a term which (in such a use) is lacking in semantic content; but we could insist that the sentence nevertheless has a sense, and expresses an intelligible proposition.

It is clear how Wittgenstein would respond to this objection, if I have been reading him correctly: he would reiterate that the possession of Sinn is of the very essence of statement-making. Since it is the Sinn of a sentence which is communicated by it (whether used in one's own thoughts or in public statements), a sentence without Sinn will lack anything to communicate. And a term without semantic content, too, must be wholly empty as a vehicle for communication. So he could concede that the philosophical use of 'is a number' might have cognitive content within the idiolect of any given speaker. (It is a further advantage of the fact that we have attributed both the notions of sense and of semantic content to Wittgenstein, that it enables us to find at least this much place for the propositions of philosophy.) But such content would merely be a matter of the subject's particular psychology. It would not be communicable, nor could the predicate 'is a number' ever be used to say anything.

A similar point can be made in connection with the idea of philosophical analysis. Consider for example Frege's proposal that statements of the form 'The number of F's = the number of G's' should be analysed as saying that the concepts F and G are one-to-one correlated with one another. (See *FA* 63.) On the *TLP* account of semantic content, there is no difficulty in explaining how such an analysis can both be correct and enlightening for a given individual. For an analysis is correct, we may suppose, just so long as Sinn is preserved, the two sentences being logically equivalent. Yet a speaker may, through attaching different cognitive contents to them both, have failed to realize that this is so. The difficulty is rather to explain how such informativeness can be communicable. For on the *TLP* account of semantic (that is, communicable) content, there is nothing that can be communicated by presenting any one such sentence as an analysis of another, since both will say the very same thing. Moreover, since differences in cognitive content which do not emerge at the level of Sinn are said to belong to the realm of the inessential in thought and language, even the information conveyed to a particular individual can have no bearing on the essence of what is said. The fact that they learn something on realizing that the one sentence is equivalent to the other is merely an inessential feature of their psychology. In short: on the *TLP* account analysis is possible, but is solipsistic and of merely psychological significance.

SUMMARY

The propositions of logic and mathematics are without semantic content (sinnlos), in that they fail to effect a directed division within the set of all possible worlds. But they are nevertheless composed of signs which have semantic content combined in syntactically legitimate ways. The propositions of philosophy and metaphysics, on the other hand, are contentless in an even stronger sense, since they contain terms lacking in semantic content. They are therefore said to be nonsensical (unsinnig).

7

Unity of Content

Our task in this chapter is to find a way for Wittgenstein to dispense with the claim that all philosophy is nonsense whilst doing the minimum possible violence to the other doctrines of *TLP*. For that claim is manifestly false.

7.1 HOW IS PHILOSOPHY POSSIBLE?

A natural suggestion would be to take the resulting philosophy-as-nonsense doctrine as a *reductio ad absurdum* of the arguments of chapter 5, which by relegating cognitive content to the realm of the inessential led to the thesis that all tautologies and contradictions say the same thing: to whit, nothing. For if we were to reinstate the Fregean idea that sense is just as crucial to communication as truth-conditions, then we could hold on to the informativeness of tautologies. This in turn would lend support to the idea that philosophical statements can have semantic content, by undermining the argument that the terms used in such statements must themselves lack semantic content.

There are at least two reasons why this suggestion should not be immediately accepted. The first is that while the arguments of chapter 5 remain in place, we cannot simply decide to deny their conclusion. At the very least we should have to discover sufficient reason for rejecting one of the premises, or for discerning a fallacy in the argument itself. Yet it is not at all obvious how this can be done. The second is that even acceptance of the Fregean position would leave us almost equally poorly placed to account for the possibility of philosophy. For recall from chapter 2 the difficulties Frege experienced in allowing for the illumination which philosophical analysis can bring. If an analysis is informative, then on the Fregean view the two sentences must have different semantic contents. But in that case the analysed proposition has not been elucidated but replaced by another. Thus Frege's problem is to find room for the possibility of even solipsistic analysis (hence the idea of philosophy as reconstruction) whereas Wittgenstein's is to explain how the results of analysis can be communicable.

It begins to look as if the only way forward, if we are to find an adequate place for philosophical analysis, would be to deny that semantic content is a unitary notion having the same identity-conditions in all different regions of discourse. Perhaps we should rather say that when engaged in doing science (or in the pursuit of factual truth generally) the concept of semantic content in operation is sameness of truth-conditions, but that when we are doing philosophy it is sameness of cognitive content.

This would enable us to steer a middle course between the *TLP* doctrine of philosophy-as-nonsense and the Fregean view of analysis as reconstruction. It would be because understanding of factual discourse is a matter of mutual knowledge of truth-conditions that one could present, as an analysis of a given statement, a sentence which is its logical equivalent. For both statements would (in scientific contexts) say the very same thing. But it would only be because we do also share knowledge of cognitive content that we could expect the realization of that equivalence to throw the same light on the understanding of others as it did on our own. And there would be communication between us, when doing philosophy, only when the sentences in our idiolects do possess the very same cognitive content. So in this context the concept of semantic content would be the Fregean one.

The same suggestion might also enable us to find room for the idea of there being terms whose use is distinctly philosophical. Such terms would be assigned a sense (cognitive content) which is intersubjective, thus fitting them for use in drawing our attention to certain essential features of language or the world. Yet they would be incapable of contributing to the semantic content of sentences employed in fact-stating discourse.

7.2 FRAGMENTARY CONTENT

The idea that the notions of communication and of semantic content might fragment into a number of different concepts has a degree of independent plausibility. And it is not just philosophical discourse for which a Fregean concept of communication would be appropriate. Thus recall the example deployed in chapter 5, of the two people who attach different senses to the connective expressing disjunction. (You will remember that the one understands 'P v Q' in terms of its truth table, the other in terms of its equivalence with '–(–P & –Q)'.) We argued that there were no grounds for claiming that they would misunderstand one another in the use of the connective in factual discourse, and that conclusion can, on our present suggestion, be allowed to stand. But notice that there is one sphere in which they definitely will misunderstand one another, and that is when they come to do logic. In particular, there will be a failure of communication over the attempt to prove the equivalence of 'P v Q' with '–(–P & –Q)'. For the one who understands the former in terms of the latter will simply not be able to see what the other is about, remaining baffled as to why they should be going through such complicated manoeuvers in order to prove something which they themselves take to have the form 'A if and only if A'.

In general it would seem that communication in the fields of both logic and mathematics requires mutual knowledge of cognitive content.[1] For only so can the participants be confident that they will all be able to follow the course of a proof, and be able to see its point and significance. So within the area of assertoric discourse (as opposed for example to the imperative) there is apparently a distinction between that which purports to be empirically based, or fact-stating, and that which purports to be *a priori* – namely discourse in logic, mathematics and philosophy. In the former case the concept of semantic content (of what is asserted) would be the *TLP* one, given by sameness of truth-conditions. But in the latter case the concept of what is asserted would be Frege's, given by sameness of cognitive content.[2]

The conditions for communication in other areas of discourse (other 'language-games') might be different again.[3] For example, suppose we ask what knowledge on the part of different speakers is essential for mutual understanding of the content of a command. (Here as before we need to bear in mind the function which communication is intended to subserve.) Clearly they at least need sufficient knowledge to be confident that, as the recipient of an order, they would know when they had reached a position which would satisfy the person who had issued it. This gives us at least a requirement of mutual knowledge of material equivalence. But since the whole point of an order is not to describe the world but to change it, we shall plausibly need conditions for communication more stringent than this. For the very act of obeying an order involving one of two predicates which would otherwise be coextensive, may bring about a situation in which those predicates fail to be coextensive after all. In which case speakers need to be confident that actions taken in obedience to a command, given their interpretation of it, would also bring about a situation which constitutes obedience as the others interpret it.

This now requires more than mutual knowledge of mere material equivalence. For from the fact that 'F' and 'G' are presently coextensive, it does not follow that success in, say, bringing home an F would also involve success in bringing home a G. For example, suppose that two Martians respectively interpret the predicate 'F' to mean 'human being' and 'featherless biped', and that each sets about complying with the order to bring home to Mars one of the smallest adult Fs. But suppose that their presence on Earth while they conduct their search causes the existence of a mutant species of featherless chicken. Then they will return home with very different creatures, and for one of them the mission will have been a failure.

Although mutual knowledge of material equivalence is clearly insufficient for communication with imperatives, it is hard to believe that anything as strong as shared knowledge of logical equivalence is required. All that is really needed is mutual knowledge of what might be called 'causal equivalence'. If two speakers are to understand one another in the use of a command, it is both necessary and (so far as the content of the command goes) sufficient, that they know of each other's interpretations that precisely the same events would be sufficient to bring about a state of affairs which would constitute obedience. Thus suppose that A and B respectively interpret the predicate 'F' to mean 'living creature (in its natural state) with a heart' and 'living creature (in its natural state) with a kidney'. Then they are always going to satisfy one another when doing what they take to be obedience to orders involving the term 'F', no matter what steps they take in the course of executing the order as they understand it. We are then left with no motive for insisting that A and B misunderstand one another, despite the fact that they do not possess mutual knowledge of logical equivalence (let alone of cognitive content).

Besides the kind of assertoric discourse – the factual – which requires mutual knowledge of truth-conditions, we appear to have found one kind – the *a priori* – which requires something stronger, namely mutual knowledge of cognitive content. And we now seem to have found a kind of discourse – the imperative – which requires something weaker, namely mutual knowledge of causal equivalence. There would even appear to be areas in which the requirement is stronger than in the *a priori* cases. For the knowledge required to understand a joke is more than shared cognitive content. A shared background of beliefs will usually be required, either about the matter to which the joke relates, or about such things as the similarities in the sounds of the expressions of the language (puns). In the same way, a shared background of belief will generally be required if you are to follow a conversation (as opposed to understanding each utterance in the course of the conversation). For only so will you be able to see the bearing of what has just been said on what was said before. A similar point might be made in connection with the understanding of live metaphors (that is to say, metaphors whose significance has not been fixed by convention).

So our suggestion – that the way to avoid the philosophy-as-nonsense doctrine is by distinguishing between different notions of semantic content – can be further defended by being fitted into a much wider picture of fragmentation.

7.3 THE CASE FOR UNITY

Our question now must be whether Wittgenstein could have adopted our suggestion – thus saving himself from what is surely his strangest and most paradoxical doctrine – or whether, on the contrary, that doctrine is too deeply grounded in his other beliefs to be excised without altering their character entirely.

Recall the point made in chapter 5, that fact-stating discourse is of the very essence of language. This idea seems very definitely to be there in *TLP*, implicit in Wittgenstein's whole approach, with its almost exclusive concentration upon those uses of language which are directed at truth. It might be thought to follow from this claim about essence, that a theory of meaning would have to begin with an analysis of the content of statements, the results of that analysis then extending smoothly to account for the contents of all other forms of linguistic act. Then from Wittgenstein's perspective there could be no question of adopting an account of the semantic content of linguistic acts belonging to the category of 'elucidation' – if that is the one to which utterances in philosophy belong – different from that provided for the contents of scientific statements.

But in reality it is one thing to claim that factual discourse is of the essence of language, and quite another to claim that the semantic content of such discourse must determine the contents of all other forms of linguistic act. We could concede that there can be no language without a truth-orientated component, and yet deny that the other (non-essential) uses of language need have their conditions for successful communication determined by the semantic content of assertions. Wittgenstein could therefore embrace the thesis that factual discourse is logically prior to all other forms, while also accepting the thesis of the fragmentation of semantic content.

There is perhaps a way of bolstering the above argument for unity. For we might introduce, in addition, a principle of compositionality of content, which is in any case required to explain the creativity of language understanding. (See 3.318, 4.027, 4.03.) This principle states that the semantic content of any sentence of the language must be a function of the semantic contents of its component parts.

Thus suppose that content were different in the various different regions of linguistic intercourse. Should we not then have to explain the contents of the component expressions of the language many times over? In explaining the meaning of a word like 'dog', for example, should we not have to fix its imperative content separately from its fact-stating content? And should we not have to do something different again to fix its content appropriate for use in *a priori* discourse? It would seem that the proposed fragmentation of semantic content stands refuted by the manifest fact that we do not need to do any such thing. Thus consider someone who is already familiar with the significance of the indicative and imperative moods: having explained the word 'dog' to them in orders such as 'Fetch the dog', we would take it for granted that they will immediately understand statements such as 'Mary has a black dog'.[4]

Although this argument appears powerful, we can in fact meet the compositionality requirement without compromising the thesis of the fragmentation of content. We merely have to distinguish between what is required for the understanding of language as a whole, and what is required for understanding any given type of utterance within it. We can concede to the Fregean that in the former case, mutual knowledge of cognitive content is required. So explanations of the individual expressions of the language should be strict: they should require the trainee to associate the very same cognitive content with those expressions as the teacher does. (Understanding of jokes and metaphors we can leave to one side as a special case, since our understanding of them – that is to say, their point rather than their literal content – is not compositional.[5] I also continue to leave the understanding of proper names for discussion in chapter 12.) But we can still maintain that when it comes to understanding individual utterances, somewhat less may be required of the trainee than is required for the understanding of language as a whole.

The idea will come out most clearly in the different ways in which the training can go wrong. Suppose that someone has taken their training with a word in such a way that their use of it is logically equivalent to that of the rest of us, but that it differs in cognitive content. Then they cannot be said to understand that word *simpliciter*, since they are not in a position to understand all forms of utterance which contain it – they will be in no position to understand philosophical claims about how the word should best be analysed, for example. But this need not prevent us from granting them a complete understanding of imperatives and factual statements which contain the word. For according to the fragmentation thesis, communication in these areas requires something less than mutual knowledge of cognitive content. Similarly, if the training results in them taking the word in a way which is only causally equivalent to ours, then we shall deny them an understanding of statements containing it. But we could still grant them an understanding of its use in imperatives.

The argument from the principle of compositionality of content is thus less than convincing. What allows us to reconcile the need to explain the creativity of linguistic understanding with the thesis of fragmentation of content is the observation that the different notions of semantic content form an hierarchy of increasing strength: from causal equivalence, through logical equivalence, to sameness of cognitive content. Then since identity of cognitive content implies, but is not implied by, logical equivalence – which in turn implies but is not implied by causal equivalence – we can put someone in a position to understand all forms of linguistic utterance by means of a training which is, from the perspective represented by some of them, an over-kill. By introducing the component expressions of the language in such a way as to ensure that speakers have mutual knowledge of cognitive content we shall thereby have secured logical and causal equivalence – which is, from the point of view of factual and imperative discourse, more than is necessary.

Although two arguments against the fragmentation thesis have failed, there certainly seems to be at least one aspect of *TLP* which conflicts with it. For not only is Wittgenstein concerned with the essence of symbolic representation in general, he also takes for granted that any given concept in language will also have an essence. There is no suggestion, for example, that an account of a concept could take any other form than a statement of conditions necessary and sufficient for its correct application. And if all concepts have essences, then this will of course hold for the concept of understanding as well. Yet according to the fragmentation thesis the concepts of understanding and of semantic content admit of no unitary characterisation. Rather, the conditions under which someone may be said to understand a proposition will vary, depending upon whether it occurs in an imperative, or in a statement of fact, or in an elucidatory remark in philosophy.

It begins to seem that the philosophy-as-nonsense doctrine might be grounded in Wittgensteins's belief that all concepts have essences. For this, when combined with other plausible assumptions such as the central place of fact-stating discourse within language, would then yield the account of linguistic understanding outlined in chapter 5; and the nonsensicality of philosophy would follow, as night follows day. It might then appear that the only obvious way of rescuing Wittgenstein from his embarrasment would be by allowing for the sorts of concepts he himself was later to characterize as 'family resemblance concepts'.[6] On this view there are at least some concepts (like that of a game) which do not possess a unitary essence, but which rather consist in a whole collection of variously overlapping characteristics. Then by placing the concept of understanding (and the associated concept of semantic content) into this category, we could say that the understanding of a philosophical remark differs from, but is related to, the understanding of a scientific statement; which in turn differs from, but is related to, the understanding of an imperative. And something similar could also be said about semantic content.

7.4 PURPOSE-RELATIVE CONTENT

If the above suggestion were correct, then the philosophy-as-nonsense doctrine would indeed be deeply embedded within the structure of Wittgenstein's ideas. Certainly if family resemblance concepts were admitted to exist, then his whole programme for analysing the propositions of ordinary language into truth-functional compounds of a class of elementary propositions would have to be given up. For that programme surely commits him to the view that all concepts can be expressed in terms of necessary and sufficient conditions of application.

But in fact there is no difficulty about giving a univocal account of the concept of understanding, consistent with all the main elements of the fragmentation thesis. We need only include within the account a reference to the purposes which are operative in the context of the utterance, thus:

> ∀x∀y∀p (x understands an utterance of 'P' by y if and only if x knows sufficiently much about y's mode of employment of 'P' for the purposes in hand).

Then when the purposes in hand are those involved in the giving and receiving of commands, sufficient knowledge will be mutual knowledge of causal equivalence; when the purposes are those involved in the acquisition of rationally grounded belief, it will be mutual knowledge of truth-conditions; and when the purposes are elucidatory, or those appropriate to logic or mathematics, it will be mutual knowledge of cognitive-content.[7] Indeed the proposal also has the merit of extending to cover the very demanding requirements for the understanding of jokes and metaphors as well.

It is arguable that many of our ordinary concepts have purpose-relative conditions of application.[8] Thus 'flat' seems to mean something like 'is flatter than enough things of the sort in question for the purposes in hand'. For when a farmer is approached by the Territorial Army asking for a flat field in which to practise tank manoeuvres he may point to one and truly say 'That one is flat'; but when he is approached by the local Bowls Club looking for a new green, he may point to the very same field and say – again truly – 'That one is not flat'. Similarly, 'knows' seems to mean something like 'has a true belief which is sufficiently reliably grounded for the purposes in hand'.[9] For compare 'Mary knows that John will be at the party – he told her so' with 'Mary knows that John is the murderer – he told her so'. The first might in many contexts be acceptable whereas the second, in a court of law, would certainly not be. The standards required for a belief to count as knowledge are raised in proportion to the seriousness of the purposes which operate in the given context. Similar points can be made in connection with words such as 'empty', 'safe', 'dry' and many others. So the above suggestion regarding the proper analysis of understanding would render the concept by no means unique.

There is thus no real problem about combining the main elements from the fragmentation doctrine with a single univocal account of understanding and of semantic content.[10] The real fault underlying the philosophy-as-nonsense doctrine is not the fact that *TLP* fails to make room for family resemblance concepts (through perhaps this is a fault), but rather the assumption that all concepts have senses which are purpose-independent. It is this which prevents Wittgenstein from seeing that the knowledge required for understanding can vary from context to context. Yet its denial would surely be consistent with all of the other doctrines of *TLP*.

I conclude that the philosophy-as-nonsense doctrine can indeed be exercised without doing violence to the body of *TLP*.[11] We can retain the commitment to concept-essences and to the programme of analysis for ordinary language. And we can hold onto the insight that the conditions for understanding within the linguistically central area of fact-stating requires mutual knowledge of logical equivalence, this being a powerful criticism of Frege's thesis that the semantic content of an assertion is the thought expressed by it. (I continue to leave the understanding of proper names to one side.) Yet we can allow that within other contexts – and particularly while doing philosophy – the requirements for mutual understanding may be more exacting.

SUMMARY

Intersubjective philosophical activity can only be possible if the semantic content of sentences (and hence the conditions for mutual understanding) can be allowed to vary from context to context. Recognition of this possibility saves *TLP* from absurdity, while leaving all its main doctrines intact.

8

Gedanken

Our task in this chapter is to elucidate Wittgenstein's use of the term 'thought' (Gedanke). At issue once again will be the extent to which the semantics of *TLP* is broadly Fregean in character.

8.1 PRELIMINARIES

As we had occasion to note in chapter 2, it is an important aspect of Frege's doctrine of sense that senses should be objective: they should have an existence which is at least intersubjective, and relations between them (such as entailment and inconsistency) should obtain wholly mind-independently. Indeed he also maintains that the senses of whole sentences, which he calls 'thoughts' (Gedanken), exist necessarily, at all times in all possible worlds.[1] He seems to have regarded this as a crucial part of his rejection of psychologism. Although conceding that there must be a mental component in any act of thinking (namely 'grasping' a Gedanke), he believes that the thought itself is not in any way dependent upon mental acts or states. And contra, for example, the imagist theory, thinking does not consist in any kind of inner mental process, but rather in a mental relation between the thinker and an objectively existing Gedanke.

It is almost certainly true that Wittgenstein rejects any belief in the necessary existence of sense. While endorsing Frege's objectivism about logic and logical relationships, he thinks (rightly, as I shall argue in chapter 9) that he can avoid Frege's heavy ontological commitments. The easiest way to see this is to reflect on the fact that the notion of sense in *TLP*, on the interpretation I have been defending, is essentially tied to the significant use of signs. (Recall that symbols are signs together with their mode of projection. There is no suggestion that the mode of projection might exist independently of the sign.) So unless he believes that signs themselves have necessary existence, he cannot believe that senses do. Yet throughout *TLP* he uses the language of construction with respect to new notations, rather than that of 'apprehending' or 'selecting' (see for example 5.475, 5.556).

Aside from the above, Wittgenstein's notion of Gedanke is much disputed. In particular, many interpret him as being opposed even to the possible intersubjectivity of Gedanken.[2] On this view, Tractarian thoughts are the link between sentences and states of affairs, those sentences only coming to represent reality via private acts of thinking. So what gives words their life, or significance, is not anything about their (potentially) public use, but rather the private mental states and acts of those who use them.

If this interpretation could be substantiated, then so far from broadly endorsing aspects of Frege's sense/reference distinction, Wittgenstein would be consigning the theory of sense to the province of psychology in a much more radical way than we have hitherto considered. For on the reading of *TLP* defended in earlier chapters, the modes of projection of signs are inessential to logic only in the sense that mutual knowledge of them is not required for factual communication. But they are at least potentially intersubjective, perhaps consisting in aspects of their public use. (And as we saw in the last chapter, the possibility of philosophy may require that they be actually so.) On the interpretation above, on the other hand, our modes of projection of signs are inessential to logic in consisting wholly of facts about the individual thinker's private psychology.

I shall be arguing for a way of taking Tractarian Gedanken which places them somewhere between a Fregean necessary existent and the above out-and-out of psychologism.[3] I shall try to show that Gedanken are abstract but temporal (supervenient) entities, which are realized in any significant arrangement of signs having truth-conditions (Sinn). On this view spoken or written signs are not supposed to get their life from internal acts of thinking. Rather, both public sentences and private thoughts stand on the same level, expressing Gedanken in virtue of consisting of signs which are used in such a way as to represent a Sinn.[4]

8.2 TEXTUAL EVIDENCE OUTSIDE *TLP*

Many have sought firm confirmation of the psychological interpretation sketched above, in Wittgenstein's 1919 letter to Russell, where he says that a Gedanke consists of psychical constituents analogous to words, which it would be the business of psychology to investigate.[5] Yet what is overlooked by these commentators is that it may have been quite clear from the way in which Russell framed his questions that he was using 'Gedanke' in the sense of 'thought-in-the-mind' (which is, after all, normal German usage), and that Wittgenstein may simply have responded in kind. Indeed there is some reason to think that this is the case.

Although Russell's original letter has not been preserved, Wittgenstein fortunately quotes from it in giving his replies. Russell's questions had apparently been (a) 'But a Gedanke is a fact: what are its constituents and components, and what is their relation to those of the pictured fact?', and (b) 'Does a Gedanke consist of words?'. It is clear, firstly, that Russell was not asking for an elucidation of any remark in *TLP*, since it is nowhere said that a Gedanke is a fact. (It is propositional signs – Satzzeichen – which are facts; see 3.14.) Rather, taking a particular use for granted, he seems to have been asking a substantive question about what Wittgenstein believes thinking to consist in. Moreover the terms in which Russell framed his questions – in such a way as to expect a unitary answer – would not even make sense unless he were thinking of a Gedanke as being a thought-in-the-mind. For of course if 'Gedanke' can cover all different forms of representation, in whatever medium (as I shall argue), then it would obviously be silly to ask what the constituents of a Gedanke are; and even sillier to ask whether it always consists of words.

It would thus be unwise to take Wittgenstein's remarks in his letter to Russell to be our guide in interpreting the *TLP* use of 'Gedanke'. Since Russell is clearly asking about thoughts-in-the-mind, Wittgenstein's reply relates not to the way in which he uses 'Gedanke' in the text, but rather to what he takes thoughts-in-the-mind to consist of. Nor would it be at all surprising that he should have failed to put Russell right on this crucial piece of *TLP* terminology. For the whole tone of the letter is one of exasperation and despair at Russell's lack of comprehension.

Moreover, Wittgenstein's statement in the letter that a

Gedanke consists of psychical constituents which have the same sort of relation to reality as words strongly suggests that he did not regard thoughts-in-the-mind as providing the link between language and reality. Had he believed this, he could hardly have used the phrase 'having the *same sort* of relation to reality'. This suggests, on the contrary, that he saw sentences and thoughts-in-the-mind as being very much on a par: each making use of ordered structures of signs to represent reality. And this is precisely the view which I believe may be discerned in *TLP* itself, as we shall see shortly.

The only other non-Tractarian evidence relevant to our topic is an isolated remark at *NB* 82, where Wittgenstein writes as follows:

> Now it is becoming clear why I thought that thinking and language were the same. For thinking is a kind of language. For a thought too is, of course, a logical picture of a proposition, and therefore it is just a kind of proposition.

This is initially puzzling. For how can a thought both picture a proposition and *be* a proposition? But the puzzle dissolves if we suppose that the first occurence of 'proposition' is Russell's use (where a proposition consists of the entities which the judgement concerns) whereas the second is his own, according to which a proposition is a significant sentence.[6] Then what remains is the claim that both private thoughts and public statements are on a par, each consisting of logical pictures of states of affairs. This gives some support to my intermediate reading of *TLP*, since there is no suggestion here that sentences come to depict via their association with private thoughts.

8.3 THE EVIDENCE OF *TLP*

There are only two remarks in *TLP* itself which appear to speak in favour of the psychological interpretation. One is 3.11, which says (in the Pears and McGuinness translation) that the method of projection for a propositional sign is to think of the Sinn of the proposition. This seems to be telling us *how* to project a sentence onto the world, telling us what such a projection would consist in. The other is 3.5 where Wittgenstein says (again in the Pears and McGuinness translation) that a propositional sign, applied and thought out, is a thought. This seems to suggest that it is the 'thinking out' – the mental projection – of a sentence which gives it its content.

Note however that in the original German version of 3.11 the definite article is used on both sides of the 'ist'. Note also that the word translated by Pears and McGuinness as 'to think' is in reality a noun ('Das Denken'). Literally translated, as Ogden does, 3.11 says that *the* method of projection of a propositional sign is *the* thought of the Sinn of the proposition.[7] Now elsewhere in their translation of *TLP* Pears and McGuinness render such uses of the definite article by the indefinite, and rightly so. For example 4, which says literally that *the* thought is *the* proposition with Sinn, they render as: *a* thought is *a* proposition with Sinn. One wonders why they departed from this practice at 3.11. Had they not done so, 3.11 would say: a method of projection for a propositional sign is a thought of the Sinn (truth-condition) of the proposition. This has quite a different flavour to it, suggesting that – rather than telling us how to project a sentence onto the world – we are being informed of a connection between the concept of such a projection and the concept of a mode of thinking of a truth-condition.

Moreover throughout *TLP*, whenever a simple is-statement occurs with the word 'ist' flanked by concept expressions governed by the definite article, I believe Wittgenstein intends to be making a statement with a form analogous to a statement of identity: a statement, that is, of the necessary co-extension of two concepts. (And wherever the word 'ist' is flanked by concept expressions governed by the definite article on the left, and by the indefinite article on the right, he intends that there be an implication from left to right but not vice versa).[8] If we adopt such a reading of 3.11 then we get the following: necessarily, something is a method of projection of a propositional sign if and only if it is a thought of the Sinn (truth-condition) of that sign. This does not even begin to lend itself to the psychological interpretation. On the contrary, it looks as if Wittgenstein is saying something like the following: each mode of projecting a sentence onto reality is, necesarily, a mode of thinking about the possible situations which constitute the truth-condition of that sentence, and vice versa. And the idea of a 'mode of thinking' could then be construed in a way which is at least very similar to a Fregean sense. For one can say that, for Frege, the sense of an expression is a mode of thinking (considered as abstract) about its referent.[9]

Confirmation of this interpretation of 3.11 may be found in

PTLP. In the passages which correspond most closely to 3.11, Wittgenstein writes as follows (translating literally):

PTLP 3.12 The method of projection [of a propositional sign] is the manner of applying the propositional sign.
PTLP 3.13 The application of a propositional sign is the thought (das Denken) of its truth-condition (Sinn).[10]

It would surely be very strange indeed to describe as an 'application' of a propositional sign an act of giving it life through associating it with a thought-in-the-mind (the psychological interpretation). Wittgenstein seems rather to be emphasizing that it is the manner of our use of signs which makes them connect with reality, as opposed to the connection consisting either in an association with a thought-in-the-mind, or in an association with a necessarily existing Gedanke. On my interpretation, he would be insisting that the sense of a sentence (its mode of projection, the mode of thinking which it expresses) consists in the conventionally determined use of its component parts (together with the conventionally determined significance of their arrangement).

As for 3.5, note that no conjunction occurs in the original German; neither is 'thought out' a literal translation of 'gedachte'. The literal translation is the one given by Ogden: The applied, thought, propositional sign is the thought. This suggests that 'applied' and 'thought' are *alternative* ways of characterizing that which makes the connection between a sentence and reality, which is in line with our reading of *PTLP* 3.12 above. The point being, that it is the (conventionally determined) use of a sentence which makes the connection with reality, and which constitutes it as expressing a mode of thinking of reality (i.e. as expressing a sense).

Now consider 3, which says, literally, that the logical picture of facts is the thought – that is, that the concept of a thought is necessarily coextensive with the concept of a logical picture of facts. Here the notion of a Gedanke appears to be introduced as a generic concept to cover all picturing of facts, whether external (spoken or written sentences, pictures, maps, etc.) or internal (thinking, imagining, etc.). Consider also 4, which says, again literally, that the thought is the proposition with Sinn. This equates the concept of a Gedanke with the concept of a proposition with a directed truth-condition. Neither of these remarks lends any support to the psychological interpretation.

Further confirmation of my intermediate interpretation may be found at 5.542. There, in the context of criticizing Russell's theory of judgement, Wittgenstein says that both 'A thinks P' and 'A says P' have the form '"P" says P'. He must therefore believe that both private acts of thinking and public sayings are similarly related to their truth-conditions (as opposed to the one being so related via the other). I take the remark to mean that neither an act of thinking nor a public saying consists in a relation between a subject (soul) and a state of affairs. Rather, both consist in ordered arrays of signs, which are used in such a way as to represent that state of affairs.

8.4 THOUGHTS AND PROPOSITIONS

One awkwardness about my reading of the *TLP* use of 'Gedanke' is that it appears to entail that thoughts-in-the-mind are *not* Gedanken. For notice that 4 tells us that something is a Gedanke if, and only if, it is a proposition with Sinn. And yet 3.1 entails that it is only perceptible signs which, together with a method of projection, can constitute a proposition. Then unless thoughts-in-the-mind are somehow perceptible, it will follow that they are not Gedanken.

However this absurdity can easily be avoided if there is sufficient reason to discover an ambiguity in the *TLP* use of 'proposition'(Satz), between a sense in which it means 'perceptible sentence plus its method of projection', and one in which it means 'complete sign – whether perceptible or imperceptible – plus its method of projection'. And indeed, just such reason is provided by 3.3, where we are told that only propositions have Sinn. For if we interpret 'proposition' here in the sense of 3.1, this tells us that only perceptible propositional signs have Sinn; thus entailing that no thought-in-the-mind could have Sinn, which would be absurd.

In general Wittgenstein uses 'proposition' in the wider sense, to cover both perceptible and imperceptible (i.e. mental) propositional signs. The narrower use, to cover the perceptible case only, is restricted to the 3.1s. And here Wittgenstein's purpose is to introduce for the first time the distinction between 'proposition' and 'propositional sign'. This can be done most easily in connection with perceptible propositions: the propositional sign being that which is immediately perceptible, the proposition itself being this together with what is not immediately perceptible, namely the use of that sign to represent reality.[11] We might then be expected to infer that there is some similar distinction to be drawn in connection with non-perceptible propositions, namely thoughts-in-the-mind.

If 'Gedanke', too, is used widely, to cover both perceptible and imperceptible propositions (as 3 and 4 suggest), then are the *TLP* notions of a thought and of a proposition one and the same? There can be no simple answer to this question, because of the possible ambiguity in the use of 'proposition' noted in chapter 4. We saw that on most of its occurrences, 'proposition' is used to mean a propositional sign together with its sense (cognitive content). On this usage propositions are symbols (signs together with their mode of projection) and there can be many different propositions with the very same truth-conditions; tautologies and contradictions counting as propositions. Understood in this way, a Gedanke is a kind of proposition, but there are propositions which are not Gedanken. For Wittgenstein is consistent in claiming that only propositions with Sinn – which mark a division within the set of all possible worlds – count as Gedanken. Thus 3.02 tells us that a Gedanke contains the possibility of the situation it represents; 4 says that a Gedanke is a proposition with Sinn; and at 6.21 we are told that a proposition of mathematics does not express a Gedanke.

However, we also noted that at a number of points in the 5s Wittgenstein uses 'proposition' in such a way that all sentences with the same truth-conditions are the same proposition, and in such a way that tautologies and contradictions, which lack Sinn, are not propositions at all. So in one respect this use of 'proposition' is closely linked to the use of 'Gedanke', since all and only sentences with truth-conditions are propositions, and are Gedanken. But in another respect it is very different, since the identity-conditions are different. For the notion of a Gedanke, unlike this notion of a proposition, belongs with the idea of a mode of determination of Sinn, rather than being closely tied to the identity of the Sinn itself. Thus on my reading there may be many different modes of thought (many different Gedanken) of one and the same Sinn (i.e. which express one and the same proposition, on this use of 'proposition').

8.5 ARE THOUGHTS ESSENTIALLY ASSERTORIC?

In discussing the *TLP* notion of a Gedanke we have come across a number of passages which apparently suggest that it is the *use* of a propositional sign which constitutes it as expressing the proposition or thought which it does. But does Wittgenstein go beyond this in believing propositions to be essentially assertoric? Does he, as some have maintained, believe that every proposition, and every Gedanke, is an act of thinking (judging) that such-and-such is the case?[12]

This interpretation is almost certainly wrong. Note to begin with that the frequent occurrences of such phrases as 'the proposition says' and 'the proposition states' (e.g. at 4.022 and 4.03) do nothing to show the essential assertiveness of the proposition. For of course a language teacher may write sentences on the blackboard and ask the class, 'What does this sentence say/state?', in circumstances which make it perfectly clear that, in another sense, nothing at all has been said (asserted). Nor does Wittgenstein's criticism of Frege's judgement-stroke at 4.442, as being logically quite meaningless (note: bedeutungslos), rest on a belief in the essential assertiveness of proposition. For what he clearly conceives of himself as rejecting is the idea that a judgement-stroke could contribute towards the semantic content of a proposition.[13] And it is entirely compatible with this that propositions may exist unjudged.

The main argument against the proposed interpretation is that Wittgenstein apparently believes propositions to have an existence which is prior to, and independent of, their being judged. Thus at 4.064 it is insisted that every proposition must already have a determinate Sinn, prior to the act of judging. And it is hard to see how this could be so unless the proposition already exists prior to being judged. That is to say: unless there already exists a propositional sign expressing that thought or proposition. Furthermore, Wittgenstein appears quite ready to believe in the existence of infinitely many propositions (4.2211, 5.43), which would be unintelligible if propositions were themselves acts of thinking or judging.

We saw at the outset of this chapter that Wittgenstein rejects the Fregean doctrine that thoughts (Gedanken) have necessary existence. Yet now, on the other hand, he does seem prepared to allow that they exist independently of being entertained or judged by a thinker. So his position must be something like the following: it is the conventionally determined use, or application, of signs which determines in advance what thought (proposition with Sinn) is expressed by any given sentence, and which thus determines its Sinn in advance. We can therefore talk of thoughts as existing in advance of being entertained. But they do not exist necessarily, since they only exist in so far as, and so long as, there are signs with an appropriately determined conventional use. We shall explore the strength of this position in the chapter which follows.

SUMMARY

A Gedanke, in the terminology of *TLP*, is any proposition (sentence together with its mode of signifying) which has Sinn. Both spoken sentences and thoughts-in-the-mind are equally Gedanken, provided that they have Sinn. But spoken sentences do not have truth-conditions in virtue of their association with a thought-in-the-mind. On the contrary, both are related to reality in the same kind of way, consisting of significant arrangements of signs with a conventionally determined use. But they do exist independently of, and prior to, being entertained by a thinking subject.

9

The Existence of Thoughts

This is the first of two chapters to employ the principle of Charity in defence of our intermediate interpretation of *TLP*, argued for on textual grounds in chapter 8. Here I shall defend Wittgenstein against the first of the twin extremes of necessary existence for thoughts, on the one hand, and psychologism about language on the other hand.

9.1 MIND-DEPENDENT THOUGHTS

In the last chapter we found Wittgenstein to be committed to the existence of thoughts as abstract types which are independent of their tokens being entertained in judgement. And since, for him, a thought is a sentence together with its mode of projection, we should also expect a commitment to the existence of abstract sign-types as well. (And indeed, 5.535 allows that there may be infinitely many names – 3.203 making clear, if further argument is needed, that in *TLP* terminology names are types and not tokens.) So both thoughts and signs have an existence as abstract types, their existence being independent of whether tokens of them are ever entertained or constructed.

Wittgenstein is committed, on the other hand, to denying Frege's doctrine that thoughts exist necessarily. Nor is there any trace of idea that thinking consists in the subject coming into some relation to (i.e. 'grasping') one of these abstract entities. On the contrary, the *TLP* doctrine is that all thinking consists in the employment of logical pictures: structured arrays of sign-tokens (whether linguistic, in speech or writing; or psychical, in private acts of thinking) which have a conventionally determined application. For Wittgenstein, acts of thinking *exemplify* thought-types, rather than consisting in the thinker standing in some *relation to* a thought-type.

Thinking is a matter of entertaining a propositional sign-token which is itself a projection of some possible state of affairs in virtue of the conventions governing the use of its component parts and their mode of combination.

Wittgenstein's position is thus apparently a species of conventionalism: the idea is that we fix rules for the primitive signs and for the significance of their modes of combination, and that the senses of all possible propositional signs of the language will thereby have been determined. (On the role of convention, see 3.315, 3.342, 4.002 and 4.0141.) Then since the relationship between the initial conventions and their consequences is thought of as being wholly objective (those conventions 'reaching ahead of us', as it were, to determine the significance of all possible combinations of signs),[1] there can be no real objection to thinking of all thought-types as existing in advance of their tokens being used by us. Yet those thought-types depend for their existence upon the initial conventions. If we had never existed, then those thoughts would never have existed either. Moreover, prior to the initial conventions being fixed, and prior to the existence of the human race, thoughts (Gedanken) did not yet exist.[2]

An analogy may help to make the position sketched here seem plausible. Consider the existence of sentence-types, and their relation to sentence-tokens. Having fixed the rules of sentence-formation for a particular language, and thinking of those rules as having determinate consequences for cases so far unconsidered, it would be entirely natural for us to think of all the possible sentences of that language as already existing, in many cases independently of tokens of them ever being employed. And indeed, this is just what we say: there are many sentences of English which no one ever has, or ever will, express. Yet we should not be tempted to think of those sentences as existing independently of the syntactic rules which govern the language. No one should think that the sentence-type exemplified by 'It is raining' existed in the year 20 million BC, or even in 200 AD. For at those times there was no such language as English. (Human languages have histories: they begin and develop and end.) Nor (probably) would that sentence ever have existed if the Normans had not invaded England, or had failed in their attempts to conquer her. Thus sentence-types are naturally thought of as abstract but mind-dependent entities, in precisely the way in which thought-types are.

Of course the analogy with sentences cannot by itself establish the mind-dependence of thoughts. For one thing, there are those who maintain that sentences themselves have necessary existence.[3] For another, it can be pointed out that one and the same thought can be expressed in many different languages. Then since thought-types have an existence which is independent of the existence of any particular language, the question arises whether they have an existence which is independent of all. But most importantly, the analogy proceeds on the assumption that thoughts are essentially linguistic. This is a large issue, which we shall consider briefly now, and return to again in the next chapter.

9.2 COULD FREGE BE RIGHT?

One point at issue is whether or not propositions have an existence which is independent of the means for their expression. Frege is apparently committed to saying that they do, since he holds Gedanken to exist necessarily (thus existing at all times in all possible worlds), whereas sentences are (presumably) temporal entities.[4] For Wittgenstein on the other hand propositions have no independent existence, since Gedanken are propositional signs in their projective relation to possible states of affairs (3.11, 3.12, 4). They thus cannot exist if no signs exist.

Frege's position gives rise to a certain tension within his philosophy, between the central place which is given to language and the study of language on the one hand, and the thesis that thoughts exist independently of language on the other.[5] Most of his philosophical effort is directed towards studying the functioning of different forms of linguistic expression, and to the construction of a logical language (Begriffsschrift) which would have those forms reflected on its surface. But if thoughts have an existence which is language-independent, whence this concentration of effort? Why can we not go straight for the nature of thought, and bypass investigation of language altogether? Frege has only two possible lines of reply. He can either concede that the study of language is not truly necessary to his enterprise, but a mere heuristic device. Or he can claim that although thoughts exist independently of language, the grasping relation is essentially linguistic, there being no other conceivable mode of access to them. Either option would stand in need of the sort of support which Frege himself never provides.

In Wittgenstein's view, on the other hand, there is no tension. If all thoughts consist of significant arrangements of signs, then all philosophy can become the philosophy of language (or at least all philosophy whose primary concern is thought; we perhaps should not accept Wittgenstein's prejudice that this is the whole of philosophy). Or better (since the term 'language' is generally used to designate a public phenomenon): all philosophy can become the philosophy of symbolism.

But of course the above argument is only *ad hominem* against Frege. It will fail to convince anyone who does not already believe that the study of language should be fundamental. And we should in any case need to explore the ideas that sentences themselves might exist necessarily, and that our mode of access to Gedanken might be necessarily linguistic, before we could take ourselves to have refuted Frege's position. It will prove more fruitful to ask whether there is anything which can be said directly against the view that thinking consists in a thinker coming to stand in a relation (grasping) to an abstract and necessarily existing entity (a thought).

The first point to note is that our acts of thinking have different causal (or at least explanatory) roles depending upon their cognitive content. It may be because I entertain the thought [that P] rather than the thought [that Q] that I reply in the negative when asked whether I am thinking that Q, even though P and Q are logically equivalent.[6] So on Frege's theory it will be the fact that I stand in R (the grasping relation) to [that P] rather than to [that Q] which differentially explains my behaviour. Now this is already hard to believe. It requires some sort of causal connection between a realm of necessarily existing abstract thoughts and human minds or brains. These connections must be of a kind hitherto unknown to science, and would force us to give up any belief in the ubiquity of physical causation. But Frege might reply that, so far, the difficulty is no worse than that faced by Cartesian Dualism, which many have, after all, brought themselves to believe in.

Suppose we now put to Frege the question whether it will always be in virtue of some non-relational psychological (or perhaps neurophysiological) facts that I stand in R to one thought rather than to another. And suppose, first, that he answers in the affirmative, claiming that whenever I stand in R to [that P] rather than to [that Q], there will be some mental event or state M in virtue of which it is true of me that I stand in R to [that P]. It can then be said that, had M not occurred, I should not at that time have grasped the thought [that P]. But now the problem for Frege is to explain why it is not these non-relational facts which are truly explanatory of my behaviour. If it is in virtue of M that I grasp [that P], then why is not M alone sufficient to explain my subsequent negative answer to the question whether I had been thinking that Q? How is Frege to prevent thoughts and grasp of thoughts from becoming explanatorily redundant?

Clearly it is not an option for him to appeal to the fact of the existence of [that P] to make the point, saying that if the thought [that P] had not existed, then M would not have resulted in the behaviour which it did. For since thoughts are supposed to have necessary existence, the counter-factual here is unintelligible. His only option is to conceive of M as being a sort of perceptual probe, sending out feelers towards [that P] rather than [that Q], and then having its subsequent causal powers determined by whatever happens at the 'surface' of [that P]. Put more prosaically, the claim would be that it is in virtue of M that I stand in R to [that P] rather than any other thought, and that there are certain non-essential properties of [that P] which exert a causal influence upon M, helping to determine its effects upon my subsequent behaviour. This at least gives us an intelligible counter-factual, despite the necessary existence of Gedanken, since it supposes that the causally efficacious properties of thoughts are non-necessary.

It is hard to know what to make of the idea that a necessarily existing abstract entity might nevertheless have contingent – perhaps changing – non-relational properties. But the real problem with the perceptual model of thinking is that it is no longer the content of the thought [that P] which explains, but some non-necessary attribute of it. So once again we get the conclusion that thoughts themselves have no real explanatory role. This must surely be unacceptable, since the whole point of introducing the idea of cognitive content was to explain fine differences in people's intentional behaviour.

It appears then that Frege must reply in the negative to our question whether the grasping relation must obtain in virtue of non-relational psychological facts, claiming rather that it is a *bare* relation. He might draw an analogy with spatial relations, which do not obtain in virtue of any non-relational facts about their subjects. And instead of the perceptual model, he might conceive of thinking by analogy with one body moving into the gravitational field of another. Just as it is the fact that an asteroid comes into close spatial proximity with the Earth, together with the constant gravitational field of the latter, which explains its subsequent motion, so it is the bare fact that I stand in R to [that P] rather than to any other thought, which explains my later behaviour.

This model does have the advantage of delivering a smooth account of how a necessarily existing thing might have a causal role. For what is contingent, on this account, is which Gedanke I grasp in thinking. And it can be true that had I not stood in R to [that P] just then, I should have answered your question differently. What remains constant is, as it were, the causal fields associated with these necessarily existing thoughts; what changes are the relations in which we stand to them.

Yet the gravitational model is bought at considerable cost. In particular it follows that two subjects (or one subject on two occasions) can be exactly similar in their non-relational psychological states and yet be entertaining distinct thoughts, no matter what sort of thought is in question.[7] Just as two asteroids can be qualitatively identical, and yet one be in the gravitational field of the Earth and one in the gravitational field of Mars, so every event in my mind can be exactly similar to yours, and yet I grasp the thought [that P] whereas you grasp the thought [that Q]. In consequence, the contents of our thoughts are removed from our direct (non-inferential) epistemic access. The only way for me to know of myself what I am thinking would be by seeing its effects on my behaviour.

Although it would be too strong to claim that the above amounts to a decisive refutation of Frege, it does mean that we ought not to believe in the necessary existence of thoughts if we can possibly avoid doing so.[8] In the sections which follow we shall consider the various possible arguments in support of Frege's position, showing that none is successful.[9]

9.3 THE ARGUMENT FROM COMMUNICATION

The argument which is closest to the surface of Frege's writings is also in fact the weakest.[10] It is that since (a) communication is possible only if thoughts are at least potentially intersubjective, whereas (b) all mental states and events are private to the individual who has them, thoughts must have an existence which is independent of such states.

In fact there are two different arguments here, depending upon whether 'private' is taken in an epistemic sense, or rather in the sense of 'inalienable'. Consider the former possibility first. Then the second premiss will claim that no one can have knowledge of the mental states of anyone besides themselves. This is false. But let that pass, for even given its truth the conclusion is not warranted.[11] For if it is knowledge of thoughts which is at issue, then the possibility of communication will require me to know what thoughts others are currently grasping. And even if thoughts themselves are genuinely objective, the grasping relation is no more open to outside observation than are the thinker's mental states. So even the thesis of mind-independence of thoughts leaves Frege no better placed to explain the possibility of communciation, so long as he believes in the epistemic privacy of the mental.

Consider then the other possible interpretation: that a person's mental states are claimed to be private in the sense that no one else can actually possess them. This is true, but still the conclusion does not follow. For the two premises are equally consistent with what I am taking to be the *TLP* view. If thoughts exist as abstract types, but supervening on the rules and conventions of some symbolic system, then thoughts will be mind-dependent (supposing that the rules and conventions are). Nevertheless it might still be true that communciation requires speakers to be grasping thoughts of the very same abstract type, and this will be so if each employs a sentence-token with the same mode of projection onto reality. Yet it will remain impossible that either of them should possess the very same thought-token entertained by the other. So the argument is invalid, on either interpretation of it.

9.4 OMNITEMPORAL AND OBJECTIVE TRUTH

Sometimes Frege argues that since (a) truth is a property of thoughts (the idea of truth being the idea of a correct representation of reality), and since (b) truth is omnitemporal (if a non-indexical thought is true at one time then it is true at all), it must follow that thoughts exist omnitemporally.[12] This argument is valid, but I can see nothing to force us to accept the second premiss. For the most that we actually have use for, in assessing predictions and historical claims, is the weaker hypothetical principle that if a thought is true, then anyone giving expression to it at any time in the past or future would give expression to a true thought.[13] This commits us, at most, to the existence of thoughts at times when there exist intelligent agents to express them.

We can grant Frege that if the thought [that sabre-tooth tigers are to be found in England in 20 million BC] were true in 40 million BC, as the omnitemporality thesis implies, then that thought would (probably) have to exist independently of the human mind. For I doubt whether any intelligent agents existed in 40 million – or indeed 20 million – BC. But we lose nothing by denying the antecedent of this conditional. In fact it consists of two independent claims: firstly, that the thought in question existed in the year 40 million BC; which we have no reason to accept in the absence of a proof of the mind-independence of thoughts. And secondly, that it is (now) a true thought that sabre-tooth tigers are to be found in England in the year 20 million BC; which merely requires that a presently existing thought can express a truth about the remote past.[14]

Frege sometimes seems to suggest that there can be objective truths about the remote past only if the thoughts with which we express those truths themselves existed at those times in the past.[15] But this is wholly unconvincing. You might just as well say that there can only be objective truths about remote regions of space if our thoughts exist at the places which they concern. For in both sorts of case we are incapable of direct verification.[16] (This would give us a thesis of the omnispatial nature of thoughts, as well as their omnitemporality.) The most plausible position is surely what I take to be the *TLP* one: that we use our presently existing thoughts to represent the remote past or remote regions of space, those thoughts being projected out to the world to determine a truth-value in a manner which is independent of our ability to verify them.[17]

9.5 THE ARGUMENT FROM ANALYTICITY

The final argument which can be discerned in Frege's writings runs as follows:

(a) There are truths which are necessary: which are true about all times in all possible worlds.
(b) Such truths are analytic, or conceptual, and are true purely in virtue of the senses of the words involved.
(c) That in virtue of which a proposition is true, must exist at any time, and in any circumstances, about which it expresses a truth.
So: Senses (and hence thoughts) must exist at all times in all possible worlds.[18]

Wittgenstein would of course have accepted both of the first two premises. Then since the argument is valid, almost the whole burden of proof falls upon premiss (c).

However, if premiss (c) is to be acceptable, then we have to regard the thought [that it is impossible for any object to be both red all over and green all over throughout the year 20 million BC] as being true in virtue of the fact that the senses of the predicates 'is red all over' and 'is green all over' *were* incompatible in the year in question (just as a thought about Jesus in 20 AD is true in virtue of the properties Jesus possessed in that year). But in fact we could equally well regard it as being true in virtue of the fact that the predicates 'is red all over throughout 20 million BC' and 'is green all over throughout 20 million BC' *are now* incompatible. We can thus reject premiss (c), in its complete generality, without having to give up either of the others. We can claim that it is relations between merely presently existing senses which constrain our talk about other times and worlds.

If Frege's argument is to be successful, then when we say that analytic propositions express truths about all times and all possible worlds, we should have to be construed as saying something which will be true (if at all) in virtue of relations which obtain between senses at all times in all possible worlds. So the necessity of 'No object is both red all over and green all over' would have to derive from a truth of something like the following form:

> For all times t, and all possible worlds w, the senses of 'is red all over' and 'is green all over' are mutually incompatible at t in w.

This would certainly give us the necessary existence of senses. But in fact we could equally well be construed as saying something which will be true in virtue of relations between merely presently existing senses, where those relations are such that they remain invariable so long as they occur in thoughts relating to the same times in the same possible worlds. Thus the necessity of 'No object is both red all over and green all over' could just as well derive from a truth of this sort:

> For all modes of thought of a time, α, and all modes of thought of a possible world, β, the senses of 'is red all over at α in β' and 'is green all over at α in β' are mutually incompatible.

Here by quantifying over modes of thought about times and worlds (that is, entities belonging to the realm of sense) we have avoided commitment to anything other than the present existence of senses.

One can thus believe, as both Frege and Wittgenstein did, that there is a class of objective analytic truths: believing that all internal relations between senses were determined, independently of us, as soon as the conventions constituting the senses of our expressions were fixed; believing, indeed, that these relations are genuine objects of discovery. And one can believe that analytic truths are necessary; constraining our talk about remote times and counter-factual worlds just as much as they constrain our talk about the present. And yet one can, consistently with both beliefs, believe that senses depend for their existence upon our existence: only coming to exist when we first begin to use a symbolic system in which those senses may be expressed.

SUMMARY

There are no good reasons in favour of Frege's belief in the necessary existence of Gedanken, and some powerful arguments against it. So it is more plausible to believe, as Wittgenstein does, that thoughts (senses) are mind-dependent entities, supervening upon the rules and conventions which govern the languages of intelligent agents.

10

Thinking and Language-using

In this chapter we continue to explore the strength of the *TLP* theory of thinking, defending it against the second of the twin extremes between which we placed Wittgenstein's position in chapter 8; namely: out-and-out psychologism.

10.1 PRELIMINARIES

The *TLP* view is that both private thinking and public speaking are on a par, each consisting of representations of possible states of affairs by means of structured arrangements of sign-tokens, where both private and public signs are projected onto the world in essentially similar ways. There are then two sides to the psychologism with which such a view contrasts, which we shall proceed to criticize in turn. On the one hand there is what might be called 'The Code-breaking Conception' of speech. This holds that our public signs derive their significance from the private acts of meaning with which they are associated, understanding the public utterances of other people being a matter of decoding them correctly into private thinkings of one's own. And on the other hand there are non-linguistic theories of thinking, which hold, in their various ways, that it is possible to characterize private thinkings and their contents without employing notions which presuppose language or grasp of a language.

It is important to be clear at the outset that our concern is only with thought in the narrow sense, in which thinkings are conscious acts in which people engage on specific occasions. This is not to be confused with the wide sense in which any propositional attitude whatever may be described as a thought.[1] This wide sense covers not only events such as wondering, judging and entertaining a supposition, but also standing states such as belief, desire and intention. It is generally agreed that these latter states may be possessed (though perhaps only in attenuated form) by non-linguistic creatures such as dogs and cats. So there is no real prospect of establishing that all thought (in the wide sense) involves structures similar to those of natural language. It may well be that there are notions of *conscious* belief and *conscious* desire which are essentially linguistic, if thinking in the narrow sense is linguistic (where a conscious belief is a belief apt to give rise to a conscious thinking with the same content); but this is something which can only be established, if at all, having first focused on thinking in the narrow sense. Indeed it is not a topic which we shall need to pursue further in the present work.[2]

As I shall understand it, thinkings are conscious mental events. But not all conscious mental events are thinkings. For example, a feeling of pain is not, the act of forming a mental image is not, and nor is the onset of a belief in perception. The first two examples are not thinkings because they lack propositional content: thinkings are mental events which can always be reported in the form 'At that moment I entertained the thought [that P]'. And the first and the third examples are not thinkings because they have a substantial sensory component. Thinkings and imaginings differ from pains and perceivings in lacking the distinctive phenomenological aspects of the latter – though whether this is a mere matter of degree, as Hume believed, or rather a difference in kind, as I believe, we need not now decide.

Although the term 'thought' needs to be taken narrowly, if the thesis that thought and language are essentially similar is to be defensible, the term 'language', on the other hand, needs to be taken widely, to include maps, pictures and diagrams. This is because of the way in which mental images can enter into the contents of our thoughts. For example I might think 'I shall arrange my office furniture thus', at the same time forming an image. This image is surely not a mere adjunct of my thinking, but rather forms a crucial part of its content. So if the thesis that thinking is linguistic is to be defensible we must allow the public analogues of images to count as language.[3] But this is in any case a reasonable extension of the term. For to take a similar example, I might say to someone 'I am going to arrange my office furniture like this', at the same time drawing them a quick sketch; and what I draw ought surely to be counted as belonging to the semantic content of my performance, since if you fail to interpret it correctly you will not have understood me. So I shall henceforward understand 'language-using' to cover all kinds of public use of symbols.

One further set of preliminary remarks: in what follows I shall abstract from a number of issues surrounding public language, which would unnecessarily complicate our discussions without, I think, affecting our main topic. One of these is the relationship between idiolectic linguistic understanding, on the one hand, and language as a public object on the other. It is this which is involved when we distinguish between what a speaker meant or intended, and what they literally said. In the present context it is idiolectic understanding which concerns us, since the notion of what is said but not meant is surely a derivative one – there could be no sayings which are not meanings, unless there were also cases in which the two of them coincide. Another issue is that of linguistic division of labour.[4] This we may safely ignore, since it appears to hold equally at the level of private thought. If I think to myself 'I must buy some gold', then I may be just as dependent upon the word of experts to identify real gold for me as I would be had I said it out loud. Then finally there are the various conventions of conversational implicature governing public speech. Some of these may operate at the level of private thinking, whereas some clearly do not.[5] But since, as we remarked in the notes to chapter 5, such conventions are not genuinely essential to language as such, we may reasonably leave the issue to one side.

10.2 THE CODE-BREAKING CONCEPTION

The simplest and most ancient form of theory which sees the content of public speech as deriving from something inner, holds that words get their life from conscious mental processes which accompany speaking or hearing. In one version, this process consists in a stream of mental images, perhaps with a single image carrying the content of each word in the spoken or heard sentence.[6] Others have held that it consists in a mixture of images and feelings.[7] But all such theories are vulnerable to an argument of the later Wittgenstein's.[8] He urges us to take an example of a meaningful utterance and to try to 'peel away' the spoken words, leaving the inner process of meaning intact. In some cases, no doubt, this can be done. I might for instance have said aloud 'I shall invite you round sometime' while actually thinking to myself 'I shall take care never to see you again'. But in many cases it cannot. Thus suppose that in the course of discussing possible locations for a holiday, I say to you 'Avignon is hot in August'. In many cases if I try to imagine a situation which is like this one in all respects except that no public utterance is made, then I find I have imagined a situation in which nothing is thought or meant either. In standard instances of public speech, it seems that the act of meaning is inseparable from the act of speaking.

There are, however, more modern versions of the Code-breaking Conception which are not similarly vulnerable. For example, there are the theories of Grice and his followers, who see the meaning of a public utterance as lying in the intentions with which it is made (it being assumed that these intentions can be characterized without mention of linguistic meaning.)[9] If I assert 'P', then what gives this its content, on such a view, is (roughly) that I utter it with the intention that my hearer should come to believe that P on the basis of recognizing this very intention. Such theories are proof against the 'peel away the utterance' argument, since it is in the nature of such an intention (called by some 'an intention in action') that it cannot exist in the absence of the utterance. If I am not in fact saying anything (or do not at least believe myself to be saying something) then I cannot intend that this utterance should induce in you a belief . . . and so on. If Grice is right, then I can no more peel away my utterance while leaving my intention in speaking intact, than I can peel away the motion of my hands at the piano while yet leaving intact the intentions imbued in their movement. But for all that, what gives public speech its content and significance are the mental states of the speaker; and understanding the words of another requires a kind of decoding, in order that one should recover from their words the belief expressed.

The main problem with these more sophisticated versions of Code-breaking Conception, however, is that their focus is almost exclusively upon the use of language to communicate. Yet the use of language in deliberating and reasoning is surely equally essential (if not equally common).[10] In the course of wondering where to go on holiday, for example, I may say aloud 'Avignon is hot in August', in the full knowledge that there is no one else present. Then in whom am I intending to induce a belief? Surely not myself, since I presumably already know myself to believe that Avignon is hot in August. Nor in anyone else, since I know myself to be alone.

Grice, in discussing examples of this sort, says that my utterance is made with the intention that it should be such as to induce the belief in an hypothetical and only vaguely specified audience.[11] But this is either false or self-defeating. It is false if it means that my use of words in soliloquy is constrained by the way in which I believe others would in fact take them. If I know my idiolect to be in some respects unique, then I may make utterances while deliberating which I know would not induce in any who overheard me the very same beliefs which I express. The account becomes self-defeating, on the other hand, if the hypothetical audience is defined as being one made up of people who would take my words in the way that I do. For this employs the notion of a 'way of taking words' which cannot be explicated in terms of intentions to communicate.

I conclude that the Code-breaking Conception is false, if taken with full generality. Not all significant speech gains its content from the underlying mental states of the speaker. Sometimes, at least, speech is a matter of thinking out loud to oneself. And in these cases (as in others) the thinking is in fact inseparable from the speaking.[12]

10.3 PROJECTING PUBLIC LANGUAGE

If our rejection of the Code-breaking Conception is to be at all satisfying, then we must show that it is possible to give an acount of the content of public speech which is not psychologistic, and which will also be equally serviceable for soliloquy as for communication. So when I say that Avignon is hot in August, what is it that makes my utterance concern heat rather than anything else? (For the sake of simplicity I confine myself to the mode of projection of predicates.)[13]

There is an answer ready to hand: it is that I associate a particular rule of classification with the word, which if correctly followed will apply to all and only places which are hot. My grasp of this rule must at least involve, even if it is not constituted by, a classificatory capacity: I must in general be capable, on finding myself in a place, of telling whether it is hot or not. (In some cases I may defer to the capacities of other people, as when I rely upon experts to identify genuine gold for me. But clearly this phenomenon cannot be a general one, on pain of vicious circularity.) It is in virtue of possessing such a capacity that I may be said to know the difference between places which are hot and those which are not.

However, there are at least two respects in which my grasp of the above rule cannot be equated with a bare disposition to employ the term 'hot' in one way rather than another. Firstly, it is essential that my capacity contain a normative element. In meaning something by the word I must have the idea that I am committing myself to a determinate pattern of application, such that there will be uses of it which are correct or incorrect irrespective of my inclinations to employ it at the time. In short, meaningful use of a term requires that the speaker have the concept of mistaken use. And secondly, we are inclined to think that the rule I grasp has consequences which outreach any capacity that I may have, determining what should be said even in cases where it may be impossible in principle that I should ever be in a position to make a judgement, such as the remote past or remote regions of space.[14]

Here we have the beginnings of a non-psychologistic account of sense, which will work for both soliloquy and communication. What makes a public utterance of mine represent the state of affairs which it does is my grasp of the rules for the use of the various signs involved, including my capacity to apply those signs to the world and to employ them in other significant sentences. And what enables such an utterance to communicate is that other people know how to employ those signs in accordance with the same, or at least logically equivalent, rules. This is, in effect, the *TLP* conception of public language: sentences consist of structured arrangements of signs which represent the world in virtue of the conventions which the speaker takes to govern the use of those signs and their mode of combination. So what makes public language significant is not any mental process, nor any associated belief or intention, but rather our capacity to use signs in a norm-governed way.[15]

10.4 NON-LINGUISTIC THEORIES OF THINKING

We turn now to consider the other half of the psychologistic enterprise: the attempt to characterize private thinking in non-linguistic terms. Here too Imagism has been, historically, the most favoured theory. Many have claimed that thinkings consist of images or sequences of images, perhaps feeling that images have a semantic transparency which makes them inevitable candidates for bearing the content of our thoughts. Yet Imagism's inadequacies are now almost universally recognized. Perhaps the best way to sum these up is to say that no image, in itself, can in fact carry the content of a proposition. No image, no matter how detailed or how schematic, can in itself carry the content of the thought [that grass is green], let alone the thought [that microscopic organisms may be discovered on Mars within the next ten or twelve years]. This is not to deny, however, that images can ever enter into the contents of our thoughts. But it will always be images used or taken in a particular way which contribute to the content of a thought, just as in the public case it is a sketch used in a particular way which contributes to the content of the utterance 'I shall arrange my furniture like this'.

The only real non-linguistic alternative to Imagism is to attempt to analyse thinking in terms of a concept which already involves the notion of propositional content, such as belief. Yet we obviously cannot say simply that thinking is believing, since thinkings are conscious events whereas beliefs are not. However, we might introduce the idea of the *activation* of a belief, by saying that an activated belief is one which is somehow engaged in the agent's current cognitive processing. Can we then say that thinking is activated belief? Again clearly not, since in any complex task there may be beliefs which enter into the control of an agent's behaviour without emerging in acts of thinking. For example, it seems likely that your beliefs about the rules of chess will be activated whenever you play, partially determining what you do without necessarily becoming conscious. Moreover, consider the significance of the thesis that perception is theory-laden: this means that our beliefs affect the content of our perceptions (and hence are activated); but without, surely, emerging in conscious thinking. The most plausible response to these objections would be to try saying that thinkings are activated *second-order* beliefs; especially since many see a connection between second-order mental states and the possession of consciousness.[16] To think to oneself that P would then be to have activated the belief that one believes that P.

I can see at least three possible lines of objection to such an account, only two of which will be pursued here. Firstly, we could challenge the whole idea that it is possible to characterize belief, and the contents of beliefs, independently of the subject's use of language.[17] The claim would be, in particular, that one cannot individuate a person's beliefs finely enough without mentioning their dispositions to use and respond to sentences in their native language. But in fact it is no easy task to make this objection stick. For some have claimed that we can explicate a fine-grained notion of belief in terms of the different ways in which even logically equivalent states can enter into cognitive processing.[18]

A second line of argument is to point out that there are all sorts of thinkings which appear to have only the most tenuous of connections with belief. If I wonder to myself whether P, or entertain in fantasy the thought that P, then I am clearly not believing myself to believe that P. But this point by itself is inconclusive, since wondering whether P, for example, might be characterized as a weak activated desire, to either believe that P or to believe that not P. And as for fantasy thinking, it would seem that this could be accounted for if we could provide an adequate explanation of the notion of 'pretending to oneself to believe'. Then thinking in fantasy that P could be identified with the activation of a pretended second-order belief that one believes that P. But in fact I doubt whether any such account can be given which does not simply help itself to the notion of thinking. For one can only be pretending to have a belief if one engages in some of the categorical actions which would manifest it. (Pretending to believe that I am in danger means starting to run away, or briefly putting on a terrified look, or something of the sort.) But in what categorical actions am I to engage when I privately pretend to believe that I believe that P, if not the act of entertaining the thought that P? For of course I may fantasize without doing anything overtly. In which case not all thinking can be reduced to the possession of propositional attitudes.

The third line of objection, however, is simple and conclusive. It is that the account gets the focus of attention of private thinking quite wrong. When I think to myself that Avignon is hot in August my attention is directed primarily towards Avignon and its likely summer temperature. Yet on the proposed account, I should in reality be concerned with my own states of belief – I should be having a belief about myself activated, that I believe Avignon to be hot in August. Thinkings would then be focused only indirectly on the world, via the content of the first-order belief involved. Their primary focus would be the self. But this is wrong. Thinking is generally world-directed, not self-directed (unless I happen to be thinking about myself). What we require is a theory of thinking (or more particularly, of that form of thinking which is judging) which presents it as a distinctive mode of activation of belief. Thinkings are conscious events having the same primary world-directedness as beliefs; my judgements somehow serving to express my beliefs without representing them. It will be my thesis that any theory meeting this *desideratum* will have to make thinking out to be essentially linguistic.

10.5 SYMBOLIC THINKING

Let us begin by asking how thinkings are related to the world. When I think to myself that Avignon is hot, what is it that links what takes place in my consciousness with heat? (Once again I concentrate upon the predicative element in thinking.) It is surely clear that any adequate answer must mention my classificatory capacities. In general, only someone who is capable of recognizing the difference between places which are hot and those which are not can entertain thoughts about heat. And they, like the person who speaks aloud about heat, must regard themselves as committed to a certain pattern of application, allowing room for the idea of misclassification. Someone only counts as entertaining a conscious thought about heat whose capacities reflect a grasp of a classificatory rule which applies to places independently of the thinker's disposition towards judgement on any given occasion. So what projects our acts of thinking into the world is not essentially different from what projects our statements: in both cases an important part of the connection is constituted by the thinker/speaker's grasp of various rules of classification, together with their attendant capacities. These capacities are exercised in thinking, just as they are exercised in the use of public language.[19]

The next point to notice is that thinkings, like sayings, are structured, being subject to the compositionality principle. Anyone who is capable of thinking that Avignon is hot in August must also be capable of thinking other thoughts which deploy the same and other elements in a variety of ways. They must be able to think that

Avignon is cold in February, that Aberdeen is cold in August, that it is hot here now, and so on – or something of the sort.[20] And as we can now say: these thinkings involve exercises of the very same capacities differently combined. Indeed thinking is unlimitedly creative, in exactly the way that language is: it is essential to thinking that new thoughts can always be formed using old materials in new ways. So any act of thinking must employ a number of component rules and capacities reflecting the structure of the thought.

Now recall that thinkings are conscious events. When I think to myself that Avignon is hot in August, there must occur in my consciousness an event which expresses the content of that thought. Since this content is structured, and is related to the world via a number of underlying rules and capacities, the conscious event must be structured as well.[21] Indeed it must consist of components corresponding to each of the underlying capacities, in such a way that one can say that, in employing one of those components in consciousness, I thereby exercise the relevant capacity. Consciously thinking that Avignon is hot could hardly involve an exercise of my capacity for recognizing hot places unless it contained an element which was systematically related to that capacity. For in general an event-type which exercises a capacity or disposition must be systematically related to it – otherwise what could pick it out as an exercise of that capacity rather than another? So the elements of the event which is the act of thinking are, in effect, 'markers' for the underlying capacities which they exercise.

What we have now found our way to is tantamount to the claim that thinking is essentially symbol-mediated. For our conclusion is that the content-conferring capacities exercised in thinking must each have individual markers in consciousness, in such a way that appropriate combinations of these markers will constitute an exercise of the corresponding capacities. Yet what is a spoken or written sign – considered as an instrument within an idiolect – except a marker, or index, for the exercise of a conceptual capacity? When I think out loud with the sentence 'Avignon is hot in August', what is the sign 'hot' except a marker whose use on this occasion is an index of the exercise of my capacity for distinguishing between places which are hot and those which are not?

Thinkings are thus world-directed in the same way that speakings are. In both cases we employ structured arrangements of events, where each component of the structure marks an exercise of a conceptual capacity, those capacities (together with their mode of combination) serving to focus the completed structure upon the world. And note that it is an advantage of our account that it is able to treat fantasy thinking in the very same way as private judging: in both cases it is structures of signs which express the content of the thinking, the difference between the two consisting in the attitude which the thinker adopts towards the completed whole. But as for what the events are which constitute the elements of our thinkings, it would be a matter for psychology to find out.[22] They might be images of spoken or of written words, or visual images of things, or a mixture of all three; perhaps differing in the case of different people. (But note that many of the images here would be functioning as mere signs, comparable to the words in a token utterance, rather than as what confers content on our thoughts, as the Imagist theory would claim.) Yet since we are allowing pictures and maps to count as part of public language, we can still maintain the isomorphism between public and private.[23]

SUMMARY

The *TLP* position outlined in chapter 8 stands vindicated as the most plausible account of the relationship between thinking and language-using. Both are on a par, consisting of arrangements of signs which represent the world in virtue of the thinker/speaker's normative capacities for their use.[24]

11

Name and Object

Our task in this chapter is to interpret the *TLP* terminology of 'name' (Name) and 'object' (Gegendstand, Ding).[1] This will determine our approach to the *TLP* semantics for sub-sentential expressions, which will occupy us throughout the remainder of this book. It will also be crucial for our understanding of the metaphysics of *TLP*, to be discussed in the sequel *MT*.

11.1 PRELIMINARIES

Our present concern is to judge between two quite different traditions of interpretation. One of these – which I shall refer to as 'the wide interpretation' – takes *TLP* names to cover not only proper names but also predicates and relational expressions.[2] Correspondingly, it takes the objects of *TLP* to include not only individuals but also properties and relations (universals). The other – narrow – interpretation takes names to cover only proper names and objects to include only individuals.[3] I shall be arguing that we ought to adopt the narrow reading.[4]

On this topic, as elsewhere, one important consideration is Charity. As will emerge in the sections which follow, the wide interpretation forces us to regard a number of Wittgenstein's remarks as seriously confused, and others as trivial. On the narrow interpretation, on the other hand, there is no appearance of confusion, and the doctrines which would otherwise be trivial become substantive and interesting. But the most important argument from Charity depends upon our assessment of the Picture Theory. As we shall see from our discussion in chapters 14 and 15, on a wide reading of 'name' the Picture Theory contains nothing of any deep philosophical significance. In effect it will merely record a contingent fact about many natural languages. On the narrow interpretation, however, it may be seen to mark a decisive step forward over the semantic theories invented by Frege. So the position argued for in this chapter can only be tentative: much will depend upon the arguments of later chapters, and the overall plausibility of the resulting reading of *TLP*.

Another general consideration against a wide reading of 'object' is that it is almost inconceivable that anyone who thought as highly of Frege as Wittgenstein did should simply have slurred over the distinction between concept and object. It is *a priori* most implausible to suppose that the writer who had acknowledged the 'great works of Frege' in *TLP*'s preface should have employed without any sort of apology an expression which simply equivocates between 'concept' and 'object'. For Frege had repeatedly insisted upon the fundamental importance of the distinction. It gets picked out as one of the three main methodological constraints in the introduction to *FA*, parallel in importance to the need to distinguish the logical from the psychological, and never to ask for the meaning of a word in isolation – both of which, it should be noted, are not only echoed in *TLP* (4.1121, 3.3), but become absorbed into Wittgenstein's general approach. (See the discussion of chapters 3 and 8, and *MT*, chapter 2.) Moreover Frege had devoted three major papers to the subject : 'Function and Concept', 'Concept and Object' and 'What is a function?'. It is just incredible that Wittgenstein might have passed all of this over as being unworthy of any explicit comment, even if, as some have argued, he believed Frege to have overestimated its importance.[5]

11.2 UNDERSTANDING THE METAPHORS

The *TLP* exposition of the Picture Theory and of the nature of elementary states of affairs abounds with metaphors of a broadly spatial character.[6] Thus a state of affairs is said to consist in a 'combination' of objects (2.01); it is said to be the changing 'configuration' of objects which produces states of affairs (2.0271–2.0272); we are told that the essence of a proposition can be seen clearly if we think of one which is expressed by a spatial arrangement of tables and chairs (3.1431); and we are told that the arrangement of names in a sentence presents a state of affairs in the manner of a *tableau vivant* (4.0311).

All this is entirely inappropriate if 'object' is intended to cover properties and relations as well as individuals, and if 'name' is to cover predicative expressions as well as proper names. For to speak of the relationship between an individual and a universal under which it falls as analogous to a spatial configuration would embody a fundamental confusion between a formal relation (which this is), and a relation proper (such as a spatial relation between two physical objects).[7] And to suggest that it is the spatial arrangement of proper names and predicative expressions in a sentence which expresses its sense, precisely conflicts with what is claimed to be the main point of the Picture Theory, on the wide interpretation: that the real sign for a relation (say) is not the relational expression itself, but rather a relation in which that expression figures (see chapter 14). Consequently those who take the wide interpretation are constrained to say that in these passages Wittgenstein is seriously confused.[8]

It might be claimed in defence of the wide reading that Wittgenstein's use of the language of spatial relations is just another of those places where he tries to say what can, on his own principles, only be shown. Yet it is hard to see even what he might be *trying* to get at in saying that a red chair is a 'configuration' of the chair and redness (2.0272) or in saying that the chair and redness 'stand in a determinate relation to one another' (2.031). On the other hand, if 'object' only covers individuals, then it is easy to see what he is trying to get across; namely, that a state of affairs will consist of individuals standing in some material relation to one another. (Although this, too, is something which cannot strictly be said, since anyone who understands an elementary proposition would already know that it describes a relation between objects.)

Some have argued that since states of affairs are said to be combinations of objects, we cannot take this to mean a genuine relation between individuals.[9] For where a state of affairs consists of a single individual possessing a property it would be nonsense to talk of the property 'combining' that object into a state of affairs. One possible line of reply would be to claim that in Wittgenstein's view there *would not be* any elementary states of affairs containing only one individual. Rather, all would consist of *relations between* individuals. Thus consider 2.0231–2.0232, where he writes as follows:

The substance of the world can only determine a form, and not any material properties. For it is only by means of propositions that material properties are represented – only by the configuration of objects that they are produced. In a manner of speaking, objects are colourless.

On the narrow reading this might naturally be taken to mean that the substance of the world – that is, the necessarily existing simple individuals[10] – does not by itself determine any fact about the world, because the only material properties possessed by such individuals consist in the relations in which they stand to other individuals. Thus individuals are, in a manner of speaking, 'colourless' in that they possess no properties except relational ones. (The corresponding semantic thesis would be that all elementary propositions consist of proper names standing in some significant relationship to one another.) These are of course of substantive and interesting claims.[11]

If we adopt this line of reply we immediately face the question of why Wittgenstein should have believed that the only properties which simple individuals possess consist of their relations to other individuals. The only possible answer is that he must have had at least the outline of a programme of analysis already in mind. Now in *MT* chapter 14 I shall put forward a model for the elementary propositions of *TLP* which enables them to meet many of the constraints which Wittgenstein lays down (notably logical independence). Since all elementary propositions on this model are relational ones, it may be that he already had it (or something like it) before his mind when writing the metaphysical remarks of *TLP*. Alternatively, since he clearly believed that even the simplest of ordinary language predicates, particularly those of colour, would turn out under analysis to contain significant logical structure (6.3751), he may have felt that there would be no need for monadic predicates to make their appearance once again at the terminal level.

However, there also exists quite another line of reply to the objection, defended by Sellars in his (1962a), which avoids having to attribute to *TLP* a doctrine of bare (propertyless) particulars. This is that Wittgenstein may have been happy to speak of monadic combinations of objects, just as Russell had been happy to speak of properties as monadic relations. So when Wittgenstein says at 2.14 that in a picture the elements (names) are related to one another in a determinate way, this would be taken to cover, as a limiting case, pictures which contain just a single name, where some property of the name itself (e.g. the style of its script) would serve to ascribe a monadic property to the individual referred to.

This is certainly a possible interpretation, though it produces a reading of the text which is far from natural. (For example, 2.03 has to be taken to cover states of affairs which contain just a single chain-link.) But it matters little for our purposes whether it is this, or rather the previous interpretation of objects as bare particulars, which is the correct one. For in fact most of the substantive doctrines of *TLP* which I shall discuss (both here and in the sequel) are consistent with either reading. Since this is so, and since the bare-particular interpretation is the more textually natural of the two, I propose to adopt it as my preferred version of the narrow reading of the *TLP* terminology of 'name' and 'object'.

Undoubtedly the most awkward metaphor to interpret, from the standpoint of the narrow reading, is 2.03. This says that the objects in a state of affairs fit into one another like the links of a chain. Given the well-known Fregean metaphor of the 'completion' of a concept by an object, it would be natural to take 2.03 as describing the (formal) relation which obtains between the objects a and b and the relation R in the state of affairs depicted by 'aRb'.[12] It would be saying that the elements in that state of affairs are related to one another immediately, that they fit together 'of themselves'. Nevertheless, we do have a powerful motive for finding an alternative interpretation of 2.03 if we can. For it is followed at 2.031 by the remark that in a state of affairs objects stand in a determinate relation to one another. This would have to be read as saying that the objects a, b and the relation R are determinately related, which is an entirely unhappy way of putting the matter if they are supposed to fit together 'of themselves'.

In fact an alternative interpretation of 2.03 is readily to hand: we can see it as a model for the material relations between the individuals in a state of affairs, designed to render intelligible the doctrine that elementary propositions are logically independent of one another. (Note that this doctrine is about to be re-introduced, at 2.061–2.062.)[13] For there is no way of making sense of it, if it is viewed through the medium of the spatial metaphors which dominate the *TLP* talk about states of affairs. Thus suppose – to take a crude example – that elementary propositions took the form 'Object a is lying on top of b'. Then the truth of this proposition would be incompatible with indefinitely many others of the same form, for instance 'Object a is lying on top of c'. For one object cannot be in two places at once. A similar point could be made in connection with any system describing spatial relations between physical objects which employs names of those objects.[14]

I suggest then that 2.03 is presenting an alternative model for states of affairs, to set alongside the spatial model of 2.031, which is to render the logical independence of states of affairs intelligible. For the image of interlocking chain-links can at least capture the idea that no elementary proposition is inconsistent with another.[15] Thus suppose that the simple names are names of chain-links, an elementary proposition 'abc' saying that a is linked to b which is linked to c. Then the truth of this proposition is compatible with the truth of any other such proposition – with 'acb', with 'ade' and so on – although in any real case, with links of determinate size and thickness, there will be physical limitations on the modes of combination available.

Note that even Wittgenstein's comment on Ogden's original translation of 2.03, which has been cited by some in support of a wide reading of 'object', is in fact ambiguous between the two.[16] Wittgenstein writes:

> Here instead of 'Hang one on another' it should be 'hang one in another' as the links of a chain *do*! The meaning is *that there isn't anything third* that connects the links but that the links *themselves* make connection with one another. So if 'in' in this place is English please put it there. If one would hang *on* the other they might also be glued together. [Emphasis in original.][17]

The sentence 'There isn't anything third that connects the links' could mean 'A formal relation is not a relation' (wide reading), or it could mean 'A material relation is not a thing' (narrow reading). In my view the reason why 'hang one on another' would be wrong is because it suggests that the relation obtaining between two individuals might be the same sort of thing as those individuals themselves, in the way that both a lump of glue and a chain-link are the same sort of thing. (However it does not follow that the *point* of the metaphor is to illustrate that this is *not* so.)

11.3 FORMS AND VARIABLES

Throughout the presentation of the Picture Theory early in *TLP*, Wittgenstein speaks of there being two very different aspects of pictures and the states of affairs pictured. There are the individual elements (the names) of the picture, corresponding to the objects in the state of affairs. And there is the form, realized in the determinate structure of the picture, which is common to both picture and state of affairs. (See 2.1–2.22.) Now there is a natural use of the term 'form' in which the form of the sentence 'aRb' is of a relational expression completed by two proper names. This is 'form' in the sense of 'logical form', on a fairly restricted (Fregean) understanding of 'logical'. On this account the sentence 'aRb' might consist of the elements (names) 'a', 'R' and 'b', and the form Øαβ. And this would, of course, count in favour of a wide reading of 'name'.[18]

In order to see the possibility of a different way of taking the name/form contrast we should turn to *NB* 98–9 – though with trepidation, since this is from the 1913 'Notes on Logic'. There Wittgenstein distinguishes, within the class of indefinable symbols, between names and forms. Here the names in 'aRb' are 'a' and 'b', and the form is the 'general indefinable' 'xRy'. So when in *TLP* Wittgenstein distinguishes between the elements and pictorial form of a picture, he may have in mind the distinction between the proper names and predicative expression in a sentence.[19] The pictorial form of an elementary proposition would then be the conventions governing which combinations of names are possible (make sense) and providing for the comparison of any possible combination of names with reality. (We shall consider such an interpretation in chapter 15.) And to say that the pictorial form is held in common between the picture and the pictured fact would be to say that both names and objects must have the same 'degrees of freedom'; i.e. that to every combination of names which makes sense corresponds a possible combination of objects, and vice versa. This would be 'logical form' in the extended sense in which one might say that although, on the Fregean approach, 'Seven is heavier than five' is well-formed (it combines two proper names with a relational expression), it is, in reality, *ill*-formed.[20]

When it comes to expressing the (Fregean) logical forms of propositions by means of variables, Wittgenstein proceeds in a way which strongly supports the narrow interpretation. Thus at 4.1272 we are told that the variable name 'x' is the proper sign for the pseudo-concept object, and 4.24 implies that it is names (simple symbols) which may be substituted for the variables 'x', 'y' and 'z'. Yet at 5.5261 he is careful to provide a distinct style of variable – namely '∅' – to range over properties. There he says that a fully generalized proposition would have the form '(∃x)(∃∅)∅x'. Yet if he really understood names to include predicates as well as proper names, and hence took the variables 'x' and 'y' to range over properties and relations as well as individuals, then it is hard to see why he should not simply have written the form of the fully generalized proposition as: '(∃x)(∃y)xy'.

4.24 goes on to say that elementary propositions, being functions of names, may be written in the form 'fx', '∅(x,y)', etc. Now since an elementary proposition is said to consist only of names, it might be thought to follow immediately from this that predicates and relational expressions are names.[21] But this would be to fail to distinguish between the expressions which an elementary proposition actually contains, and the ways in which one might *represent* its form. Thus suppose that elementary propositions describe the linking together of chain-links, the sentence 'abc' saying that a is linked to b which is linked to c. The only *words* which such a sentence would contain would be the proper names 'a', 'b' and 'c'. But of course there is absolutely nothing to prevent us from representing it as having the form 'Fx', or 'Gxy', or even 'Hxyz'. And indeed, we shall need to treat the sentence as having these forms in order to explain the validity of different patterns of argument involving generality.[22]

11.4 FURTHER *TLP* EVIDENCE

The fact that Wittgenstein is clearly prepared to quantify over properties and relations, as he does at 5.5261, might suggest that he recognizes them within his basic ontology. And then they could hardly avoid mention in elementary propositions, given the general reductive programme of *TLP*. This would give us reason to assume that elementary propositions, consisting only of names, must include names of properties and relations.[23] But in fact the system of quantification employed in *TLP* is quasi-substitutional (5.501, 5.52). So which ontology our quantifications commit us to will depend upon the way in which the substitutions are explained. And as we shall see in chapter 16, this can be done in such a way as to legitimize second-order quantification without commitment to the existence of universals. We shall also see in chapters 15 and 16 that there is a case for saying that *TLP* embraces a form of Conceptual Nominalism, which can be defended powerfully against its Realist rivals.

At 4.123, in the course of discussing the distinction between internal and external properties and relations, Wittgenstein writes as follows:

> (This shade of blue and that one stand, eo ipso, in the internal relation of lighter to darker. It is unthinkable that *these* two objects should not stand in this relation.) [Emphasis in the original.]

This certainly seems to suggest that shades of blue (i.e. properties) are being counted as objects. But in fact Wittgenstein immediately goes on to write the following:

> (Here the shifting use of the word 'object' corresponds to the shifting use of the words 'property' and 'relation'.)[24]

Given the narrow reading of the *TLP* use of 'object', this can be interpreted to mean that when he speaks in the previous remark of 'two objects standing in this relation' he is talking non-standardly, having in mind two properties standing in an internal relation to one another – the shift in the use of 'relation' from external to internal being accompanied by a shift in the use of 'object' from individual to property.[25] So 4.123 need raise no problem for the narrow reading. Given the wide reading, on the other hand, it is not at all obvious how Wittgenstein's qualifying statement should be understood. For when we shift from speaking of two 'objects' (e.g. an individual and a universal) standing in some external relation to one another, to speaking of two 'objects' (e.g. two universals) standing in an internal relation, it is far from clear why there should be a corresponding shift in the sense of 'object'.

One further set of remarks speaking strongly in favour of the narrow interpretation is 3.323–3.324, which runs as follows:

> (In the proposition 'Green is green' – where the first word is a proper name of a person and the last an adjective – these words do not merely have different Bedeutungen: they are *different symbols*.) In this way the most fundamental confusions are easily produced (the whole of philosophy is full of them). [Emphasis in original.]

By 'different symbols' here – and throughout 3.321–3.325, as we saw in chapter 4 – it is clear that Wittgenstein means not just 'signs having different senses', but rather 'signs having different *kinds* of sense, different *kinds* of use'. It would then be simply extraordinary that he should, on the one hand, believe that the most fundamental confusions can be produced by slurring over the different kinds of use that proper names and predicates have, and yet that he should, on the other hand, use the term 'name' in such a way as to do precisely that.[26]

A final remark supporting the narrow reading is 5.535, where Wittgenstein says that what Russell's axiom of infinity tried to say would express itself in language though the use of infinitely many names with different Bedeutungen. For Russell's axiom had concerned the existence of infinitely many distinct *individuals*.[27] So if 'name' here were taken widely, then what Wittgenstein says would be straightforwardly false. For a language containing infinitely many predicates would, on such an account, contain infinitely many names. Yet it would not even begin to show the truth of the axiom of infinity. So once again we have the choice of either taking 'name' to be ambiguous, or taking Wittgenstein to be foolish, or adopting the narrow reading throughout.

The only place in *TLP* where Wittgenstein unequivocally uses 'name' in the wide sense is 5.02, where he gives as an example of an affix to a name, Russell's use of 'c' as an affix to the sign '+'; thus implying that '+' is itself a name.[28] But I can see no reason why we should take this to be anything other than a non-literal illustration of what he is basically getting at, namely the essential compositeness of sentences. For it is clear that the whole point of the passage is to distinguish between signs which are, and signs which are not, essentially composite – '–p' belonging to the first category (contra Frege's doctrine that sentences are names) whereas both 'Julius Caesar' and '$+_c$' belong to the second. Moreover, when speaking directly about the simple sign which could replace '$+_c$', Wittgenstein is careful to describe it only as a sign (Zeichen) rather than a name.

11.5 EVIDENCE OUTSIDE OF *TLP*

The evidence of *NB* is equivocal, though in general it supports the narrow reading. In particular, it is one of the earliest themes of the pre-*TLP* writings that it would be a complete mistake to think of proper names and predicative expressions as functioning in anything like the same way. (See *NB* 10, 98–9, 104–5, 111, 121.) It is this early concern which finally culminates in the Picture Theory, on my interpretation of it. (See chapter 15.) Moreover there are many passages where Wittgenstein uses 'object' and 'name' in such a way as to contrast with 'property' and 'predicate'. See for example *NB* 65, where he talks of the ideas of thing, relation and property in the plural. See also *NB* 115, where he talks of 'the name of a property (to speak loosely)'.

On the other hand there are two (but only two) places in the early writings where 'object' is definitely used in such a way as to cover properties and relations. The first is at *NB* 61, which reads as follows:

> What seems to be given us *a priori* is the concept: *This*. – Identical with the concept of the *object*. Relations and properties, etc. are *objects* too.[29] [Emphasis in original.]

These remarks occur in a particularly exploratory – and often poorly expressed – sequence of passages: on analysis, on the extent to which ordinary objects can be regarded as simple, on whether there really do have to be simple objects, and so on. I can therefore see no reason why they should not be read as a conditional, embodying a criticism of Russell. That is to say: if the concept 'object' is given to us as 'whatever can be picked out by means of a demonstrative' (as Russell thinks), then properties and relations would be objects too (which Russell did not think). We might then be expected to contrapose, and say that since properties and relations are obviously not objects, the concept 'object' cannot be given to us in this way. Certainly Wittgenstein never makes anything further of the fundamental role of demonstratives, presupposed by an unconditional reading of the above remarks. (And in the very next passage on p. 61 he is to be found speaking of propositions containing names *and* relations.)

The second place is at *NB* 69, where Wittgenstein says that in the inference from 'All men are mortal' and 'Socrates is a man' to 'Socrates is mortal', both Socrates and the property of mortality are functioning as simple objects. But I can see no reason why this need be taken at face value either. For it is clear from the context that what is interesting him here is the fact that one can apply the principles of logic to the ordinary – unanalysed – propositions of natural language. So in this context, to treat something as a simple object is merely to behave as if it had, itself, no logical structure. All he is saying, in effect, is that for some purposes we can treat 'Socrates is mortal' as if it were an elementary proposition.

Finally, there is a certain amount of post-*TLP* evidence – mostly anecdotal – that years later Wittgenstein himself adopted the wide reading of the terminology of 'name' and 'object' in *TLP*.[30] But in accordance with the general principles of interpretation argued for in chapter 1, I propose to accord this no independent weight.

SUMMARY

There are many arguments supporting the narrow reading, and there is no insuperable textual evidence against it. But in the end the question comes down to a matter of judgement: does the narrow reading, or does it not, make *TLP* more plausible and interesting than the alternative? In this chapter I have set out part (but only part) of the case for thinking that it does. This issue will remain with us for the remainder of this book.

12

Names, Knowledge and Identity

Armed now with the idea that 'name' in *TLP* covers only proper names, we can return to consider what Wittgenstein has to say about their semantics, considering also how this issue relates to his treatment of identity.

12.1 THE *TLP* THEORY OF NAMES

In chapter 3 we argued that 3.203 should be read as saying that the object to which a proper name refers constitutes its semantic content (Bedeutung), it being the referent itself which figures in the truth-conditions (Sinn) of sentences in which the name occurs (4.1211). But then we argued in chapter 4 that 3.3411 should be seen as committing Wittgenstein to the idea that names have sense as well as reference: each significant name constituting a symbol, having associated with it in the idiolects of particular speakers some mode of thinking about, or way of determining, the object to which the name refers. Yet differences in symbol (either within or across idiolects) which do not emerge at the level of reference are said to be inessential, making no difference to the semantic content of sentences in which they occur.

It is easy to see the point of this combination of views. Wittgenstein is accepting Frege's theories of idiolectic understanding and of how reference gets fixed, but is rejecting his theory of the role of proper names in communication. He is accepting that speakers must associate a sense – a mode of thinking of the referent – with every proper name which they understand, it being in virtue of expressing such a sense that the name comes to have the reference which it does within their idiolects. But he is denying that mutual knowledge of modes of thinking is required for communication through the use of a name. On the contrary, speakers may be said to understand one another so long as they know that they each use the name to refer to the very same thing, irrespective of any differences in the sense they associate with it (provided, of course, that they have mutual knowledge of whatever is required for understanding the predicative element in the sentence). And all sentences which differ only in that one co-referring name has been substituted for another may be said to have the same truth-condition (Sinn), and to say the very same thing.

The claim that the semantic content of a name is exhausted by its referent ought more accurately to be expressed by saying that names for different things belonging to the same sortal category differ from one another in semantic content only in so far they differ in reference. For there will of course be much more involved in the understanding of a name, which will be common to all competent speakers irrespective of idiolect, than the bare knowledge of its referent. In particular, speakers will need to know how that name may fit together with other words to form a sentence, and the kinds of things which can significantly be said of its referent – they must know, in a phrase, the 'logical grammar' of the name. To this extent, at least, names may be said to have public senses. But all names belonging to the same sortal category will have the same public sense, the distinctive contribution of any given individual name to the semantic content of sentences in which it occurs being exhausted by its referent.

It is important to note that Wittgenstein's view is not that a speaker's knowledge of the logical grammar of a name is to be 'read off' from their direct acquaintance with the nature of the referent, as some have claimed.[1] On the contrary, he is emphatic that the significance, or otherwise, of various different combinations of words is a feature of the symbols involved, which in this context means their public senses; maintaining that we cannot attempt to justify those combinations by appealing to features of their reference (3.317). His view is thus that understanding a name involves knowing its logical grammar (its public sense), as well as possessing some means or other of determining its reference; but different speakers may employ different means of determining the reference of a name and yet continue to communicate.[2]

If we took the above account to apply to the proper names of ordinary discourse, then we might allow the modes of thinking associated with the names in an idiolect to take the form of a definite description, or to consist in a non-descriptive recognitional capacity, or even to take the form of a memory-based demonstrative (e.g. 'By "Mary" I mean that woman I met then'). Our thesis would be that in order to understand another's statement involving a name you would have to possess some such mode of thinking of the referent. But this need not be the same mode of thinking as that employed by the speaker, nor need you know what sense the other employs. Indeed the account might also be extended to cover all singular referring expressions including indexicals (with due deference to the differences in their logical grammar). The role of any such expression in communication would simply be to present its referent as a topic of discussion (mutual knowledge of reference sufficing for understanding) not to convey any particular way of thinking of it.[3]

In chapter 13 we shall defend just such a view of the semantics of ordinary proper names. For the present we shall continue our discussion of Wittgenstein's views, considering first some objections to our interpretation, which arise out of his remarks on the notion of knowledge of reference.

12.2 NAMES AND KNOWLEDGE

In the early sections of *TLP* where Wittgenstein talks of our knowledge of simple objects – the objects which form the referents of the simple names – he employs the verb 'kennen' rather than 'wissen' (2.0123–2.01231). Since this word can mean 'to be acquainted with' as well as 'to know', it might be suggested that he is here putting forward the thesis that knowledge of the reference of a simple name is a matter of direct acquaintance, rather than knowledge in virtue of a Fregean mode of thinking as my interpretation implies.[4]

The suggestion is weak however. It is sufficient to explain the use of the verb 'kennen' that Wittgenstein is here talking of knowledge of the internal (non-contingent) attributes of objects. He is emphasizing that in order to know an object (referent of a name) one must fully grasp its logical status and characteristics. So he is talking of knowledge of *what* an object *is*, rather than of knowledge *that* such and such is contingently true of it (compare 5.552). Now the showing/saying doctrine implies that this is not the sort of knowledge which could be expressed in a significant proposition. So the choice of terminology may merely serve to stress the fact, since the object of 'kennen' can be non-propositional too. He could maintain perfectly consistently that one may refer to an object by virtue of possessing a recognitional capacity for it, or via a memory-based demonstrative. He could even hold that reference may be effected through some contingent description or other, or through some uniquely identifying essential characteristic.[5] All of these would be versions of the Fregean theory of how reference gets fixed.

In addition, the specific features of Wittgenstein's metaphysics would make a direct-acquaintance doctrine extremely hard to believe, for reasons similar to those we raised against the Fregean theory of thinking in chapter 9. For the simple objects of *TLP* exist necessarily, being constituents of all possible worlds (2.02–2.0272).[6] And whatever the merits of the Russellian doctrine of acquaintance in connection with names for fleeting mental states of the thinking subject (sense-data), it is wholly implausible if the names are to designate necessarily existing (and hence mind-independent) things. Since such entities obviously cannot themselves enter into the thinker's consciousness, we should have to suppose the acquaintance-relation (like Frege's grasping-relation) to obtain directly between a changing mind and a necessarily existing thing, this relation somehow being sufficient to explain the thinker's knowledge of what that thing is (which will emerge, for example, in what sentences they acknowledge to be significant). Besides remaining completely mysterious, this relation, too, would have to be removed from the thinker's conscious access.[7]

There is one further passage in *TLP* dealing with knowledge of objects which appears to cast doubt upon our quasi-Fregean interpretation. This is 4.243, which implies that one cannot understand two names without knowing whether their reference is the same or different. For such a thesis would surely be untenable if to understand a name were to associate with it some mode of determining its referent, such that there might be a number of different modes of thinking which determine the very same referent. For then one might understand two names, which express two different senses, without knowing that they have the same bearer; and it would be informative to learn that this is the case.[8]

In fact it is not merely our interpretation of the *TLP* doctrine of names for which 4.243 raises a problem. For the passage goes on to apply the transparency thesis, not just to the proper names of a fully analysed language, but even to words in ordinary speech. It claims that if I understand a word of English and a word of German which in fact mean the same, then it is impossible for me not to know that they do. This is of course implausible. It is a matter of common experience that one can believe two words to mean the same although there are in fact sentence-constructions in which their use would be different, or possible circumstances in which the one would be appropriate but the other not. Therefore one might obviously doubt that two words, which one understands, mean the same when in fact they do. So in charity to Wittgenstein we should seek some other interpretation of 4.243.

One suggestion is that Wittgenstein does not use 'know' ('wissen') in quite its standard sense. This would receive some support from 5.5562, where he says that if we know on logical grounds that there must be elementary propositions, then everyone who understands propositions in their unanalysed form must know it. This is simply absurd if 'know' is used in such a way as to imply 'belief'. For whatever else may be the case, speakers of ordinary language neither believe nor disbelieve in the existence of a class of logically independent elementary propositions consisting of names of simple, necessarily existing objects. So Charity requires us, if we can, to interpret the *TLP* use of 'know' in such a way that knowledge does not have to involve belief.

Evidence for just such an interpretation may be found at 5.136–5.1362, where Wittgenstein implies that because we cannot *infer* future events from those of the present, we cannot have knowledge of the future either. (See also 6.36311.) This suggests that to know something, on Wittgenstein's view, might be to possess a logically necessary warrant for it – to be in a position to deduce, on the basis of other things which one knows (justifiably and truly believes), that it must be the case. This would of course explain why he thinks that ordinary speakers know of the existence of elementary propositions: for they are capable (if Wittgenstein is right) of deducing it. They have merely not yet constructed the necessary arguments. It would also explain his views on translation, assuming he held that translation-manuals can be constructed *a priori* by anyone who is bilingual. (And note that he does gloss his remark at 4.243, about knowing that an English and a German word mean the same, by saying that he must be *capable* of translating the one into the other.)

It might be objected that 5.1362 only really implies that a logical warrant for a truth is a necessary condition for knowledge of it, not that such a warrant is sufficient – it being left open that belief may also be required for knowledge. But in fact the final bracketed sentence of 5.1362 clinches our interpretation. This says that 'A knows that P' is senseless (sinnlos) if 'P' is a tautology. For recall from chapter 6 that 'senseless' is the term used to characterize the status of tautologies and contradictions, suggesting that 'A knows that P' will be tautological whenever 'P' itself is. And indeed this is explicitly stated at *PTLP* 5.04441. In which case, since it is obviously possible for 'P' to be a tautology without my believing it (as 6.1262 recognizes), knowledge must here be understood as not implying belief.[9]

The fact that Wittgenstein's use of 'know' is non-standard is of some help in defending our interpretation of the *TLP* doctrine of names against the transparency thesis expressed at 4.243, but it is still not sufficient. For there is no guarantee that someone who employs two names with different senses which in fact refer to the very same thing will always be able to establish that this is so *a priori*. Quite the contrary. So we cannot explain Wittgenstein's saying that anyone who understands two such names must know that they have the same referent simply by pointing out that by 'know' he means 'is in a position to deduce'. We need in addition to suppose that he has in mind a specific programme of analysis. We need to suppose that he believed that the names in a fully analysed language would have to be introduced by means of some general rule, rather in the way that the names of the numbers are introduced. For then anyone who understands two such systems of names, and who understands names from the different systems which in fact refer to the same things without believing that they do, will nevertheless be in a position to work out *a priori* that they do – just as someone who understands both 'XCIII' and '93' without realizing that they designate the same number must still be capable of working it out.

Is there then any reason to suppose Wittgenstein to have believed that the names of a fully analysed language would be introduced by a general rule? Notice first, that it somehow has to be guaranteed that there is a name for every single object if his substitutional account of quantification is to be adequate, according to which '∃xFx' is defined as the negation of the joint-negation of all sentences which result from completing the predicate 'Fx' with a proper name (5.501, 5.52). This surely requires that those names be produced in accordance with some systematic rule. Furthermore, he certainly thought it possible for such a language to contain infinitely many names: see 4.2211 and 5.535. Indeed there is reason to think he believed that it actually would do so. For at 4.463 he speaks positively of logical space being infinite, and logical space is defined by the set of elementary propositions (3.42). So either there must be infinitely many names, or there are infinitely many modes of combining names (infinitely many different forms of elementary propositions). Yet it is hard to see how there could be infinitely many names in a language, for a non-Platonist like Wittgenstein, unless they were introduced by a general rule. A language surely could not contain infinitely many names by accident, so to speak.

Moreover, the model for elementary propositions which I shall explain in *MT* chapter 14 will have precisely this feature: infinitely many names introduced by a general rule. So it may be that Wittgenstein already had something like this model in mind when he wrote 4.243. At any rate, this will prove to be a likely enough possibility to save our interpretation of the *TLP* doctrine of names, especially given the intrinsic implausibility of the alternative: that he believed in direct acquaintance with a class of necessarily existing simple objects.

12.3 ORDINARY NAMES

Thus far we have been expounding Wittgenstein's view of simple names (the names which will mark the end-point of analysis – 3.202). Our question now is what view he took of our ordinary proper names. Did he, like Russell, espouse some version of description-theory, thus giving what I shall argue is a false account of their semantics? Or did he believe that there is some way of extending his doctrine of simple names to cover all proper names?

The evidence for a description-theory is apparently quite strong. For 3.24 tells us that any proposition which mentions a complex object must contain a description of it. Not only that, but the description must apparently enumerate all of its parts, since Wittgenstein says that a proposition about a complex entails propositions about its constituents. (Compare *NB* 62: 'To say that one thing is part of another is always a tautology'.) So he appears not only to have held a description-theory of ordinary proper names, but also to have had quite specific views about the form which such a description would take: it would designate the individual parts of the complex object and describe their relations to one another.[10]

This would of course be absurd as an account of the modes of thought (senses) employed by individual speakers. When I think about Mary I certainly do not think of each of the individual parts of her body, let alone each cell and atom. Indeed Wittgenstein was aware of as much, since at *NB* 64 he remarks that he might refer to a particular watch without having the least knowledge of a wheel which is one of its components. So the thesis of 3.24 would certainly be unacceptable as an account of the senses which ordinary proper names possess. But then since he thinks that differences amongst modes of determining the same reference belong to the realm of the inessential in language, he would hardly have devoted an important paragraph to them anyway. Rather, we should treat 3.24 as an account of the semantic content of an ordinary name.

We argued above that the *TLP* view is that the semantic content of a name is simply the object for which it stands, knowledge of which object is being talked about sufficing for understanding. Let us suppose that he wished such an account to apply to the proper names of ordinary language. Then there need be no conflict here if he also held a thesis of essentiality of composition. For in that case knowledge of the parts and their arrangement would be knowledge of something which is, necessarily, the object talked about. And conversely, knowledge of the reference of the name would be knowledge of something which is, necessarily, made up of those parts. Indeed a proposition containing a proper name would be logically equivalent to a proposition containing a description of the parts of the bearer of the name, and so both would, on the *TLP* account of the semantic content, say the very same thing.

The thesis of essentiality of composition can easily seem plausible in its own right. For consider a particular physical artefact, say an individual table. Could this very table have been made out of different parts? Could it have existed if its parts had never existed? Surely not. For what, in that case, would have made it true that it was this very table which existed rather than another? Of course it would hardly be plausible to maintain that every single part of an object is essential to it, for the table could surely have existed had a different piece of wood been used for one of its legs. And we also need to make some provision for the replacement of parts over time. What is perhaps essential to the individual table is that it should have been made up of most of the parts from which it was originally constructed, arranged in something like the way in which they were.[11]

The *TLP* doctrine of ordinary proper names might then be seen as follows. Speakers will employ some means of determining the reference of any name which they understand. These modes of thinking may vary from person to person, and their discovery and description would be the business of psychology. From the point of view of successful communication all that matters is the reference: so long as speakers know themselves to be speaking of the very same things they will understand one another. But in virtue of the thesis of essentiality of composition for complex objects, each such name will be logically equivalent to a description of the composition of its referent. Consequently sentences containing such a description will be logically equivalent to the corresponding sentences which contain the ordinary proper names. So they will say the very same things, and the former may be regarded as an analysis of the latter.

Such an account cannot be generally acceptable however. For essentiality of composition is not indefinitely transitive, nor does it apply to all categories of object. Thus although it may be essential to this table that it should have been made out of the pieces of wood of which it was, it could surely have consisted of quite different atoms and molecules. For suppose that the trees which had supplied the planks had been fed on nutrients consistng of qualitatively similar but numerically distinct molecules throughout their lives. Then the table would still have consisted of the very same pieces of wood (and indeed the planks would still have derived from the very same trees – in the case of living things it is their point of origin, not their composition, which is essential to their identity),[12] and would thus still have been the very same, despite consisting of different microscopic parts. So a sentence involving a name for that table would not, after all, be logically equivalent to a sentence enumerating its simple parts.

It might be doubted whether essentiality of composition is really necessary to Wittgenstein's case. For suppose that ordinary proper names are rigid designators, as Kripke and others have argued, referring to the same individuals with respect to all possible worlds.

And suppose that their analyses in *TLP* employed descriptions of parts having the form 'The thing which is in fact made up of the following parts . . . ', the role of the 'in fact' being to index the description to its reference in the actual world. Then such a description will, if accurate, have the same reference as the corresponding name with respect to all possible worlds, the two then being logically equivalent.

This suggestion is an advance on the previous one, successfully reconciling a form of description-theory of names with the thesis that the semantic content of an ordinary name is exhausted by its bearer. Yet if we suppose Wittgenstein to have adopted either it or the previous suggestion, then he must be mistaken in his view that the relationship between the *analysans* containing the ordinary name and the *analysandum* enumerating the parts of its referent would be a logical (tautologous) one, and hence one which for him must be dependent upon the symbols alone (6.113, 6.126). For it is not in virtue of being the symbol which it is (having the sense which it does) that a proper name will be equivalent to a world-indexed description accurately describing the component parts of its referent. Rather, this will be true in virtue of the nature of its reference. Nor could such a truth be known *a priori*, through reflection on sense alone. So what Wittgenstein needs is to find a place for a distinctively metaphysical rather than narrowly conceptual species of necessity.[13] Now I shall argue in *MT* chapter 3 that there is nothing in his approach to metaphysics in general which stands in the way of his recognizing the category of metaphysical necessity. But it would of course mean that his programme of analysis, as well as his attempt to reduce all necessity to tautology, would have to be abandoned.

There is therefore no wholly satisfactory way of interpreting Wittgenstein's version of description-theory for ordinary names. Construed as a theory of sense it is manifestly absurd. And although construed as a theory of semantic content it may be in one respect acceptable, it nevertheless requires the backing of a distinction between metaphysical and conceptual necessity, which would put it entirely at odds with the programme of analysis within which the theory itself is placed. As to the question what might have motivated him to embrace a form of description-theory of any sort, the answer will have to wait on my investigation in *MT* of the *TLP* programme of analysis and the argument to Simples.

12.4 IDENTITY

We may now see how the above ideas fit together in the *TLP* treatment of identity. If true identity-statements involving two simple names are both necessary and knowable *a priori*, and if all ordinary proper names are analysable into a description of the simple component parts of their referents, then the identity-sign will only ever figure significantly in sentences where it occurs within the scope of a quantifier. What Wittgenstein notices, and explains at 5.53–5.534, is that it is then possible to do without such a sign altogether. Its use can rather be absorbed into the quantifier notation, by means of the convention that different variables within the scope of a quantifier are always to be replaced by names for different things. Thus 'b = The F', where 'b' is an ordinary proper name, will in fact have the form '$\exists x(Gx \mathbin{\&} \forall y(Gy \rightarrow y = \text{The F}))$', where 'Gx' is a description of the simple component parts of b. And this in turn, employing the above convention, may be expressed as '$\exists x(Gx \mathbin{\&} (\exists xGx \rightarrow \text{The F is G}) \mathbin{\&} -\exists x\exists y(Gx \mathbin{\&} Gy))$'. So as Wittgenstein remarks at 5.533, the identity-sign would not be an essential ingredient in a conceptual notation (Begriffsschrift), thus giving sense to the claim that identity is not a relation (5.5301).[14]

How much of this could survive our excision of the *TLP* claim that ordinary proper names may be analysed into a description of component parts? Clearly it would no longer be possible to say that the identity-sign will only ever occur significantly within the scope of a quantifier, and so the argument for the inessential nature of such a sign would collapse. But a slightly weaker thesis might remain, as we shall see in a moment.

Supposing that the semantic content of an ordinary name may be identified with its bearer (as we shall argue in the next chapter that it should) then how ought we to respond to Frege's original argument for his full-blown theory, premised upon the informativeness of identity-statements? Clearly we must deny that the cognitive content (the sense) of such statements will in general be intersubjective. Rather, since different speakers may associate different senses with the names involved, the information to be gleaned from the truth of an identity-statement will vary from person to person. Yet since we are agreeing with Frege that names at least have idiolectic senses, we can hold on to his insight that it is only possible to explain the differing cognitive content of 'a = a' and 'a = b' if we accept that names express modes of thinking in addition to possessing a referent.

We should, nevertheless, be committed to the claim that there is no difference in semantic content (Sinn) between 'a = a' and 'a = b'. And this can easily seem counter-intuitive. For if I assert that Jekyll is Hyde, have I not said something different from when I assert that Jekyll is Jekyll? Indeed if you misheard me, and took me to be saying that Jekyll is Jekyll, would you not have misunderstood me? Since we are committed to answering these questions in the negative, we need somehow to explain away the temptation to think the opposite. Here the familiar distinction between semantics and pragmatics can come to our aid – the distinction being between what speakers literally and soberly say, and what they would be understood to be trying to communicate in saying what they do. On the semantic level there is no difference, I claim, between 'Jekyll is Hyde' and 'Jekyll is Jekyll'. But obviously what someone would be trying to communicate by asserting the former would differ from what, if anything, they would be trying to communicate in asserting the latter. An identity-statement is only ever made, in general, when the speaker presumes that their hearer will attach different senses to the names involved. And what, pragmatically, they will be trying to communicate is that both of those modes of thinking (whatever they are – the speaker need have no precise knowledge of them) in fact pick out one and the same individual.[15]

Returning now to the question of the role of the identity–sign on such a view, the point to notice is that it will only ever figure in sentences whose semantic content differs from that of 'a = a' (or '–(a = a)') when it occurs within the scope of a quantifier. This is not quite the same as saying, with Wittgenstein, that the identity-sign is dispensable. For in any language which allows there to be names with different modes of determining what may be the same referent, we shall have need of a sign to express such a fact. But its usefulness will be confined to the cognitive contents expressible within the idiolects of particular speakers. The identity-sign will make no distinctive contribution to the semantic (literally communicable) content of sentences.

SUMMARY

The *TLP* semantics for simple names is that they express senses which are merely idiolectic, their semantic content being exhausted by their bearers.[16] As for ordinary proper names, Wittgenstein is best read as wishing to extend his thesis to them, but as having been misled into thinking that this would be consistent with subjecting their semantic content to analysis. Thus interpreted, he is still able to retain most of his views on identity as well as to reply to Frege's argument from the informativeness of identity–statements.

13

Proper Name Semantics

Our task in this chapter is to deploy Charity in defence of the reading outlined in chapter 12, sketching out how Wittgenstein's position – construed as an account of the semantics of ordinary proper names – is more powerful than any of its rivals.

13.1 THE SEMANTIC CONTENT OF NAMES

Consider first the thesis that the semantic content of a name is exhausted by its bearer, which contrasts with any form of full Fregean theory, that mutual knowledge of speakers' modes of determining the reference of a name is required for communication.

The most plausible version of Fregean theory is the so-called 'Cluster Theory' of names.[1] This holds that the public sense of a name will be a body of information about its bearer, consisting of both definite and indefinite descriptions, comprising all beliefs within that name-using community which are more or less truisms about the bearer. In order to allow for the possibility that some of this information may turn out to be false of the bearer without the name being deprived of reference, the theory holds that the sense of a name will take the form 'The thing of which most of the following body of information is true . . . . '. The criterion of sameness of sense for names is also to be construed loosely, in such a way that names may be said to have the same sense although the clusters of information associated with them do not precisely coincide. This allows a name to retain the same sense through a degree of change in its associated cluster, resulting either from addition or subtraction of information. It also permits speakers to be said to know the sense of the name although they do not themselves possess the full body of information associated with it. (Not everyone who is competent in the use of the name 'Moses' knows that he was found in the bullrushes by Pharoah's daughter.)

The Cluster Theory is at its most plausible in connection with names of historical and public figures and places, such as 'Moses', 'Margaret Thatcher' and 'Hiroshima'. For in such cases there does seem to be a body of public, truistic, information available, which most competent users of the name in the language-community will know most of. It is much less plausible in connection with names of private individuals and out-of-the-way places. For in these cases different users of the name may possess quite different – perhaps non-overlapping – bodies of information. Of course this fact in itself is not decisive, since Cluster Theorists can respond by claiming that the language-community for such a name in fact fragments into many different communities, each of which associates a different sense with it. But then they are constrained to say that speakers from these different name-communities will fail to understand one another in the use of the name, even if they know that they are talking about the very same thing, since they do not know what sense the other associates with it. Yet this is extremely implausible.

For example, someone who knew me well at school but who knows beyond this only that I went on to teach philosophy at Essex, and someone who knows my writing but who otherwise only knows my place of affiliation, may surely understand one another in the use of the name 'Peter Carruthers', and go on to exchange information about me successfully, as soon as they learn of the one piece of identifying information which they hold in common. They do not have to know the majority of the information which the other associates with the name before they can be said to communicate. It is natural to claim, on the contrary, that it is sufficient for understanding that the speakers know they are talking about the very same person – which is precisely the *TLP* thesis that the semantic content of a name is exhausted by its referent.

Faced with examples of this sort there is only one possible line for Fregean theorists to take: they must hold a shifting-sense theory, allowing the sense of a name to vary from context to context in accordance with the information held in common between the speakers.[2] But even this will not do, since it is possible for speakers to know that they are talking about the same thing without knowing anything at all about one another's mode of determining the reference of a name, and yet we should be strongly inclined to say that they fully understand one another in its use. Any example of the following schematic sort will do:[3] A and B know that they each associate some piece of identifying information, α, with the name 'N'; B and C know that they share a piece of identifying information, β, of what is in fact the same thing, also associated with 'N'; where the modes of thinking α and β do not in any way overlap. Then imagine that when A and B have been talking about N, B says to C as the latter enters the room 'We were just talking about N'. This gives both A and C sufficient reason to believe that they will use the name 'N', at least on this occasion, to refer to the very same thing. Then if A remarks 'I was just saying that N is now 64 years old', C surely understands this, despite knowing nothing whatever of A's mode of thinking of N. Here it can only be the mere fact of mutual knowledge of reference which suffices for understanding.

It is easy to see how these intuitive judgements about mutual understanding can be underpinned if we recall that the purpose of successful communication, in factual discourse, is to facilitate the acquisition of rationally grounded beliefs about the world. For it suffices to give me reason to add a belief to my stock of information about an individual if I know that your assertion concerns that very same thing. And this reason-giving force will remain unaffected whether or not I know the manner in which you are thinking of it. Moreover, in contrast with the case of predicates and molecular and general statements discussed in chapter 5, even the practice of challenging and providing evidence for statements leaves the position unchanged. For a challenge to the truth of an atomic statement will hardly ever concern the existence of a bearer for one of the names involved. This is because we rarely have occasion to introduce a new name until the existence of its intended bearer is known for certain, and because a piece of information will not be added to a speaker's mode of identifying the bearer until it has for them the status of a truism about that thing. So there is no special pressure on us to try to secure mutual knowledge of one another's modes of identification (especially since the task would in many cases be onerous); on the contrary, mutual knowledge of reference will suffice.

13.2 INDIRECT DISCOURSE

If we are to provide an adequate defence of the *TLP* theory of names, then we should not rest content with raising objections against its rivals, but should also show how it can respond to the arguments deployed in their support. We saw at the end of chapter 12 how the sting can be drawn from Frege's argument from the informativeness of identity-statements. But what of his other main argument, that the notion of intersubjective sense is needed to explain the role of names within indirect discourse, for example within reports of belief?[4] Frege's view is that names here refer to the senses which they ordinarily express, these senses serving as a partial specification of the content of the subject's propositional attitude. Obviously we are prevented from offering any such account, since we are denying that there is in general any such thing as the intersubjective sense of a name. But in that case what is it that I assert when I say 'Mary believes that Reagan is kindly'?

Here we need to advert once again to the two different perspectives we can take towards belief-description, mentioned briefly in chapter 5. Sometimes our interest in reports of belief is itself belief-acquisitive, the fact that someone else reportedly believes something giving me some reason to believe it myself. From this perspective a report of belief has only to respect the semantic content of the belief in question, which in the case of names means only that reference is to be preserved. So reports of belief from this perspective are *de re*, and it matters not how you choose to refer to whatever the belief is about. Yet even so it is implied that the believer has some particular mode of thinking about that thing, though it is not specified what their mode of thinking is. Thus when our primary interest is belief-acquisitive, 'Mary believes that Reagan is kindly' may be understood to say the following: 'There is some mode of thinking α, which is such that it is uniquely about Reagan, and Mary believes [that α is kindly]'.[5]

The other major perspective which we take towards belief-description is explanatory. Here it is crucial that the report should respect the mode of thinking employed by the believer themself, or at least be sufficiently close to it for the explanatory purpose in hand. In general the criterion of accuracy will be sameness of cognitive content (idiolectic sense): the sentence used in the report being required to have the very same cognitive content as the thinker's belief, or otherwise to describe that content. This immediately raises a problem for us. For since we deny that names have inter-subjective senses, they are unfitted for use in communicating cognitive content. But I do not see that this is any real objection to our account. For it is independently plausible that one has to be careful in using proper names if we wish to specify the precise content of someone's belief.[6]

One way of using names to convey the content of a belief is indirect, drawing on our background knowledge of the believer's situation to enable us to recover from that report sufficient information about their mode of thinking. For example Kripke, in telling us the story of Pierre in his (1979), in fact gives us enough information to be able to approximate to the content of the beliefs reported by 'Pierre believes that London is pretty' and 'Pierre believes that London is not pretty' respectively. (The story is that having lived all his life in France, Pierre has acquired sufficient information about London for him to be inclined to assert 'Londres est jolie'. He then moves to England, settling in what is in fact part of London, and learns English by the direct method. Then, without having given up his earlier belief, he is inclined to assert 'London is not pretty'.) In the first case we know him to be thinking of London by description, presumably including such information as that it is the capital city of England, with many ancient buildings and parks and so on. In the second case we know him to be thinking of London through his acquaintance with the part of it in which he lives. This information is of course not strictly asserted by the reports of Pierre's belief, but is recoverable from them by those who know the story.[7]

In cases where there is no such background knowledge about the believer's situation, a proper name will only be of service in describing the content of a belief from the explanatory standpoint in contexts where it can reasonably be presumed that we and our hearers (and of course the believer in question) associate sufficiently similar modes of thinking with it. Thus if I say to a philosophical colleague 'Mary believes that Michael Dummett lives in Oxford', then this should be construed as saying the following: 'There is a mode of thinking α, which is uniquely about Michael Dummett and is close enough to our mode of thinking of him for the explanatory purpose in hand, such that Mary believes [that α lives in Oxford]'. Whereas if I wish to describe Mary's belief to someone who has met Dummett at a party without realizing that he is a philosopher, then I may have to adopt a more indirect mode of description, such as 'Mary, who knows of Michael Dummett as a famous philosopher, believes that he lives in Oxford'.

13.3 LACK OF EXISTENCE

Perhaps the strongest objection to the *TLP* account concerns names such as 'Vulcan' (intended to be the name of a supposed intra-Mercurial planet) which lack a bearer.[8] For it commits us to the view that sentences containing such names are without semantic content – utterances of them saying nothing (being unsinnig: 3.24), there being nothing which counts as understanding them. Yet is this not extremely counter-intuitive? For two scientists discussing the likely velocity of Vulcan or the temperature on its surface may surely understand one another and succeed in communicating.

In reply we only need to draw a distinction between understanding an utterance and understanding the person who makes the utterance. If Mary says to Peter 'Vulcan is hot', then on our account she has in fact said nothing, and nothing that Peter can do will count as understanding it (knowing its semantic content) since it is without semantic content. That sentence will nevertheless serve, in Mary's mouth, to express a particular belief (described from the explanatory standpoint). For we are conceding that names (even bearerless ones) have idiolectic senses, expressing for their users determinate modes of thinking. Peter will of course know that this is so, and in context may have a fair idea of what Mary's mode of thinking is. So when she says 'Vulcan is hot' he may be said to understand her, in that he knows (roughly) why she has uttered that sentence: he knows (roughly) what belief it expresses for her. This gives us a sense in which the two of them may be said to communicate despite the fact that their utterances are without semantic content (have no literal meaning). It is sufficient, for example, to distinguish their conversation from a random sequence of noises, and to explain how the various moves which each makes in the course of the conversation can be intelligible to the other. Nevertheless, considered as a piece of putatively fact-orientated discourse, the whole conversation must be regarded as abortive.

A closely related problem concerns the semantics of negative singular existentials. If I say 'There is no such planet as Vulcan' (which we may represent either as having the form '$-Eb$' or the form '$-\exists x(x = b)$'),[9] then I surely succeed in asserting something. Yet how can this be, it the name 'Vulcan' is without semantic content? We might try responding to this difficulty by denying that such statements have a determinate content, pointing out that our characteristic response to them is to ask 'How do you mean?'[10] But this is not very persuasive. Although it is true that if someone says 'There is no such person as Margaret Thatcher' my immediate response will be to ask 'What do you mean?', it does not follow from this that the statement lacks determinate content, since my response would be the same if it had been said instead 'Margaret Thatcher was never Prime Minister'. The question 'What do you mean?' in such cases is not so much a demand to specify a content, as a request to explain how we could have been so seriously mistaken.

What is right about the above suggestion is that a negative existential should be regarded as an hiatus in the normal use of a proper name.[11] But rather than denying it semantic content altogether, a better response to the problem is again to make use of the idea that bearerless names, while lacking semantic content, will still express idiolectic senses. We can then interpret the negative existential '$-\exists x(x = b)$' (or '$-Eb$') to say this: 'For all modes of identifying a thing α: if α is associated by us with this use of the name "b", then the thought [that $\exists x(x = \alpha)$] is false'. So in the case of the statement 'There is no such planet as Vulcan' we can regard this as saying: 'For all modes of uniquely identifying a planet α, associated by us with the name "Vulcan", the thought [that α exists] is false'. This provides a semantic content for negative singular existentials while remaining faithful to the thesis that in normal discourse the semantic content of a name is its bearer.

13.4 FIT VERSUS ORIGIN

Many have agreed with Wittgenstein in rejecting Frege's theory of the semantic content of names. But few others have combined this with an acceptance of Frege's account of the manner in which reference gets fixed.[12] This is that the reference of a name, within the idiolect of a given speaker, is determined by the mode of thinking – the sense – which that speaker associates with it. Most who have held the view that the semantic content of name is exhausted by its referent have seen reference as being fixed by something external to the speaker, generally a causal chain linking the speaker's use of the name, via the uses of it by other members of the speech community, to some baptismal or information-gathering episode involving the referent.[13] The difference can be summarized by saying that for Wittgenstein reference is determined as what best *fits* the mode of thinking which a speaker associates with a name, whereas for others it is determined by the *causal origin* of the speaker's use of it.

In the version of causal theory proposed by Kripke, the causal chain is to lead back to the first occasion on which the name was used. This can have counter-intuitive consequences. For example, suppose that the baby which was in fact baptized 'Margaret Thatcher' was switched soon afterwards with another without anyone knowing. Then according to Kripke we should all of us now be speaking of someone other than the 1989 Prime Minister when we use that name, and most of our beliefs involving the name would be false. But the causal theory also admits of more sophisticated forms, for example that the referent of a name is to be the causal source of most of the information which a speaker associates with it.[14] This has the desired consequence in the example above, that we are indeed speaking of the 1989 Prime Minister when we use the name 'Margaret Thatcher'. Yet what all forms of the causal theory agree on is that reference is determined by something outside of the speaker's thought and consciousness.

I confess that I find this difficult to understand. For reference is not – unlike parenthood – the sort of relation which we find ready-made in the world, our only tasks being to label it and investigate its nature scientifically, perhaps discovering *a posteriori* that it is causal. On the contrary, if causal origin has a role to play in determining reference this can only be because we as speakers intend that it should do so. It is these intentions which would find their expression in our intuitive judgements about who, in the sorts of example used to support the causal theory, has succeeded in referring to what. But then it would no longer be something external which determines reference, but rather the speaker's intention to refer to the causal origin of the information which they associate with the name; which is just a more sophisticated version of the theory that reference is determined by *fit* with the speaker's mode of thinking.

The main problem for causal theorists is this: what if speakers were to dig their heels in when faced with the sort of example used to support the causal theory, and were to insist that no, they had not been referring to that thing (the thing which is in fact the causal origin of their use of the name), but rather to the one and only thing which is such-and-such? True enough, this does not tend to happen (the examples have a strong intuitive appeal); but what if it did? Would causal theorists really be prepared to override the speaker's own clear statement of what it is that they meant?[15]

So much for the theoretical case against the causal theory of referring. Defenders of the causal theory generally assume that their opponents are committed to the view that the sense of a name will always take the form of a definite description. But as we saw in chapter 12, this is false. Any plausible version of the theory that reference is determined by *fit* should maintain that the idiolectic sense of a name can consist – partially if not wholly – in a recognitional capacity. All the same it is worth considering the arguments of causal theorists on their own terms.

13.5 KRIPKE'S ARGUMENTS

One of the main arguments used against description-theories turns on the behaviour of proper names within modal contexts.[16] In particular, for any proper name 'N', it will be true that N might not have been F, where 'F' is any description which could plausibly be thought to constitute its sense. In contrast 'The F might not have been F' will generally be false. Kripke sums this up in the claim that proper names are rigid designators – they designate the very same individuals with respect to all possible worlds – whereas descriptions designate non-rigidly, their reference with respect to a given world depending upon the thing in that world which happens to satisfy (fit) the description. It follows, Kripke thinks, that the description-theory of reference-fixing for names must be false, since the logical behaviour of names and descriptions is so different.

The argument is unsound however. Notice to begin with that there is a way of reading 'The F might not have been F' according to which it comes out true, namely where we understand the definite description to fall outside the scope of the counter-factual, being indexed, as it were, to the thing which is in fact the F in the actual world. For example, 'The Queen might never have become a monarch' would naturally be understood as saying that the person who is in fact Queen in the actual world in some other possible world lives her life without ever ascending to the throne (e.g. because she has an elder brother). So in order to rebut the argument it is formally sufficient to claim that there is a convention according to which the modal operator in a sentence containing a proper name is always understood to have narrow scope, so that the name is indexed to its reference in the actual world.[17]

Of course it is one thing to make such a claim, and another thing to motivate it properly. But in fact the combination of views we are attributing to Wittgenstein means that a defence of our claim is not far to seek.[18] For in the absence of the above convention, the truth-value of a modal statement – and hence of course its semantic content – would vary depending upon what descriptive information is associated by the speaker with the proper names involved. Then since speakers do not in general know the modes of determining reference which others employ, this would mean that in modal discourse we should constantly be misunderstanding one another. If Wittgenstein is right that the semantic content of a name in transparent contexts is exhausted by its referent – different speakers differing over the modes of determining reference they employ – then a convention whose effect is to retain the same semantic content for names in modal contexts is almost inevitable, else we should continually be having to exchange descriptions before we could understand one another's counter-factual and other modal statements.[19]

Kripke's other major argument against description-theories of reference-fixing turns on the fact that a speaker may succeed in referring via the use of a name, despite the fact that all of the information which they associate with the name is in fact false of its bearer. In which case it follows, he thinks, that it cannot be the associated information which determines the reference. For instance, consider his famous Gödel/Schmidt example.[20] Suppose that my only identifying information about Gödel is that he was the first to prove the incompleteness of arithmetic. But suppose that, unknown to me, it was in fact a little-known Austrian called

'Schmidt' who first constructed such a proof, Gödel having stolen his result and published it under his own name. Despite this, we should surely wish to maintain that I say something true when I assert 'Gödel is now living in America', which requires that my use of the name 'Gödel' has somehow succeeded in referring to Gödel, and not to Schmidt who still lives in Austria.

Of course there is one further identifying description available to me in this example, namely 'The person referred to as "Gödel" by those from whom I derived this use of the name'. If it were this rather than the previous description which determined my reference, then I should after all have been talking about Gödel, just as intuition suggests. This would be sufficient to save the description-theory from Kripke's counter-example.[21] But what needs to be shown is that speakers do indeed employ such descriptions; and it needs to be explained why they should allow these other-dependent descriptions to override their identifying information, serving ultimately to determine what they refer to.

The important feature of Kripke's example is that both the belief and the name in question are derived from hearsay, since it is an obvious piece of common sense that the information which we base upon the word of others is very often wrong. For consider the risks that we would run if we allowed information gained through hearsay to determine the reference of names which are introduced to us in that way. Firstly, as we built up our dossier of information around the name we should risk failing to refer at all, since there may be no person, or no one person, of whom most of that information is true. Secondly, we may end up referring (as in the example above) to someone other than was referred to by those from whom we derived our use of the name, thus entirely undercutting any warrant which their assertions may have given us for our beliefs. The only way for us to safeguard reference, and to maximize the opportunities for successful communication, is to hold ourselves responsible, in the use of the name, to the reference which it has for those from whom we derived it.

In fact the users of a proper name may be divided into producers and consumers, as Evans suggests.[22] The producers are the primary users of the name, who are acquainted with its bearer and refer to it by virtue of that acquaintance. This gives pride of place to recognitional capacities amongst the senses of names, since it seems very likely that such capacities must play a crucial part in a producer's mode of thinking of the bearer of a name. The consumers are secondary users, deriving their use of a name (either directly, or indirectly through other consumers) from that of the producers, and holding themselves responsible to the reference which the name has for those producers from whom they derived it.

The sense which a consumer of the name 'N' will associate with it, will therefore be such as to imply the following description: N is the thing referred to by those from whom I derived this use of the name 'N' (where the use of the name in question is individuated by means of the dossier of information associated with it). Notice that I say that the consumer-sense will imply, rather than be identical with, such a description. For if a consumer thinks 'N is bald', it would in general be implausible to identify the cognitive content of their thought with the content of a thought involving a description of the above form. One reason is that their thought is surely focused outwards on the person N, not inwards on the dossier of beliefs which they associate with the name 'N'. Nor is it very plausible to claim that they are explicitly thinking about causality. But this need not prevent their thought from implying such a description, as will emerge from the fact that they are disposed to take themselves to be committed to certain other thoughts and beliefs. Indeed our intuitive response to Kripke's own examples is evidence of just such a situation.

So when I entertain the thought 'Gödel is in America' the cognitive content of what I think cannot be expressed by any sentence which employs a definite description in place of the name 'Gödel'. But the fact that I respond to Kripke's hypothetical example by saying that I should nevertheless have been thinking about Gödel, and not Schmidt who lives in Austria, is sufficient to show that I understand the name in such a way as to commit myself to the description 'The person referred to by those from whom I acquired this use of the name "Gödel"'. Thus a consumer-name has an idiolectic sense which implies a definite description mentioning causality, and the name comes to have the reference which it does in virtue of there being a unique thing which fits the implied description; and yet the cognitive content of the name is not expressible by means of any such description.[23]

Note that there is nothing incoherent about the sense of a name implying a description which mentions the reference which that name has for others, so long as the chain of dependent usage comes to an end somewhere. For remember that we are not concerned with the public, intersubjective, senses of names (it really would be incoherent to claim that all speakers employ a name with an other-dependent sense). Indeed we are engaged in defending a thesis which denies that there are any such senses. Our claim is only about how any given speaker's use of a name comes to refer: namely, that reference is effected by virtue of a unique object fitting the mode of thinking which the speaker associates with it, the consumer-sense of a name always having an other-dependent form.

Turning now to consider the producer-sense of a name, we should notice that there are examples which are formally analogous to the ones we have been discussing. These force on us a parallel modification in the form which such a sense will take. Thus suppose that when I first meet and am introduced to Gödel he is (unknown to me) heavily made up for a part in a play, in fact closely resembling Schmidt. I might thereafter take my use of the name 'Gödel' to be founded on a recognitional capacity when really it is not. For although I should be disposed to 'recognize' Schmidt as Gödel, I would surely succeed in referring to Gödel when I use the name. This raises a prima facie difficulty for the thesis that the reference of a producer-name is determined by *fit*. But here I have available the further description 'The man through acquaintance with whom I acquired this use of the name "Gödel"' (the use in question being individuated by my 'recognitional' disposition).[24] And we can explain why this description should be allowed to override my supposed recognitional capacity in determining the reference of my use of 'Gödel' in a manner similar to the other-dependent case. For since it is a matter of common sense that defects in perception and recognition can occur, and that the appearance of objects can change very greatly over time, if I were to allow reference to be determined by whatever fits my recognitional capacity I should risk referring to things which I was never in fact acquainted with, thus undercutting the rational basis for my beliefs.[25]

We can therefore continue to maintain that reference is determined by *fit* rather than mere causal origin in the face of Kripke's counter-examples; our account having the additional advantage that both the consumer and producer senses of a name are of a form such that the things fitting their implied descriptions will in fact be the causal origin of those uses of the name, thus explaining the intuitive appeal of the examples.

SUMMARY

A semantic theory of names of the sort which we have attributed to Wittgenstein is to be preferred, on the one hand, to Frege's theory that communication requires mutual knowledge of modes of determining reference, and on the other hand to theories which require reference to be determined by something other than *fit* with the modes of thinking associated with a name.

14

Isomorphic Representation

In this chapter we begin our consideration of the Picture Theory of the proposition, outlining and assessing the interpretation which lies closest to the surface of Wittgenstein's text: namely that sentences represent isomorphically; a relation between two individuals, for example, being represented by a relation between two proper names.

14.1 EARLY INSIGHTS

In January 1913 Wittgenstein wrote a letter to Russell in which he claimed to have made a new discovery: that qualities and relations are all copulae (*NB* 120–1). Instead of thinking of the state of affairs of Socrates being mortal as consisting of Socrates and mortality linked to one another by a special sort of relation (a two-place copula), he now wishes to analyse it into Socrates and 'something is mortal'. The motivation for the change of view, he says, is that there cannot be different types of things. On his old way of looking at the matter, both 'Socrates' and 'mortal' get treated as kinds of name, and then a theory of types is necessary to explain why 'Mortality is Socrates' is nonsense. But his new analysis, he thinks, renders a theory of types superflous by making it impossible to substitute the wrong way round, since the two symbols are themselves of different kinds.

Here, then, was clear expression of an idea which remains associated with the Picture Theory throughout its development, as we shall see. The problem of sentential significance – of what makes 'Socrates is mortal' significant but 'Mortality is Socrates' and 'Socrates Plato' not – is to be solved by distinguishing between different kinds of symbols, one of which itself is (or contains) a copula. It is also the earliest expression of the doctrine that logic (and the theory of symbolism generally) has priority over metaphysics, to be discussed fully in *MT*. For the mistake in the doctrine of the copula, Wittgenstein thinks, is that it then requires the backing of a metaphysical theory of types to explain sentential significance. There is also some suggestion in this early letter that it is a mistake to think of a predicative expression as being related to reality in anything like the way that a proper name is, it being this that gives rise to the illusion that objects and properties are merely different kinds of thing.

By the time of writing the 'Notes on Logic', in September of the same year, Wittgenstein's ideas had sharpened considerably. He now distinguishes between names and *forms* (general indefinables), the proposition 'aRb' being analysed into the names 'a' and 'b' and the indefinable form 'xRy' (*NB* 98). So he still thinks that it is the relational expression itself which contains the copula. But he also insists, for the first time, that a proposition is a fact (*NB* 98). This is certainly one aspect of the mature Picture Theory, where it is supposed to be the fact that the elements in a sentence are related to one another in a particular way which enables it to represent a configuration of objects. (See 2.14–2.15, 3.14–3.1432.) Not only this, but he also says that what symbolizes the relation in 'aRb' is not the sign 'R' itself, but rather a relation between the signs 'a' and 'b', of which the sign 'R' forms only a part (*NB* 99,105). This too is an aspect of the mature Picture Theory. (See in particular 3.1432.)

However this time the ideas are not introduced as providing a solution to the problem of sentential significance, but rather to explain how it is possible for us to understand new sentences, Wittgenstein insisting that there must be general indefinable symbols if it is to be possible for us to understand propositions which we have never heard before (*NB* 98).[1] This too survives into the mature Picture Theory, since it is said to be the fact that we can understand new propositions without them having to be explained to us which shows that a proposition is a picture (4.015–4.02).

Wittgenstein's doctrine would then appear to be that what symbolizes in the proposition 'Socrates is mortal' is a certain fact, namely the fact that the name 'Socrates' has a certain property (the property of having the sign 'is mortal' written immediately to the right of it). Similarly, what symbolizes in the proposition 'Socrates loves Plato' is a certain fact, namely that the names 'Socrates' and

'Plato' stand to one another in the relation of being written one on the left and one on the right of the sign 'loves'. The idea is thus that representation is isomorphic, the predicative fact that Socrates is mortal being symbolized by the fact that the name 'Socrates' (itself an individual thing) has a certain property, and the relational fact that Socrates loves Plato being symbolized by the fact that the names 'Socrates' and 'Plato' (again individual things) stand to one another in a certain relation, and so on.

Note that at this early stage, at least, Wittgenstein thinks that both names and forms signify elements of reality (have reference). For he speaks of the relation which figures in 'aRb' being related to the relation R in a way which is in some respects analogous to the way in which a name is related to a thing (*NB* 99). And in a particularly revealing remark in the 'Notes dictated to Moore', he says that propositions are related to reality by virtue of (a) their names being names of simples, and (b) their relations having quite a different sort of relation to relations (*NB* 111). (Nothing further is said here about what the 'difference in sort' might be.) So at this stage the doctrine is not just that relational facts, for example, are symbolized by relational facts; it is also that each distinct element in the representation – i.e. the two names, as well as the relation between them – refers to a distinct aspect of reality; namely, to two simple individuals and a relation.

It is easy to see how the thesis of isomorphic representation might help with the problem of sentential significance. For if what symbolizes loving, in 'Socrates loves Plato', is the relation which exists between two names written on either side of the sign 'loves', then it is obvious why 'Loves Socrates Plato' is nonsense. For in this sequence of signs the relation in question simply does not occur. Similarly, 'Socrates Plato' is nonsense because no significance has been attached to the relation which exists between two names when one is written immediately after the other.

It is not nearly so obvious, on the other hand, how the thesis could help solve the problem of the new sentence. For the task here is to explain how we can know the meaning of a previously unencountered sentence in virtue of knowing the meanings of its component parts. Now according to the isomorphism thesis, the component parts of 'Socrates loves Plato' are two names and a relation between them. So I know that 'Socrates' stands for Socrates, that 'Plato' stands for Plato, and that the relation between the two names stands for the relation of loving. But this does not by itself give me an understanding of the sentence: I must also know that a whole consisting of three such parts says that the things which the names stand for are related to one another by means of the relation for which the relation stands.[2] I must know, in fact, that the sentence purports to be an isomorphic representation: that if I come across a sentence (a fact) in which two names stand in a certain relation to one another, then the sentence will say that the things which the names stand for are related to one another by means of the relation signified by the relation between them.

According to the isomorphism thesis there must then be two distinct aspects to the knowledge which enables us to understand new sentences: on the one hand there is the knowledge of the reference of the component parts of the sentence, the names and relations involved; and on the other hand there is the knowledge that this sentence, like any other, purports to be an isomorphic representation of a fact, saying that the referents of the component parts stand to one another in a manner isomorphic to the arrangement of those parts themselves. Yet this is precisely *not* to solve the problem of the new sentence, which was to explain our understanding of new sentences on the basis of our understanding of their component parts alone.

If we had been allowed to introduce an additional item of knowledge into the explanation like this, then we could have solved the problem of the new sentence without embracing the isomorphism thesis (though we might still have needed that thesis to solve the problem of sentential significance). We could have said that we understand 'Socrates loves Plato' by virtue of knowing (besides the reference of 'Socrates', 'loves' and 'Plato') that whenever a sentence consists of a name of a thing, followed by a name of a relation, followed by a name of another thing, then the whole sentence says that the first thing stands in the relation named by the relation-sign to the second thing. Now admittedly, the extra item of knowledge enabling us to understand 'Socrates is mortal' would have to be rather different. It would have to be the knowledge that whenever a sentence consists of a name of a thing followed by a name of a property, the sentence then says that the thing has the property. So it might be claimed as an advantage of the isomorphism thesis that it reduces the additional knowledge required for understanding new sentences to a single item, the same for all forms of sentence. But this advantage is minor, being comparable to the introduction of a notation which enables us to replace all the different forms of copulae (two-place, three place, etc.) with a single ubiquitous copula. We should still be left claiming that there is more required for the understanding of a new sentence than can be derived from the meanings of its component parts alone, just as the ubiquitous copula would still leave us having to deny (contra Wittgenstein) that predicates and relational expressions are themselves copulae.

The position so far is as follows: as early as the years 1913–14 Wittgenstein had arrived at the thesis of isomorphic representation, developing ideas which were to continue to be associated with the Picture Theory in *TLP*: that a sentence is a fact, and that the expression for the relation in 'aRb' is not the sign 'R' itself, but rather a relation of which that sign forms only a part. These ideas were introduced to subserve two distinct purposes: to solve both the problem of sentential significance and the problem of the new sentence. They can indeed solve the former problem (though we shall return to question the depth of this solution later). But they do not really help us with the latter.

14.2 SOME DISTINCTIONS

It is important to distinguish between a weak and a strong version of the thesis of isomorphic representation. For one might hold that sentences are isomorphic representations of facts without holding that every significant element of a sentence must stand in a relation of reference to an element of the fact.[3] In particular, one might accept that it is the relation obtaining between the names in 'Socrates loves Plato', rather than the sign 'loves' itself, which enables the sentence to express the fact that Socrates loves Plato, without holding that the relation between the names itself designates, or refers to, a relation. So from the fact that the Wittgenstein of *TLP* undoubtedly endorsed some version of the thesis, it does not follow that he believed that predicative expressions, like proper names, have reference. It may be that between the years 1914 and 1918 he moved from the strong version of the thesis – believing, as we have seen, that a relation between names serves to refer to a relation – to the weaker version, endorsing isomorphism without holding that the relation between the names itself refers to the relation obtaining between the things.

It is equally important to distinguish between the isomorphism thesis, on the one hand, and the doctrine that a sentence is a fact, on the other. Consider the possibility of a language containing no proper names but only predicates and relational expressions, individuals being signified by properties of the predicative expressions. For example, there could be a convention according to which differences in the style of script in which a predicate is written would be used to signify the individual being said to possess the corresponding property.[4] Thus 'TALL' might say that Plato is tall, 'tall' that Socrates is tall, 'TALLER than' that Plato is taller than Socrates, 'taller THAN' that Socrates is taller than Plato, and so on. With respect to this language the isomorphism thesis would fail, since the fact that Plato stands in a certain relation to Socrates would not be signified by a relation between their two names, but rather by a relational sign possessing two distinct attributes. Yet the doctrine that a sentence is a fact would still be correct. For it would not be the relational sign itself, but rather the fact that it is written in the two distinct styles of script, which would represent the situation in question.

This distinction is important because it turns out to be the doctrine that a sentence is a fact, rather than the thesis of isomorphism (in either of its versions) which really solves the problem of sentential significance. For in the language imagined above, the reason why 'taLL' would fail to constitute a sentence, for example, would be that no significance has been attached to the fact of that word being written in two distinct styles of script. (Just as in English 'Plato Socrates' fails to constitute a sentence because no significance has been attached to the fact of two proper names being written one after the other.) So what makes a sign into a sentence is that it constitutes a significant fact. It can be left open whether or not significant facts must be ones which are isomorphic with the situations depicted.

It might be thought that even the doctrine that a sentence is a fact stands easily refuted by the possibility of codes in which, for example, 'Marmalade' means 'I have passed on the microfilm'. But to this there are at least two effective replies. The first is that the existence of such codes must necessarily be parasitic upon notations in which sentences are facts, if we are to regain the potentially infinite expressive power of natural language. Only languages whose sentences consist of distinct elements combined in significant ways admit of the possibility of constructing unlimitedly many significant sentences. So we might say that a sentence, if it is to be part of a language with unlimited expressive power, must be a fact.[5]

The second possible reply to the objection would rely on the *TLP* identification of semantic content with logical equivalence. Since 'Marmalade' and 'I have passed on the microfilm' are here logically equivalent, they both possess the very same semantic content. And since the latter obviously contains a more explicit representation of their shared truth-condition than the former, it may be regarded as an anlysis of it. (See *MT* chapter 7 for a discussion of this idea of analysis.) So we could say that any sentence is (essentially) a fact, in that it will always be analysable into a sentence which is *manifestly* a fact.

14.3 ISOMORPHISM IN *TLP*

We have already noted that there is sufficient textual evidence to find in *TLP*, not only the doctrine that a sentence is a fact, but also the weak version (at least) of the thesis of isomorphic representation. But there are two quite distinct ways in which the latter thesis could be grounded in the text, depending upon whether we adopt the wide or the narrow reading of Wittgenstein's use of 'name'.

On the wide reading, the elementary sentences which constitute the end-point of analysis (and which consist only of 'names' in immediate concatenation) would contain both proper names and predicative expressions.[6] So here the isomorphism thesis would apply in the manner indicated at 3.1432: what really enables an elementary sentence to represent a relational state of affairs would not be the relational expression itself, but rather the relation which obtains between the proper names involved in the sentence, which exists when they are written on either side of the relational-sign. So on a wide reading of 'name' the isomorphism thesis would be true in precisely the same way for both elementary sentences and the sentences of ordinary language: the relational expressions occurring in such sentences would figure only as parts of relations between proper names.

It is worth recalling just how awkward the wide reading is as an interpretation of many of the crucial remarks of *TLP*. Consider 2.15, for example, which tells us that it is the fact that the elements of a picture are related to one another in a determinate way which represents that things are related to one another in the same way.[7] Given the wide reading of 'name' (in this context 'element') together with the isomorphism thesis, the 'elements' of a picture would include not only the proper names involved, but also the relations obtaining between them. So 2.15 would say that it is the determinate relation obtaining between two names and the relation between them (for example) which represents that two individuals and a relation stand in a determinate relation to one another. This is not only awkward in itself, but looks like a return to the doctrine of the copula; which was, as we have seen, what the isomorphism thesis was originally intended to eradicate.

It is also important to note that on the wide reading, the isomorphism thesis, together with the associated doctrine that a sentence is a fact, must constitute the whole of the Picture Theory.[8] Whereas if the narrow reading is adopted, as we shall see in the next chapter, there is the possibility of finding in the Picture Theory an additional thesis, namely that predicates and relational expressions do not have reference. In which case much may depend upon our assessment of the worth of the isomorphism thesis. If, as I shall argue in the next section, that thesis is relatively trivial and uninteresting, then Charity will provide us with a powerful motive to find some additional interpretation of the Picture Theory if we can – and this will mean adopting the narrow reading of 'name'.

The narrow reading is equally consistent with either of the two versions of isomorphism thesis. But it means that they would apply in a different way to elementary propositions (which consist only of proper names) than to the propositions of ordinary language. In connection with elementary propositions the truth (at least of the weak version of the thesis) would be apparent on the surface. Since such a proposition would consist only of proper names standing in some significant relation to one another, it would be manifest that relations between objects are being symbolized by relations between names.[9] Indeed it would be manifest that both states of affairs and the sentences which describe them consist of individual objects (the same number in each case) standing in some relation to one another, just as the isomorphism thesis requires. This might then be supposed to reveal to us something of the essence of ordinary propositions, showing that here too (and despite appearances to the contrary) it is relations between names which do the symbolizing, rather than the relational signs themselves.[10]

14.14 DEPTH OR TRIVIALITY?

We have already seen how we might construct a language which would represent contramorphically, rather than isomorphically. Objects would be signified, not by individual names, but rather by properties of predicative expressions, through the use of distinct styles of script. And properties and relations would be signified by individual objects (signs), rather than by properties of, and relations between, signs. So the isomorphism thesis cannot be supposed to be a necessary truth about linguistic representation as such. Rather, it will be a contingent – if ubiquitous – fact about natural language.

We might be tempted to wonder whether it is even that. For why can we not turn the *TLP* account of what symbolizes in 'aRb' on its head? What is to prevent us saying that what signifies the relation here is the relation sign 'R' itself, and that what signifies the objects a and b are not the signs 'a' and 'b' themselves, but rather the relational properties which exist when those signs are written in some significant relation to a relational sign? But the answer to this is obvious: there is in fact no one such property in connection with any given name, since there are no rules governing where a proper name must occur in a sentence. What signifies the object b in 'aRb' cannot be the property which the sign 'R' has when 'b' is written immediately to the right of it, since the sentence 'bRa', equally, contains a designation of that object.

So what emerges is that the real substance of the isomorphism thesis is merely this: that in natural language the rules governing the ordering of proper names, predicates and relational expressions in a sentence go along, not with the names, but with the predicates and relational expressions.[11] In general, if you want to know whether or not a string of words constitutes a sentence, then it is no good looking to your understanding of the names involved. Rather, you must look to your understanding of the predicative expressions. For it is to these, rather than to the proper names, that belong the rules governing what is to constitute a significant ordering of the appropriate number of words in a sentence – the rules which make that ordering, in the relevant sense, a fact rather than a mere string.

However (quite apart from the possible notations imagined above) it appears to be an entirely contingent, inessential, feature of natural language that we have rules of word-order at all. With simple predicates and symmetrical relational expressions anyway, we could have a convention according to which word-order is indifferent – it being equally permissable to write 'a is next to b' or 'b a is next to'. All that would be required to constitute a well-formed sentence would be that the appropriate number of names and predicative expressions should occur in some immediate linear relation to one another – which removes all temptation to think that there is something special about predicative expressions.

It might be felt that things are different when we consider directional relational expressions. Of course we could have a convention on which we could write indifferently 'a loves b', 'a b loves' or 'loves a b'. But it might be thought that some convention governing the relative ordering of the names 'a' and 'b' would be needed to show direction of the relation. However, we could in fact get by equally well with the use of active and passive suffixes to the proper names.[12] Then both 'a_a loves b_p' and 'b_p a_a loves' would say that a loves b. So once again there would be no motive to single out the relational expression for special treatment.

I suspect that the reason why we have conventions governing word-order at all, in the construction of simple atomic sentences, is that in spoken language we use such conventions in lieu of punctuation – it helps us to know when one sentence ends and another begins. And although there must be some convention to show which words go with which in the construction of complex sentences, we might be able to get by with a simple 'proximity convention' – words which occur together belonging together. (On this convention 'Ate John big apple' would be simply ambiguous between 'Big John ate an apple' and 'John ate a big apple'.)

There are thus two respects in which the isomorphism thesis is merely contingent. Firstly, it is contingent that we use individual signs to designate individual objects, rather than using properties of other signs (such as styles of script) to perform that function. Secondly, even given the use of individual proper names, it is contingent that we employ rules of word-order, and so contingent that relations get represented by relations between names, rather than by the relation-signs themselves.

SUMMARY

A weak thesis of isomorphic representation, at least, is endorsed in *TLP* (entailing the more general doctrine that a sentence is a fact). But if this is all that there is to the Picture Theory of the proposition, then that theory is almost devoid of philosophical interest.

15

The Picture Theory

Our task in this chapter is to argue for an interpretation of the mature Picture Theory which goes rather deeper than the thesis of isomorphic representation.

15.1 WITTGENSTEIN DISSATISFIED

We have already noted that as early as April 1914 Wittgenstein felt that the relations between the names in a sentence must have quite a different sort of relation to the relations between the corresponding things, than those names themselves have to their bearers (*NB* 111). This belief in a fundamental difference in mode of signifying between names and predicative expressions seems certainly to have survived into *TLP*. For as we had occasion to note in chapter 4, at 3.323 Wittgenstein remarks that proper names and adjectives do not merely have different Bedeutungen, but are *different symbols* (emphasis in original); the context making it clear that by this he means that they are associated with different kinds of modes of signification, their contributions to the truth-conditions of sentences in which they occur perhaps being as different in kind as is the contribution of a predicate from that of a quantifier.

Now notice that the strong isomorphism thesis fails to bring out such a difference. It does emphasize a distinction between names and predicative expressions, but one belonging wholly to the level of the sign rather than to the manner of signifying. It says only that the true sign for a relation is not (unlike a proper name) itself an object, but is rather a relation between signs, of which the relational sign forms only a part (call this 'a significant relation'). It remains silent on the question of the sort of referring effected by significant relations. So far as the strong isomorphism thesis goes, the kind of reference involved might be entirely analogous to that which obtains between a name and its bearer. We might therefore expect that Wittgenstein would either have become dissatisfied with his early endorsement of the thesis, or would at least have wished to see it supplemented.

The evidence of Wittgenstein's dissatisfaction with early versions of the Picture Theory is striking. In September 1914 he is to be found identifying the question of how relations are correlated with relations, with the problem of truth (*NB* 6). A few days later he then articulates the Picture Theory of the proposition, for the first time using the analogies of pictures and models.[1] He then writes:

> This must yield the nature of truth straight away (*if I were not blind*). [*NB* 7. Emphasis mine.]

He also remarks that it must be *possible* (my emphasis) to demonstrate everything essential by considering examples of picture-writing. So on the one hand he seems to feel that the analogy with pictures ought to provide a complete solution to the problem of truth; and yet on the other, he is unable to see how it does. Then in October of the same year he writes this:

> Are we misled into assuming 'relations between relations' merely through the apparent analogy between the expressions: 'relations between things' and 'relations between relations'? *In all these considerations I am somewhere making some sort of* FUNDAMENTAL MISTAKE. [*NB* 10. Emphasis in original.]

From the use of the phrase 'relations between relations' in this passage, it is evident that he has in mind his thesis of strong isomorphism. So he has apparently come to feel that there is something very misleading about treating the semantics of significant relations as being analogous to the name/bearer relation (this relation being a 'relation between things').

What we have so far then, is firstly a feeling on Wittgenstein's part that the analogy between propositions and pictures ought to be able to provide the solution to the problem of representation; and secondly, an indication that he takes the strong isomorphism thesis to be in some respect fundamentally mistaken.[2] Now the interpretation of the mature Picture Theory which I shall provide in section 15.3 brings both of these strands together: the analogy with pictures being used to illustrate a thesis which would deny reference to predicative expressions altogether, at the same time providing a satisfying solution to the problem of the new sentence.

It therefore seems possible, at least, that in the autumn of 1914 Wittgenstein was taking his first tentative steps away from the strong isomorphism thesis, and towards a quite different version of Picture Theory. Indeed in his continued discussions of pictures and of the problem of representation through October and November, he does articulate suggestions in which we can see the beginnings of what I take to be the mature theory, as will emerge below.[3]

15.2 RELATIONS BETWEEN RELATIONS

It is likely that the source of Wittgenstein's dissatisfaction with the strong isomorphism thesis is (partly) a feeling that names and significant relations have quite different modes of signifying. But there are also hints of a rather more precise source of worry. For on the day after he first presents the analogy between propositions and pictures he remarks:

> A picture can present relations which do not exist! How is that possible? Now once more it looks as if all relations must be logical in order for their existence to be guaranteed by that of the sign. [*NB* 8.]

A couple of months later he again returns to the idea. Having compared the way in which a proposition will present a possible connection between objects to a *tableau vivant*, he then asks:

> But when I say: the connection of the propositional components must be possible for the represented things – does this not contain the whole problem? How can a non-existent connection between objects be possible? [*NB* 26.]

Although these remarks are hardly perspicuous, we can at least take it that there is supposed to be a problem for the Picture Theory (at this stage, for strong isomorphism) in explaining the possibility of falsehood: in explaining how a proposition can describe relations between objects, which fail to exist.

I believe we may here see Wittgenstein as setting himself a dilemma, arrived at by asking precisely what it is that the relation in 'aRb' is supposed to refer to. Is it, on the one hand, to refer to the relation R in general – a relation in which any number of different pairs of things might stand to one another? Or is it, on the other hand, supposed to refer to a particular instantiation (or token) of the relation R, which can obtain between the individuals a and b alone? It is the second horn of this dilemma which appears to make falsity impossible. For if 'aRb' is false, then that particular token of the relation R does not exist, and so the relation between the names in 'aRb' would refer to nothing. Since this is obviously unacceptable – depriving false sentences of semantic content – what we need to understand is why the opposite horn of the dilemma would have been equally unacceptable.

Suppose, then, that the relation in 'aRb' refers to the relation R in general – to a relation-type, or universal. Since the relation referred to is general, and since it might have existed independently of the objects a and b (had 'aRb' happened to be false), there must surely be something which in fact connects the relation R with those objects. Since the relationship between the relation-type and the objects is not a logical ('internal') one, it must presumably be contingent. But then it looks as if we must be back with the doctrine of the copula once again: there must be some three-place relation-token obtaining in this case, linking the objects a and b to the relation-type R. So if there were no question of us believing in the copula, we should be forced to deny that significant relations refer to a relation-types – unless we could somehow overcome resistance to the idea that the relationship between R and a and b is an internal one. (Hence Wittgenstein's remark about it seeming as if all relations must be logical.)

What, then, is so wrong with the doctrine of the copula? Suppose, firstly, that we tried to combine such a doctrine with a version of isomorphism thesis. In that case just as the state of affairs aRb would be thought to contain four entities: the objects a and b, the relation-type R, and a three-place relation (copula) relating the other three; so too the sentence 'aRb' would be thought to contain the signs 'a', 'R' and 'b', together with a three-place signifying relation which holds between the other three signs.[4] But now we can set just the same dilemma as before: if this significant relation refers to a three-place relation-token, then we shall be unable to explain how the sentence can have semantic content but be false; but if it refers to a relation-type, on the other hand, then there must be yet another relation, serving in this case to relate this relation-type to the other three elements in the state of affairs, and we shall be launched on a vicious regress.[5]

Then suppose, secondly, that we dropped the isomorphism thesis, maintaining that whereas the sentence 'aRb' consists of just three elements (the signs 'a' and 'b', and the significant relation which holds between them), the state of affairs depicted consists of four (the objects a and b, the relation-type R, and the three-place copula). The trouble with this view, for Wittgenstein, would be that it conflicts with his belief in the priority of logic over metaphysics, to be discussed in detail in *MT*. For the freedom of movement allowed to items in the world would no longer be guaranteed by the set of significant combinations of their signs. Thus although 'bRa' is for us a significant sentence, it may be that there is some feature peculiar to the three-place copula which makes this combination of things metaphysically impossible. In which case, if we suppose ourselves to know that this is not the case, we should have to maintain that we possess a faculty of metaphysical insight, giving us language-independent access to the possibilities and necessities in nature. Wittgenstein's view, on the contrary, is that our knowledge of what constitutes a genuinely significant sentence (and hence a genuine possibility in the world) must flow from our understanding of the symbols involved.[6]

Either way then, the doctrine of the copula is for Wittgenstein untenable. What emerges is that, in so far as he still endorses the strong isomorphism thesis, he is caught on the horns of a dilemma. On the one hand he cannot have the significant relation in a sentence referring to a relation-type, on pain of needing to reintroduce the doctrine of the copula. But on the other hand he cannot have it refer to a relation-token either, or he will be incapable of explaining how a proposition can be both meaningful and false.[7]

15.3 RULES OF PROJECTION

Towards the end of October 1914 Wittgenstein began to write a sequence of remarks in which he talks about there being a method for comparing reality with a picture/proposition (*NB* 20–3). More particularly, he draws an analogy between the manner in which a proposition symbolizes, and a system of coordinates which projects a situation into a proposition (*NB* 20). These remarks are extremely suggestive, though there is no evidence that Wittgenstein at the time developed them in the way that I am about to do.

Think, for example, of how we might designate a particular point on a flat surface using a two-dimensional system of coordinates.[8]

We might refer to it as 'the point ab', where 'a' and 'b' name lines on different axes. It is immediately apparent that there are two quite different aspects to such a designation: there are the individual names, referring to lines on the surface; and then there is the background rule of projection, which enables us to map this arrangement of names onto the surface in question. This is a rule telling us that a sign of the form 'xy' is to refer to the point where the lines x and y intersect. It is natural then to wonder whether this divergence in aspect might not find an analogue in propositions, in the distinction between proper names and predicative expressions: the proper names serving to refer to individual things, the predicative expression carrying with it a rule for determining, of the things referred to, whether or not the sentence expresses a truth about them.[9]

The idea of a rule of projection finds a place in *TLP*, at the heart of the exposition of the Picture Theory. At 4.0141 Wittgenstein writes as follows:

> There is a general rule by means of which the musician can obtain the symphony from the score. . . . And that rule is the law of projection which projects the symphony into the language of musical notation.

The natural way to take this analogy for how an arrangement of names in a proposition manages to depict a possible state of affairs, is to treat the individual notes on the score as names of sounds of a particular pitch and duration. Then the general rule (the 'law of projection') will be one telling you that the linear arrangement of notes is to be transformed into a temporal sequence of the corresponding sounds. So there are two distinct aspects to the functioning of the score: there is reference to individual sounds (a task performed by the notes on the stave), and there is the general rule which enables you to map a given arrangement of notes onto a particular sequence of sounds.[10]

Think now of the spatial images which dominate the *TLP* presentation of the Picture Theory: the image of an arrangement of names presenting a situation like 'a *tableau vivant*' (4.0311), or the image of a proposition consisting of a spatial arrangement of tables, chairs and books (3.1431). If we read the *TLP* use of 'name' narrowly, so that the names involved here are proper names, then the natural way to take these images is as follows. Suppose I say 'Look, let this table stand for Paul, this chair for John, that chair for

George, and this book for Ringo; now *this* is how the Beatles used to stand relative to one another on stage' (arranging the objects on the floor of my office). In order for you to know what arrangement of objects is being represented here, you have to know two different sorts of thing: you have to know the referents of the individual elements, and you have to know the general rule that spatial arrangements of elements are to be taken to represent a similar arrangement of their referents, according to a certain (vaguely specified) scale. It is this general rule which would enable you to compare the model with the objects modelled, and which would thus enable you to assess the correctness (truth) of the model. It would then be this latter item of information which would correspond to the predicative element in a sentence.

The suggestion is that there are, on Wittgenstein's mature view, two very different aspects to picturing. On the one hand there is referring – a task which falls to the individual elements of the picture (the proper names). And on the other hand there are the rules for projecting pictures onto reality – i.e. for determining, of any given picture, whether or not it correctly represents the relations between the referents of its elements. If the suggestion that these rules are the analogue of the predicative element in a proposition is correct, then the idea is that the mode of signifying of such an expression is a rule for determining, with respect to the objects referred to in any atomic sentence in which it occurs, whether or not that sentence expresses a truth about them. And the mode of signifying of a simple predicate will consist in a rule for determining, of any given object, whether or not that predicate correctly applies to it.[11]

If this account of the distinction between names and predicative expressions were correct, then a two-tier (referential) semantics would be unnecessary for the latter. Their semantic content would not be an item in the real world (a referent) which would determine, in conjunction with the referents of any names involved, the truth-value of the sentence. Rather it would consist in a rule (whose existence, note, is mind-dependent) for determining, with respect to any atomic sentence in which that expression occurs, whether or not it is a truth about the referents of the names involved. And the sense of a predicative expression would be similar: not a mode of determining an item in reality as referent, but rather a rule for mapping objects onto truth-values.

This is not to say, however, that on Wittgenstein's account there would be no room for a symbol/Bedeutung distinction in connection with predicative expressions. On the contrary, this is one of those places where the distinction between Bedeutung (semantic content, contribution to Sinn) and reference comes into its own. Wittgenstein is, on the above interpretation, rejecting the notion of reference for predicates. But this still leaves him able to say that there may be a number of distinct predicative symbols with the same Bedeutung – and not just because of mere differences in sign, either. For a number of distinct (cognitively distinct) rules may nevertheless be logically equivalent, making the very same contribution to the truth-conditions of sentences in which they occur; in which case they may all be said to possess the same semantic content.

15.4 STATES OF AFFAIRS

Clearly we cannot simply say that names refer to objects and predicates express rules for classifying those objects, and leave it at that. For consider the sentence 'Susan has freckles'. Suppose it is true. Then our account will claim that this is so in virtue of the fact that the rule of classification expressed by 'has freckles' applies to Susan. But there must be more to it than this. It cannot merely be Susan herself who exists on the referential end of things, since after all she would still be there whether she had freckles or not. Rather, there must be some difference *in Susan* between the case where she has freckles and the case where she does not. It must be in virtue of something about her that the rule of classification applies (or does not). So our account must at least recognize the existence of property- and relation-*tokens*, such as the particular instance of freckledness which is present in Susan, or the particular case of loving which obtains between Socrates and Plato. Note that these tokens are unique, Paul's case of freckles being different from Susan's no matter how similar. They are also spatiotemporal entities: being located in space, and having a beginning and an ending in time. Thus the token of freckledness present in Susan is positioned wherever she is, moving around with her. And it did not exist before she did (perhaps not until puberty), and will cease to exist when she dies or has a skin graft.

This idea can also be approached by considering the semantics of whole sentences. To understand a sentence is, we are supposing, to know its truth-condition. But if an atomic sentence is true, then there must be something in the world which makes it so. So understanding such a sentence is a matter of knowing what, in the world, would make it true. Call this 'a state of affairs'.[12] Then what sort of state of affairs would render 'Fb' true? Clearly the state of affairs of b being F – of the object b possessing a token of the property Fness. For even if we supposed the predicate 'F' to refer to the universal Fness, there would still have to be something present in b in virtue of which it participates in that universal. (Even Platonists are obliged to bring property-tokens into their ontology.) In which case, to understand 'Fb' is to know that it would be made true by the state of affairs of b being F. And to understand the component predicate is to grasp a rule of classification which applies, or fails to apply, to things in virtue of the property-tokens they do or do not possess. (But as we saw earlier, this is not to say that the predicate may then be thought of as referring to those tokens.)[13]

The ontology yielded by our semantics is thus that the world contains both individuals and the states of affairs into which they enter, where a state of affairs consists of one or more individuals together with a property or relation token.

15.5 ARGUMENTS FOR THE INTERPRETATION

As we have seen, our interpretation of the Picture Theory gives us a fairly natural reading of 4.0141, where Wittgenstein talks about rules of projection. It also gives us an explanation of why he should have felt the comparison between a proposition and a picture to be so illuminating. For it would enable him to encapsulate the claim that there are two very different aspects of statement making: on the one hand referring, which falls to the individual elements (the names) of the picture; and on the other hand the rules for determining, of the referents of those elements, whether or not they stand to one another in the way represented by the picture (this task falling to predicates).

A further argument for the interpretation is this. We have already seen chapter 11 that there is a strong case for taking the terminology of 'name' and 'object' in *TLP* narrowly, to cover only proper names and individual things respectively. But then it might seem puzzling that Wittgenstein should have been so confident that his programme of analysis would 'obviously' bring us, in the end, to propositions consisting only of proper names (4.22–4.221). For since he was not actually in a position to provide such an analysis, how could he have been so confident? Who could have said where analysis would eventually lead us? (See 5.55–5.5571.) But this would be to overlook the fact that analysis, on Wittgenstein's conception of it, is not just a matter of constructing ever more detailed representations of the truth-conditions of sentences. As we shall see in *MT* chapter 7, he agrees with Frege and Russell in thinking it is also a matter of constructing notations which will be logically, or philosophically, perspicuous (3.325).

Here, then, is the reason why analysis must produce a sign-language which will enable us to do without the use of any predicative expressions: it is because we are overly tempted, as philosophers, to assimilate the use of such expressions to the use of proper names.[14] (See 3.32–3.325.) It is only when we see the possibility of a language which contains, in addition to logical connectives, only proper names (a language in which it is manifest that propositions are models of reality), that it will become transparent that there are two completely different aspects to statement making: referring, and the rules for comparing sentences with reality. We should then be supposed to see that it is this latter role which is performed, in natural language, by predicates and relational expressions.

Another argument for the interpretation is that it enables us to explain (in a way that the isomorphism thesis does not) why Wittgenstein should think that the Picture Theory can provide a solution to the problem of the new sentence (4.02). We are capable of understanding new sentences, on this account, because the form of our understanding of the predicative expressions of the language already contains generality within it. For remember, the idea is that the semantic content of a predicate will consist in a rule for determining, of any given object (of the appropriate sort), whether or not that predicate applies to it. And this rule would, of course, be something which a competent speaker would know: for it is something linguistic, as opposed to extralinguistic. Indeed it is the analogue of the sense of a proper name rather than its reference, in that any competent speaker will govern their use of the predicate in accordance with that (or a logically equivalent) rule. Then given Wittgenstein's belief that the relationship between a rule and its application is wholly objective (as we shall see in *MT* chapter 4) the truth-condition of each new sentence would be rendered entirely determinate in advance. And the speaker may then be thought of as knowing that truth-condition by virtue of their grasp of the rule.

The comparison between a proposition and a picture provides a graphic illustration of the point. Consider the famous example of the use of models in the Paris law-courts to depict traffic accidents (*NB* 7). Here, as before, there are two different kinds of thing which you have to know in order to understand such representations. You have to know what things in reality are designated by the various elements in the depiction (this model pram stands for the pram, this model car stands for the taxi, that one the car driven by the defendant, and so on). And you have to know the general method of representation – for instance that the relative spatial positions of the objects at a certain time and place are to be represented by the relative spatial positions of the models on the surface of the desk, in accordance with a certain scale. Once you know all this (once you understand the predicate) then of course any new combination of the models on the desk will show you what combination of objects is being represented *without more ado*.

Our interpretation of the Picture Theory is certainly consistent with the text of *TLP*, and enables us to explain aspects of Wittgenstein's thought which would otherwise remain puzzling – that elementary propositions are to consist only of proper names, and that the Picture Theory is intended to solve the problem of the new sentence. But the strongest argument in its support is once again the principle of Charity. As we shall see in the chapter which follows, there are powerful arguments for denying reference to predicative expressions. So adopting the proposed interpretation will enable us to see *TLP* as marking a decisive advance over the semantic theories of Frege and Russell.

SUMMARY

We have set out the evidence that Wittgenstein was dissatisfied with the strong isomorphism thesis, and have developed and argued for an interpretation of the Picture Theory which would involve its rejection. The idea is that the predicative expression in a sentence serves not (as names do) to refer to an item in reality, but to provide the mode of comparison between the sentence and the world.

16

Predicate Semantics

Our task in this chapter is to deploy Charity in support of our interpretation of the Picture Theory, arguing for a non-referential account of the semantics of predicative expressions. For the sake of simplicity the discussion will be confined to one-place predicates, but our conclusions would be readily generalizable.

16.1 PRELIMINARIES

Recall from chapter 2 that the sense/reference distinction embodies a principle of semantic ordering. If an expression has both sense and reference then there is a non-symmetric dependence of truth-value upon reference, and of reference upon sense – it will be in virtue of the fact that the expression has the sense that it does that it has the reference that it does, and it will be in virtue of having the reference that it does that sentences containing it have the truth-values that they do. Put differently (with slightly misleading temporal connotations) you could say that to apply the sense/reference distinction to an expression is to claim that its contribution to the truth-values of sentences in which it occurs will be a *two-step process*: sense determining reference determining truth-value. Then applying the distinction to predicates as well as proper names will yield an account of the semantics of an atomic sentence 'Fb' which looks like this: the sense of the name 'b' determines an individual as its bearer; the sense of the predicate 'F' determines some entity as its referent; then the bearer of the name somehow fits (or fails to fit) together with the referent of the predicate to determine that the sentence is true (or false).

We might represent such an account diagrammatically thus (where the arrows represent non-symmetric dependence):

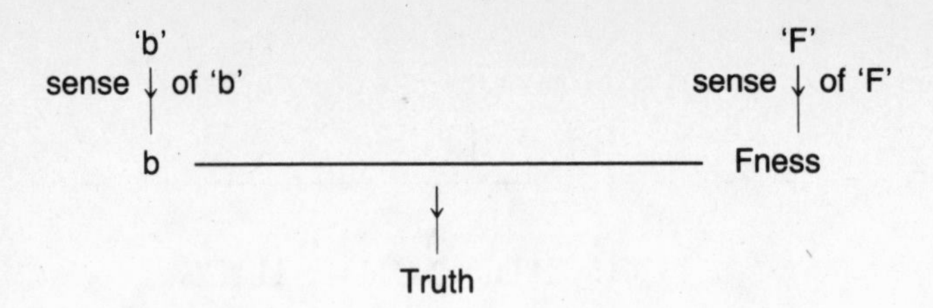

We shall consider shortly the various different proposals which might be made concerning the nature of reference for predicates (the nature of Fness). But notice for the moment that any such view must contrast with the sort of non-referential semantics sketched in the last chapter, which might be represented diagrammatically thus:

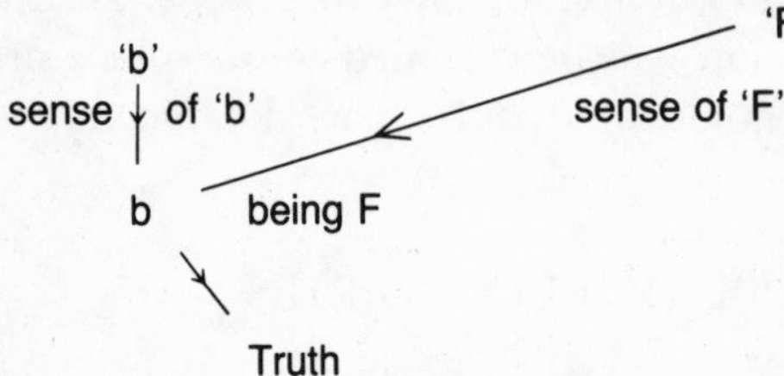

The idea here is that the sense of a predicate is not, as the referential view would have it, a mode of thinking about a referent. It is rather a rule of classification, applying directly to the referent of the name in virtue of some property-token which that thing possesses. On such a view, to understand a predicate 'F' is to know the difference between things which are F and things which are not F, where this knowledge consists in grasp of the rule of classification which constitutes the sense of 'F'. (Remembering – in accordance with the arguments of chapter 9 – that rules are mind-dependent entities, supervening on human dispositions.)

In the next section we shall consider, and respond to, the main argument supporting a referential semantics for predicates. Then in the sections following I shall argue against each of the various forms which such a semantics might take.

16.2 SECOND-LEVEL QUANTIFICATION

The most obvious objection to a semantic ontology consisting only of individuals and property- and relation-tokens is that if we accept as true that there is something which Susan and Mary both are (namely freckled), then we are committed to the existence of property-types as well. In which case the most natural treatment of quantification (here an existence-statement of second-level) will oblige us to accept property-types as the referents of predicates.

What is at issue in this argument is not just whether or not we can accept a non-referential semantics for predicates, but also the plausibility of attributing such an account to Wittgenstein. For there is no evidence to suggest that he thought there to be anything untoward about second-level quantification. Indeed there are a number of remarks in *TLP* which appear to show that he regards such quantification as perfectly legitimate.[1] How else, for example, are we to make sense of his claim at 4.0411, that if we tried to express universal quantification over objects by writing 'Gen.Fx' we should not know what was being generalized? (See also 5.5261.) At the very least there would be some difficulty in attributing to Wittgenstein a conception of the role of a predicate which would render quantification over properties either false or unintelligible. But in fact there is no reason why our account of the semantics of predicates should not leave room for an adequate theory of second-level quantification – indeed a theory modelled on the explicit *TLP* account of first-level quantification.

Wittgenstein's account of first-order quantification is a substitutional one, the quantifiers being introduced by means of applications of the N-operator to the set of all propositions of a certain form. Thus 'Something is F' gets expressed as '$N(N(\overline{Fx}))$' – that is to say, as the negation of the joint negation of all propositions which result from completing the predicate 'Fx' with a proper name; saying in effect that it is not the case that 'Fx' is true of nothing. In these terms it will be quite simple to express 'There is something which Susan and Mary both are'. It will come out as '$N(N(\overline{\emptyset \text{Susan} \; \& \; \emptyset \text{Mary}})$'. That is: as the negation of the joint negation of all sentences which result from completing the open sentence '∅Susan & ∅Mary' with particular predicates. And note that nothing whatever is implied here about whether or not predicates have reference.

Of course the *TLP* account requires that there be a name for every object, and is therefore only workable in a fully-analysed language (supposing the analysis provides some general rule for generating names for all objects). But in fact nothing essential to the account would be lost if we interpreted the phrase 'all sentences of a certain form' to mean 'all *possible* sentences of a certain form'. We could then explain the truth-condition of 'Something is F' as the denial that 'Fa' is false for every possible assignment of an object in the domain to the name 'a'. This is, in effect, the way in which first-level quantification is introduced in many modern textbooks.[2]

We can now provide an exactly parallel account of the truth-condition of 'There is something that Susan and Mary both are'. Only instead of talking about possible assignments of properties to the predicate 'F' (which would commit us to a referential semantics), we can construct the account in terms of possible rules of classification governing its use. In fact we can give the truth-condition thus: it is possible to fix a rule for the use of the predicate 'F' such that the sentence 'FSusan & FMary' would be true. Slightly more formally: There is a possible world w, which differs (if at all) from the actual world only in whatever is required to fix a rule for the use of 'F', such that 'FSusan & FMary' expresses, in w, a truth about the actual world.

It counts in favour of this quasi-substitutional approach to second-level quantification that it explains our feeling that 'There is something that Susan and Mary both are' is vacuous, in a way that 'There is something that is red' is not. For *of course* there will be some possible rule of classification which will apply to both Susan and Mary.[3] Any two objects (belonging to the same sortal category anyway) will always turn out to have something in common. But on the other hand, it is not at all trivial that there should be some possible assignment of an object in the domain to the name 'a' such that 'a is red' will turn out to be a truth.

It might be objected against our account that we accept second-level quantification with respect to worlds in which there are no human beings, and so no one to fix a rule for any predicate. Yet rules are supposed to be contingent, mind-dependent entities. For example, is it not the case that even if there had never been any human beings there would still have been something that nothing is (namely a unicorn)? But in fact this need cause us no problem. On our account its truth-condition may be expressed as follows: ∀v ((v differs from the actual world only in containing no humans) → ∃w(w differs from actual, if at all, only in whatever is required to fix a rule for 'Fx', such that 'Nothing is F' expresses, in w, a truth about v)).

This is sufficient to defuse the argument from second-level quantification. We can accept that there are truths of second-level without being committed to a referential semantics for predicates by (in effect) interpreting the second-level quantifier as ranging over possible rules of classification.

16.3 EXTENSIONAL REFERENCE

Some philosophers maintain that the reference of a predicate is a set of individuals, namely its extension. But of course no one would say that the relationship between a predicate and its extension can be direct. Rather, a predicate will in addition serve to express a sense – a mode of thinking about the extension – in virtue of which it comes to have the reference which it has.

On this account the truth-value of a sentence of the form 'Fb' will get fixed like this: the sense of the name 'b' determines a particular individual as its bearer; the sense of the predicate 'F' determines a particular class of individuals as its extension; and the whole sentence is true if and only if the bearer of the name belongs within the extension of the predicate. We might represent such an account diagrammatically as follows (for a particular case of true sentence 'Fb'):

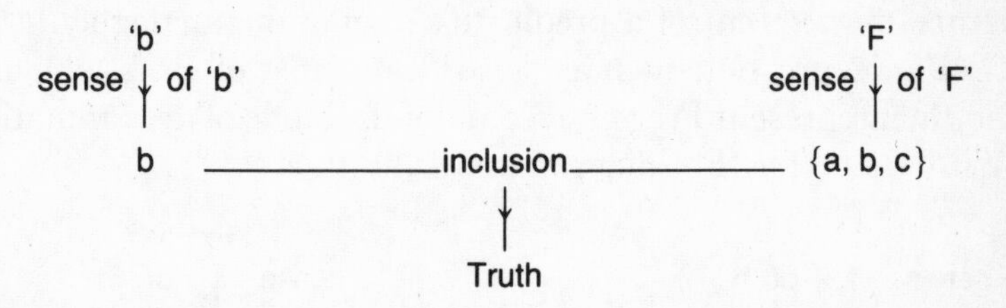

As before, the arrows here correspond to the direction of non-symmetric dependence.

But now let us ask: how exactly does the predicate 'F' come to have as its extension the set {a, b, c}? Indeed, what is it for a predicate to determine an extension at all? The answer surely is (and can only be) that a predicate comes to have a given extension by virtue of being *true* of each individual member of the set. There is simply no other way of rendering intelligible the association between a predicate and a set of individuals. But now we have a conflict with the principle of semantic ordering. For if 'F' only comes to 'refer' to the set {a, b, c} because it is true of a and true of b and true of c, then it does not contribute to the truth of 'Fb' via the determination of a referent, as that principle requires. On the contrary, it only comes to have the extension which it does by virtue of the truth of the possible sentences 'Fa', 'Fb' and 'Fc' – which is as much as to say that predicates do not have their extensions as their referents.

The argument here is best presented as a trilemma. Either (1) we can reject the principle of semantic ordering. But in that case we should lose our grip of the intended significance of the sense/reference distinction. Or (2) we could deny that a predicate comes to have a set of individuals as its extension by virtue of being true of each member of the set. But in that case it would be left wholly unintelligible how the connection is supposed to have been set up. Or (3) we could accept that predicates do not refer to their extensions. This is left as the only viable alternative.

It is clear that an exactly parallel argument can be deployed against Frege's view that the reference of a predicate is an 'incomplete' but purely extensional entity.[4] On this account the reference of 'Fx' would not be a set, since sets are, in his view, individual things. Rather, he thinks that the referent, like the predicate itself, must contain a 'gap' in it. Nevertheless the reference of a predicate is to be extensional: all predicates having the same extension sharing the same incomplete entity as referent. We therefore have to picture the referent of a predicate as being the analogue in the world of an expression such as '. . . is a member of {a, b, c}', and we can then represent Frege's account of the mode of determination of a truth-value for 'Fb' diagrammatically thus:

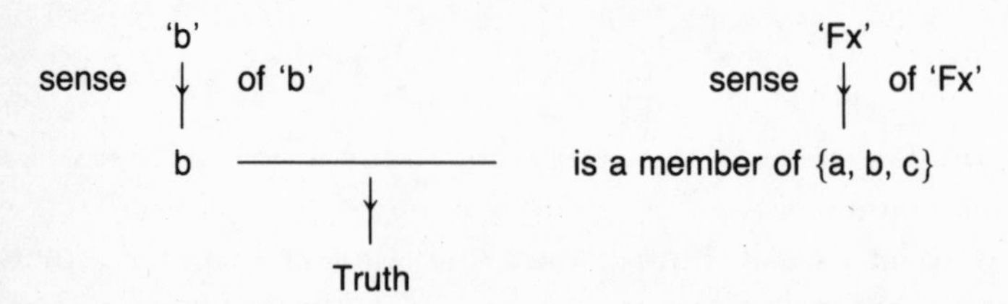

Yet this gives rise to just the same problem as before. For how are we to explain what it is for a predicate to refer to such an incomplete entity, except in terms of it being true of each individual member of the component set? How are we to explain how predicates with such obviously different senses as 'is human' and 'is a featherless biped' can nevertheless have the same incomplete entity as reference – where they share the same referent just in case they share the same extension – except in terms of them both being true of each individual member of their extensions? So once again, if it is not to become wholly unintelligible that a predicate should come to have the 'referent' that it has, our account of the matter must proceed via the truth-values possessed by certain (possible) atomic sentences. Which is as much as to say that predicates do not have extensional reference, unless we could find some way of explaining the sense/reference distinction without recourse to the principle of semantic ordering.

What these arguments establish is that if a sense/reference distinction applies to predicates to all, then the notion of reference involved cannot be given a purely extensional characterization. But it is important to distinguish here between a notion of reference which might be sufficient for the purposes of a logician – to provide an interpretation of the symbols in a formalized language, fit to validate the rules of inference and to figure in consistency proofs (formal semantics) – and the notion of reference which enters into an account of what it is for a speaker to understand a language (semantics proper). On the former conception it is entirely anodyne to say that predicates have reference, and perhaps true that their reference is purely extensional. But on the latter conception – the conception which is to figure in an account of a speaker's knowledge of the truth-conditions of their sentences – it is incoherent to ascribe extensional reference to predicates, as we have seen. It may be that many of those who have defended extensional reference for predicates have failed to keep this distinction in mind.[5]

The arguments above against extensional reference are insufficient to show that predicates do not have reference at all. There remains the possibility of saying that a predicate has as referent a given universal, provided that two predicates can be co-extensive and yet refer to distinct universals. But there are in fact two quite different versions of this possibility, depending upon whether universals are thought to be transcendent (Platonic) entities, or rather immanent (Aristotelian) ones. We shall now consider each of these two theories in turn.

16.4 TRANSCENDENT UNIVERSALS

Suppose first of all that our Platonist accepts the sense/reference distinction. Then their account of the manner in which the truth-value of 'Fb' gets determined will proceed as follows: the sense of the name 'b' determines an individual object as referent; the sense of the predicate 'F' determines a given universal (Fness) as referent; and the whole sentence is true if and only if the object then participates in (is copulated with) the universal. Represented diagrammatically:

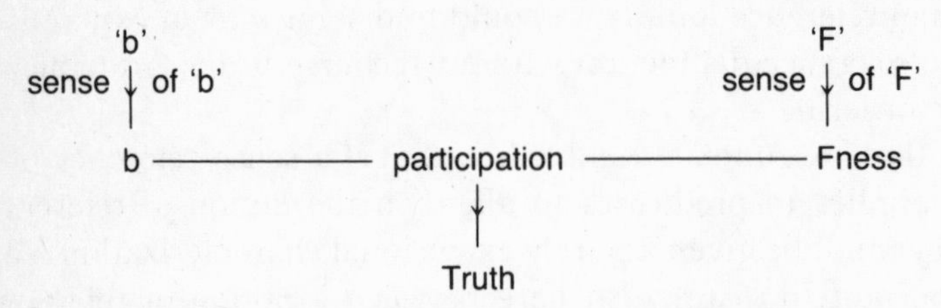

In chapter 15 we noted some serious problems involved in the idea of a copula. But here I shall present an additional argument, involving what I call 'The Principle of Semantic Relevance'.

The principle which I have in mind is this: if reference is to be attributed to an expression, then the evidence which speakers would take to bear on the truth of sentences containing it (particularly, where available, anything they would count as a canonical mode of verification) should display sensitivity to the existence and nature of the referent. The idea is that a semantic theory should reflect the main features of the use of an expression – in verifying, falsifying and offering evidence. Since truth is to depend upon reference, evidence of truth should as it were 'point towards' the referent; especially where the evidence is of the most direct sort, where we may think of the truth of the sentence being *manifest* to us. Note, however, that the principle of Semantic Relevance is not the same thing as Ideal Verificationism. The claim is not that to understand a sentence is to know how an ideally situated intelligence would be able to verify it. Rather, the claim is that there must be a degree of isomorphism between the truth-condition of a sentence and the main features of what we count as evidence for its truth. For evidence of truth is, after all, evidence that the truth-condition is fulfilled.

It follows that to claim that the semantics for a certain class of expression should be a two-tier one is to present a particular model of the canonical mode of verifying sentences in which it occurs. The first step will be for the speaker, relying upon their grasp of the sense of the expression, to identify some entity as the referent. Then the second step will be to see whether that referent fits together with the semantic content of the other component expressions of the sentence in the way required for truth. Our use of proper names does appear to fit this model quite well. The canonical way to verify a sentence 'Fb' is first to locate and identify the individual b, and then to establish whether or not that object has the appropriate property. But there is nothing corresponding to these two stages in our use of predicates. Having located the individual b there are not then two further steps remaining: to identify the universal Fness, and to establish whether or not b participates in it. On the contrary, there is only one step remaining: to establish whether b is F. To understand a predicate is not to have a means of identifying and thinking about a universal, but is rather to know the difference between things which are F and things which are not: it is to grasp a rule of classification.

Consider how one would, ideally, set about establishing the truth of 'Susan has freckles'. The first step is to locate and identify Susan. Then you look to see whether her face is freckled. Nowhere in this process would there occur a distinct step which might be described as 'the identification of the universal freckledness'. Nor is there anything in the evidence which we might present for the truth of the sentence which bears on the existence of that universal. It is therefore otiose to propose a Platonist semantics for predicates which distinguishes between their sense and reference.

Yet there remains the possibility of a purely referential Platonist semantics for predicates. This is Russell's view: that predicates refer to transcendent universals, not via a mode of presentation (a sense) but directly, through immediate acquaintance. Such a doctrine is immune to the argument from Semantic Relevance, since Russell too can claim that acquaintance with the universal Fness is a matter of knowing the difference between things which are F and things which are not, thus enabling the speaker to judge directly (in 'one step') whether or not an atomic sentence containing the predicate 'F' is true. But there is a danger, at this point, of the dispute becoming merely verbal. For if to be acquainted with the universal Fness is to know the difference between being F and not being F, then it is not at all clear how such an account would differ from the sort of non-referential semantics we have attributed to Wittgenstein. We could try marking the distinction by saying that for Russell the difference between being F and not being F is something which we talk *about* – something belonging to the realm of reference – whereas for Wittgenstein it is rather a *mode of thinking about* reality (something belonging to the realm of sense). Yet it remains far from obvious, on the face of it, how this distinction could obtain any purchase upon our linguistic practices. For both sides are agreed about what actually takes place in the canonical verification of an atomic sentence: we find the individual spoken of and judge whether or not it falls within the appropriate classification.

In fact the difference between a purely-referential and a non-referential semantics amounts to this: that for Russell (and for Platonists generally) universals have necessary, or at least mind-independent, existence; whereas for Wittgenstein rules are mind-dependent entities. For Russell, to know the difference between being F and not being F is to be acquainted with something extra-linguistic, something belonging to the real world independently of us and our dispositions. Yet such an account would run into many of the difficulties we raised for the Fregean account of thinking in chapter 9. In particular, we should want to know the structure of the mental faculty which is supposed to enable us to become acquainted with these things. Is there a unique species of causality involved, and if so how can it operate between a necessarily existing abstract universal and the human mind? Or is there supposed to be a way of knowing things in the real world which is not causal at all?[6] These problems do not arise for a non-referential account, since the idea here is that our use of a predicate is guided by our grasp of a rule of classification whose existence supervenes upon our normative linguistic practices and dispositions.[7] Since the account retains all of the advantages of the Russellian view without the need for any special faculty of intuition, it is by far the more reasonable.

16.5 IMMANENT UNIVERSALS

The only remaining version of referential semantics for predicates implies the claim that universals (if they are instantiated) are immanent in the physical world. On this account there is really something (in the world) in common between Susan and Mary, which is present in them both, in virtue of which they both fall under the rule of classification which constitutes the sense of the predicate 'has freckles'. In fact they are said to be related to one another by virtue of a kind of identity, since part of the universal freckledness is present in each of them; it being this universal which is said to be the referent of the predicate.[8]

Such a view does not obviously run into trouble with the principle of Semantic Relevance, since in establishing that Susan has freckles (which on this account, as on Wittgenstein's, is a matter of classifying her as freckled in virtue of her possession of an appropriate property-token) we can be said to be establishing the presence of freckledness in her. Since the relationship between the property-token which plays a direct part in the process of verification and the immanent universal which is supposed to be the referent of the predicate is one of partial identity, there is no need for a distinct step – 'locating the universal' – in the canonical verification of the sentence 'Susan has freckles'.

Troubles with such a view, however, arise over those predicates – such as 'is a unicorn' and 'is a round square' – which fail to be instantiated. For in these cases there can be no immanent universal to serve as their reference. Yet they certainly seem capable of figuring in sentences which are determinately true. For example, 'Susan is not a unicorn' is true, as is 'No one has ever succeeded in drawing a round square'. But how could this be? For if an expression is supposed to have reference, then the truth-value of sentences containing it ought surely to be sensitive to facts about the referent. In particular, no atomic sentence containing it can be true unless that expression does have a referent.

The only possible response to this argument would be to interpret the negation-sign in 'Susan is not a unicorn' as occurring external to the predicate, in such a way that the resulting sentence can be true even though that predicate lacks a reference. Compare, for example, 'It is not the case that Zeus is wise'. Some have wished to distinguish this sharply from 'Zeus is not wise', claiming that the former can be true despite the fact that 'Zeus' lacks reference. However, the problem with such a response is that uninstantiated predicates can just as well figure in truths where they clearly do not fall within the scope of the negation-sign, such as 'Unicorness is not present in Susan' (or less barbarically, 'Being a unicorn is not something that Susan is'). The only way to save the account now, would be to claim that even here, and despite appearances to the contrary, the predicate actually falls within the intended scope of the negation. In fact it would have to be claimed that it is impossible to find anything to contrast with external negation in connection with predicates. But this would be utterly mysterious. For if (some) predicates really did have reference, then what could prevent us asserting, of the referent itself, that it is not instantiated in some given individual?

Although a semantic theory which takes immanent universals to be the referents of predicates is not generally adequate, this is not to say that there might not be any purposes for which we are required to recognize their existence. For example, Armstrong has argued that they are needed to form part of an adequate theory of causation.[9] Rejecting both Humean and Covering Law theories, he thinks that we should explain how two things can share the same causal power by appealing to the presence, in them, of an identical nature (the very same immanent universal). But there is nothing in what we have said above, nor in a non-referential semantics for predicates, which is inconsistent with such an account. For it is one thing to claim that immanent universals exist, and quite another to claim that they enter into semantics as the referents of predicates.[10]

Moreover, it may need to be conceded that some types of predicate – namely natural kind terms – do refer to immanent universals. For suppose we agree that nothing could be water which was not in fact made of H_2O, no matter how much it resembled it in everyday properties.[11] Then the sense of 'water' must imply a description of the form 'has the same fundamental constitution as most of the stuff normally identified as water', and the canonical mode of verifying 'The Thames consists of water' would be to locate the Thames, to identify the internal constitution of most of the stuff normally called 'water', and then to establish whether the Thames had that very constitution. This would fit the referential model exactly.[12]

SUMMARY

A non-referential view of predicates is able to account for the intelligibility of second-level quantification just as well as its rivals. Yet it does not suffer from any of the difficulties which beset the alternatives. Hence the Picture Theory, as we have interpreted it, marks a decisive advance over the semantic theories of other philosophers, including Frege and Russell.

Conclusion

I have been concerned to argue that *TLP* contains a set of semantic doctrines which are actually correct, and which are at least sufficiently plausible that they collectively deserve to be accorded the status of a semantic paradigm – serving, like the Fregean paradigm, as a focus for contemporary discussion and debate. Tractarian semantics are best presented in the form six interconnected doctrines.

1 There is a distinction between semantic content on the one hand (which is both that of which knowledge is required for understanding, and that which is conveyed in literal communication) and senses on the other (which are the cognitive contents expressed in the idiolects of particular speakers, in virtue of the confluence of which an expression has the semantic content which it does). In one respect the sense of an expression is merely psychological, in that it may vary from person to person, and since mutual knowledge of it is not required for linguistic understanding. But it is nevertheless essential that anyone who understands an expression should associate with it some sense or other. For one cannot think about or refer to elements of reality directly, but can only do so via some mode of representation. The Tractarian paradigm thus combines an acceptance of Frege's view that sense determines truth-conditions, with rejection of his idea that mutual knowledge of sense is required for communication.

2 The identity-condition for semantic content, at least within factual discourse, is sameness of truth-condition (or of contribution to truth-conditions). Hence all analytically equivalent sentences, and all atomic sentences making equivalent predications of the very same individuals, possess the same semantic content (say the very same thing). Mutual knowledge of truth-conditions then suffices for

understanding, despite the fact that speakers may attach widely differing senses to their sentences. The Tractarian paradigm thus combines referential and possible-worlds semantics on the one hand, with the claim that semantic content is determined by speakers' modes of thinking on the other.

3 Platonism is false, whether about propositions (senses) or universals. Thinking cannot consist in the subject coming to grasp a necessarily existing proposition, since there is no way of rendering intelligible how such an entity could guide a thinker's behaviour in the manner in which a cognitive content is supposed to do. Nor can thought involve reference to necessarily existing universals, both because of the problem of cognitive access between such entities and the human mind, and because universals fail to figure in the canonical modes of verification of atomic sentences, thus running foul of the principle of Semantic Relevance.

4 Private thinking and public language-using are isomorphic. Both are on a par with one another, consisting in structured arrangements of sign-tokens which are projected onto the world by virtue of the thinker/speaker's classificatory and identificatory capacities. Neither is logically prior to the other: it is not conceptually impossible for there to be a creature lacking a public language who is capable of conscious thinking, but nor are public utterances rendered meaningful by the thoughts which accompany them. In both cases the connection with the world is effected by the subject's capacities for the use of the component signs. (Whether such an account of the manner in which truth-conditions are determined is capable of underpinning our belief in the objectivity of truth, will be investigated in the sequel to this book, where I argue for a positive reply. See *MT* chapter 15.)

5 As for proper names (and singular referring expressions generally), besides possessing a logical grammar which may be shared by many different names, the distinctive semantic content of any particular name is exhausted by its reference. Yet each name will express a sense – a mode of thinking about its bearer – in the idiolect of any speaker who understands it, in virtue of which it comes to have, for that speaker, the reference which it does. So

reference is determined by *fit* with the mode of thinking which a speaker associates with a name, which may include recognitional capacities as well as implying definite and indefinite descriptions. Yet mutual knowledge of (any aspect of) modes of thinking is unnecessary for communication.

6 Predicates and relational expressions (and indeed all other types of word which make a contribution to semantic content, except singular referring expressions, and perhaps also natural kind terms) lack reference. They serve rather to express rules for determining the truth-values of sentences; one-place predicates, for example, expressing rules for mapping objects onto truth-values in virtue of the property-tokens which those objects possess. Yet even here the distinction between sense and semantic content can be made out, since there may be a number of predicates which differ in cognitive content while nevertheless being analytically equivalent; in which case the differences between them will have no significance for factual communication.

I have argued, in as much detail as space has permitted, that these six doctrines are actually correct. At any rate they are clearly defensible, and are indeed superior to the doctrines of the Fregean paradigm with which they should be contrasted. However, in the above presentation of Tractarian semantics I have engaged in the fiction that its claims are restricted to factual discourse. This is false to Wittgenstein's intentions, but necessary to preserve truth. If we are to extend the theory to cover the contents of sentences belonging to all forms of discourse, then we need a concept of semantic content which is purpose-relative. I therefore propose that the Tractarian paradigm should be emended through the addition of a seventh doctrine.

7 The semantic content of a token utterance is relative to the purposes operative in the context of that utterance. In order to understand (know the semantic content of) someone's utterance on a given occasion, it is both necessary and sufficient that you know sufficiently much about the mode of thinking expressed by that utterance for the purposes in hand. In *a priori* discourse the condition for understanding will be mutual knowledge of sense

(cognitive content); in imperative discourse it will be mutual knowledge of causal equivalence; and in other modes of discourse, and in other contexts, the identity-conditions for semantic content may be different again.

Thus emended, the one respect in which the semantics of *TLP* deviates from the above paradigm concerns its treatment of ordinary proper names. For at the same time as endorsing thesis 5 above, Wittgenstein thinks that the semantic content of ordinary names may be subjected to analysis, holding that they may be replaced by descriptions of the manner in which their bearers are constructed out of their parts. Here he overlooks the distinction between conceptual and metaphysical necessity. For while it may plausibly be claimed in connection with at least some types of physical object that the manner of their construction out of their parts is metaphysically necessary, it certainly is not conceptually or analytically so. This additional doctrine of Wittgenstein's is thus best quietly dropped, the question of why he might have felt himself obliged to maintain it being held over to the sequel. The answer in fact lies deep within the foundations of the *TLP* programme of analysis (see *MT* chapters 7 and 12).

Notes

PREFACE

1 I here assume that there are issues and problems which are a-historical, at least in the limited sense of being the common property of philosophers belonging to different philosophical eras. But this is not to say, of course, that all issues are a-historical in this sense. Sometimes coming to understand a past philosopher's treatment of (what one takes to be) a given issue, one will discover that it was not really *that* issue they were addressing, but rather one which is now of merely historical interest.

2 It is remarkable how many commentators have undervalued the influence of Frege on *TLP*, as a glance at the comparative frequency with which Frege and Russell are mentioned in their indexes will reveal. In some cases – e.g. Malcolm (1986) – he is not even mentioned at all. Distinguished exceptions to this trend are Anscombe (1959) and Griffin (1964).

3 I strongly disagree with McDonough (1986), who believes that all the main features of Wittgenstein's semantic system can be demonstrated from the thesis that the logical connectives do not refer, together with a characterization of the nature of tautologies. One telling point against him, is that the argument he attributes to Wittgenstein simply helps itself to the thesis that all necessary propositions are tautologies; whereas this clearly needs arguing for, and indeed presupposes a whole programme of analysis which must receive its justification from elsewhere (see *MT* chs. 7 and 13). Another point is that even granting McDonough's account of the nature of tautologies (which is in fact only partly accurate – see ch. 6), his attempt to demonstrate all the other features of *TLP* is extremely weak. For example, his argument to show that all genuine propositions are contingent (ibid. pp. 77–9) can only succeed by making assumptions about what it is to say something which would need to be independently argued for; and once such an argument is provided, we can in fact derive the thesis that all genuine propositions are contingent without having to appeal to the nature of tautologies (see chs. 5–7).

4 Fogelin points out in his (1976) that Wittgenstein's account of the quantifiers is expressively inadequate, there being no way in which the N-operator can be used to construct propositions of mixed multiple generality, such as '$\exists x \forall y Fxy$'; although Geach shows in his (1981) how this defect may easily be remedied. More seriously, Fogelin also shows

that some of Wittgenstein's doctrines concerning the N-operator commit him the existence of a decision-procedure for predicate logic; whereas there is demonstrably no such thing.

5 Wittgenstein clearly thinks that we are required to employ just a single logical connective in order to avoid the illegitimate procedure of piecemeal definition (5.451, 5.46, 5.47). He thinks that if we had to employ a plurality of connectives, then there would be insuperable problems over the order in which they should be introduced. For if we introduce one connective in advance of another, then we should not be able to take the latter for granted in giving the former's definition. Yet any adequate explanation of a connective must get across the significance, not just of attaching it to elementary propositions (or, in the case of the quantifiers, to elementary propositional functions), but also to propositions (and propositional functions), which themselves contain logical connectives. It seems that we should first have to explain the negation-sign as it applies to elementary propositions, for example, and then later redefine it as applying to general propositions once the quantifiers have been introduced; which is precisely piecemeal definition.

There is a perfectly real problem here, which had barely been recognized at the time when *TLP* was written. But it is simply false that we need a single ubiquitous connective in order to overcome it. For as has now long been recognized, we can achieve the same effect through the use of definitions which are *recursive*. (This was pointed out to me by Jack Copeland.)

CHAPTER 1 PRINCIPLES OF INTERPRETATION

1 Here I am in agreement with Stenius (1960), ch. 1. See also the appendix in Favrholdt (1964).

2 I do not necessarily mean here *our* interests. For it may be that the author is not addressing issues with which we ourselves are concerned. I intend Charity to be a principle of historical interpretation rather than of rational reconstruction (a distinction I get from Janaway, 1988). Sometimes maximizing the interest of a text from the point of view of the author's contemporaries may mean minimizing its interest to us. But not, I think, in the case of *TLP*.

3 See ch. 4 for some examples.

4 In a letter to the publisher Ficker, Wittgenstein describes *TLP* as 'strictly philosophical and at the same time literary'. Quoted in McGuinness (1988), p. 288.

5 See the letter from Russell quoted by Blackwell (1981), p. 8 .

6 See von Wright's 'Historical Introduction' in *PTLP*. McGuinness (1988, p. 265), however, conjectures the *PTLP* may have been written in the autumn of 1917.

7 For the conversations with Waismann, see Waismann (1979). For notes

taken at Wittgenstein's Cambridge lectures, see Lee (1980), as well as Ambrose (1979) and Diamond (1976).

8 Wittgenstein's remark in the preface to *PI* explaining his desire to see *PI* and *TLP* published together in a single volume is certainly insufficient to establish that *TLP* can be identified with the 'Augustinian picture' which forms the target of attack throughout the early sections of *PI*. That *PI* can only be understood in contrast with *TLP* (with which I agree) does not mean that all its early remarks about Simples, names and so on necessarily refer to *TLP* doctrines. On the contrary, Wittgenstein may have used the 'Augustinian picture' as a convenient focus to bring out points both of agreement and disagreement with *TLP*. For further discussion see my (1984a).

9 See the Editor's preface to Wittgenstein (1979), pp. 12 and 15, and Wittgenstein (1974), pp. 114–18.

10 See von Wright's 'Historical Introduction' *PTLP*.

11 McGuinness (1988) argues that at the beginning of the summer Wittgenstein had been bent on suicide, only being disuaded from it by a chance meeting with his uncle Paul, who took an interest in his philosophy, and who offered him a home at Hallein in which to work (ibid. p. 264). This is consistent both with my claim of urgency, and with the corollary that Wittgenstein was not writing in a relaxed and leisurely frame of mind.

12 See von Wright's 'Biographical Sketch' in Malcolm (1958), pp. 12–13. See also the topics covered in *PR*, written between 1929 and 1930.

Of course it is controversial to claim that Phenomenalism was a new interest, since some interpret the simple objects of *TLP* to be sense-data. Arguments against this reading will be given in *MT* ch. 8.

13 The assessment is von Wright's, and is clearly correct. See Malcolm (1958), p. 20.

14 My impression is that Wittgenstein was always partly contemptuous of Russell as a philosopher; whereas Frege he revered from the beginning to the very end of his career.

CHAPTER 2 BACKGROUND: FREGE AND RUSSELL

1 Moore is mentioned at 5.541, Whitehead at 5.252 and 5.452, Kant at 6.36111 and Hertz at 4.04 and 6.361.

2 See his 1912 letter to Russell, Wittgenstein (1974), p. 9.

3 See von Wright's 'Biographical Sketch', in Malcolm (1958), p. 5. However Pears (1987) makes a convincing case for a direct influence – at least in point of phraseology – of Schopenhauer on a number of the remarks in *TLP* and *NB*.

4 See Griffin (1964), ch. VIII. But it is possible that Wittgenstein only knew of Hertz's work via the account provided by Russell in ch. LIX of *The Principles of Mathematics*.

5 The details of the evidence are as follows. In the case of Russell, not only are both *The Principles of Mathematics* and *Principia Mathematica* mentioned explicitly in *TLP* (at 5.5351 and 5.452 respectively), but there is also evidence that Wittgenstein was unhappy with the inexactness of the proofs provided in *Principia*, and proposed to rewrite the first eleven chapters – see Blackwell (1981), pp. 12–13; and see appendix I of Coope et al. (1971) for a table of correspondences between *TLP* and *The Principles of Mathematics*. We also know from Russell's letters that Wittgenstein read, and apparently disliked, *The Problems of Philosophy* – see Blackwell (1981), p. 16. Moreover there is an admiring reference to Russell's *Philosophical Essays* (containing 'On the Nature of Truth and Falsehood') in the letter to Russell mentioned in note 2 above. Beyond this we know nothing for sure, though it seems highly likely that Wittgenstein would have got to know Russell's papers from the period which immediately precedes the time of their association in Cambridge (between autumn 1911 and autumn 1913), particularly 'On the Relations of Universals and Particulars' and 'Knowledge by Acquaintance and Knowledge by Description' (reproduced in Russell, 1956 and 1918 respectively).

As for Frege, only *BLA* is explicitly mentioned in *TLP*, at 5.451. But it is safe to assume that Wittgenstein would have read Frege's earlier masterpiece *FA* (especially since *TLP* 3.3 is very nearly a quotation from *FA* 60 and 62), as well as those of Frege's writings mentioned by Russell in his appendix on Frege in *The Principles of Mathematics*: including *Begriffsschrift* (reproduced in Frege, 1972), 'Function and Concept', 'On Concept and Object' and 'On Sense and Reference' (all reproduced in Frege, 1984). For so far as we can gather, it was through reading this appendix that Wittgenstein came to study Frege in the first place – see Malcolm (1958), p. 4. In addition, 3.263 closely echoes the remarks on explaining primitive signs in Frege's 'Foundations of Geometry 2' – see Frege (1984), pp. 300–1.

6 See Blackwell (1981), p. 16.

7 See Wittgenstein (1974), p. 111.

8 See in particular Dummett (1973) and (1981b).

9 Most notably in Sluga (1980) and Baker and Hacker (1984).

10 See Frege (1984), pp. 157–63.

11 However, the means of identification need not, in Frege's view, be an effective one; see *BLA* 56.

12 Frege's actual view is that the reference of a predicate is an 'incomplete' but purely extensional entity. See his (1979), p. 118ff.

13 See Frege (1984), pp. 145, 162 and 185–7.

14 See Frege (1984), pp. 159–60. Of course he would allow that there can be understanding where idiolects diverge, provided that speakers know what sense the others attach to their expressions.

15 This use of 'semantic content' is very similar to Salmon's use of 'information content' – see his (1986), p. 13. In both cases the intention is to designate that which is communicated by the literal

meaning of a statement, or that which must be known by one who understands it. However, Salmon's choice of terminology is unfortunate, since there is an already established use of 'information content' to mean what I am here calling 'cognitive content'.

16 See Russell (1917), p. 159, and (1912), p. 32.

17 See Russell (1917), pp. 153–5, and (1912), pp. 26–8.

18 See 'On Denoting' in Russell (1957), as well as his (1917), p. 162–6.

19 See the introductions to Frege's *FA* and *BLA*, as well as his paper 'Thoughts' in his (1984) and the second of the two papers entitled 'Logic' in his (1979). But the terminology of possible worlds is not Frege's.

20 See Dummett's discussion of this issue in ch. 3 of his (1981b).

21 See the second of the two papers which bear that title in Frege's (1979).

22 See the final essay of Russell's (1910a).

23 See Russell's (1912), p. 58.

24 This is emphasized by Currie in his (1982a).

25 See Frege (1979), pp. 207–12. As Currie points out in his (1982b), these difficulties occassionally lead Frege to employ a notion of sense for which the criterion of identity is logical equivalence; which had also been the notion of content employed in his earlier *Begriffsschrift*. See for example Frege (1984), p. 143.

26 See Frege (1984), p. 148 and (1952), p. 159.

27 The terminology is introduced in Tugendhat (1970) and taken up by Dummett in his (1973).

28 See Russell (1912), p. 28.

29 See Russell (1917), pp. 156–8.

CHAPTER 3 SINN AND BEDEUTUNG

1 See for example Kenny (1973), pp. 60–2 and Pears (1987), pp. 75 and 110. This is also the line apparently taken by Anscombe, who proposes that 'Bedeutung' in *TLP* should be translated by 'reference' (with our knowledge of reference being a matter of acquaintance) and 'Sinn' by 'sense'; explicitly asserting that Wittgenstein's conception of sense is the same as Frege's (see her 1959, pp. 17 and 26). But in fact she does not go as far wrong as this would suggest, for she herself goes on to use 'sense' to mean 'truth-conditions' in expounding *TLP* (ibid., pp. 59–63), which is the view I shall adopt myself. This is because she badly misunderstands Frege. She correctly notes (p. 60) that for Frege the sense of a sentence – a thought – is the thought that its truth-condition is fulfilled (see *BLA* 32), but wrongly takes this to mean that the thought may be identified with the truth-condition. Rather, for Frege there may be many different thoughts of – many different ways of

presenting – one and the same truth-condition. (It is clear from the context of *BLA* 32 that we fix the truth-condition of a sentence by assigning referents to each of its component terms, implying that he takes truth-conditions to belong, not at the level of sense, but of reference.)

2 See *TLP* 5.54–5.5422 and Wittgenstein (1974), p. 23. See also the excellent reconstruction of the debate between Wittgenstein and Russell in Blackwell's (1981), especially pp. 18–24.

3 See for example Dummett (1973), pp. 590, 663 and 680.

4 Frege had of course maintained that predicates and concepts are essentially 'incomplete' whereas names are not – see his 'Function and Concept'. But it does not follow that there is nothing of significance left of this doctrine once we accept that all words are incomplete sentences – see my (1983b) where I extract a number of different strands from the incompleteness-metaphor. Nor does it follow that Wittgenstein is then free to reject Frege's distinction between concepts and objects as some have held (for example Allaire, 1963, p. 336).

5 See Frege (1984), p. 158.

6 As we saw in note 1 above, Anscombe falls into this trap.

7 This is urged by Anscombe (1959), p. 17.

8 '$+_c$' is Russell's addition-sign restricted to the case of cardinal numbers.

9 I here slip past the *TLP* distinction between senselessness and nonsense, which I will be expounded in ch. 6.

10 This suggestion should be distinguished sharply from the one made by McGuinness in his (1981), that 'Bedeutung' in *TLP* is best explicated in terms of Tugendhat's (1970) notion of semantic role or truth-value potential. On this account two expressions may be said to possess the same Bedeutung just in case they always produce sentences with the same truth-value when combined with the same expressions; and to say that an expression has Bedeutung is just to say that it does figure in true or false sentences. Here the Bedeutung of an expression is wholly a matter of its contribution to truth-value, whereas on my account it is its contribution to the content communicated by sentences containing it.

One thing wrong with McGuinness' suggestion is that it ignores the realism involved in saying that the Bedeutung of a name is an object (and is intended by him to do so). On this matter I am in agreement with Malcolm (1986) and Pears (1987), both of whom discuss this issue extensively – the objects of *TLP*, which make up the unchanging substance of the world and exist in all possible worlds, are wholly independent of the human mind and of language. But another thing wrong with the McGuinness suggestion is that it implies that the Bedeutungen of all types of expression are purely extensional. Whereas I shall argue in ch. 5 that the criterion of sameness of Bedeutung for all other types of expression besides proper names is logical equivalence.

11 The theses in question are (1) that the objects occurring in states of affairs have necessary existence, (2) that elementary propositions are logically independent of one another and (3) that a complete assignment of truth-values to the set of all elementary propositions gives a complete description of a possible world. Then when an elementary proposition directs us to the existence of a particular state of affairs we are in fact directed towards the set of all worlds in which that state of affairs exists and away from the remainder. And if we are directed towards the set of all worlds in which a given state of affairs exists, then we are directed towards the existence of that state of affairs itself and away from its non-existence.
12 See Russell (1910a), p. 158.
13 Anscombe, too, notices the directional connotations of 'Sinn'; see her (1959), p. 17.

CHAPTER 4 IN SEARCH OF SENSE

1 This temptation will eventually be vindicated by the discussion which follows in this and succeeding chapters. Quite a different temptation is to say that what gives life to the perceptible sign – what turns it into a symbol – is an imperceptible act of thinking on the part of the user of the sign. See for example McDonough (1986), pp. 62–5 and Malcolm (1986), ch. 4. In my view this interpretation is certainly incorrect, and it will be countered in ch. 8–10.
2 See Frege (1984), p. 158.
3 On this issue I am in broad agreement with Griffin. See his (1964), p. 95ff.
4 However, this should not be taken to imply that for Wittgenstein (as for Frege) senses are detachable from sentences; see ch. 8.
5 As Blackwell shows in his (1981), Wittgenstein's main criticism of Russell's theory of judgement was that the latter could not allow for the integrity – the wholeness or completeness – of the judged proposition (ibid. p. 23). For in order to account for the possibility of falsehood whilst holding onto the idea that judgement involves a direct relation to the things which the judgement concerns, Russell had been forced to construe it as a relation between the thinker and an ordered set of individuals and universals, thus losing hold of the essential wholeness of what is judged. I think Wittgenstein came to feel that the only solution was to give up the idea that judgement can be a direct relation to things in the world, moving rather towards the Fregean view that it always involves a mode of presentation of them. This then surfaces in non-Russellian use of 'proposition' throughout most of *TLP*, the integrity of the contents of judgements being preserved at the level of symbols (sign plus sense), in the wholeness of the propositions which thinkers employ to express their judgements.
6 Goldstein does have other arguments for this same conclusion. But

many of them are suspect, in that they make unreflective use of Wittgenstein's early Notebooks and later writings to establish claims about *TLP*. Moreover many of the passages in *TLP* which he cites, in fact do not obviously support his case. For example, he cites 3.3 in support of the claim that every Satz has Sinn (which he translates as 'sense'), when 3.3 merely says that *only* Sätze have Sinn (ibid. p. 46). And he cites 5.143 in support of the claim that tautologies and contradictions are not Sätze, omitting from his quotation that 5.143 says that 'in a manner of speaking' contradictions vanish outside all Sätze (ibid. p. 48).

7 In addition to the evidence mentioned above, it is worth also noting 3.13, where Wittgenstein writes: '('The content of a proposition' means the content of a proposition that has Sinn.)' The qualification here is redundant unless there can be propositions which lack Sinn (and so lack content). Note also 5.5351, where Wittgenstein uses 'non-proposition' in such a way as to imply that non-propositions are nonsensical sentences, as opposed to those which are merely senseless (such as contradictions and tautologies).

CHAPTER 5 ESSENTIAL SENSE

1 Since the *TLP* thesis is that the semantic contents of names are exhausted by their bearers, and since names are rigid designators (referring to the same individuals with respect to all possible worlds) it might be suggested that the *TLP* account of semantic content can be characterized in terms of logical equivalence for all categories of expression without restriction. For then if two names have the same bearer (and so the same semantic content), sentences which differ only in that the one has been substituted for the other will share the same truth-value with respect to every possible world. Note, however, that such an equivalence is metaphysical rather than conceptual or analytic – having to be established by empirical investigation. Whereas the argument which I shall give shortly would only warrant equating sameness of semantic content (for expressions other than proper names) with analytic equivalence. So it is better to characterize the *TLP* position by saying that understanding requires mutual knowledge of truth-conditions – where two names make the same contribution to truth-conditions just in case they have the same reference, whereas all other types of expression make the same contribution to truth-conditions just in case they are analytically equivalent.

2 This is loose because, in the normal terminology of *TLP*, propositions are sentences with their modes of projection (their Fregean senses), and propositions can be distinct from one another whilst being logically equivalent.

3 This my reply to the charge Dummett makes against the Wittgenstein of *TLP*, that by taking sameness of Sinn to be given by analytic

equivalence he is prevented from giving any account of linguistic understanding (see Dummett 1973, pp. 633–4). On the contrary, Wittgenstein's contribution lies in distinguising sharply between speaker understanding (idiolectic sense) and the knowledge required for communication (semantic content). It is only the latter which may be characterized in terms of analytic equivalence.

4 I owe the ideas expressed in this paragraph to Dummett. See his (1978), pp. 3 and 435. For further discussion see my (1987b).

5 This example ought properly to be somewhat more complicated, since there is no simple correspondence between perceived colours and wavelengths of light. But this in no way affects the point being made.

6 Note that their understandings are certainly not more than materially equivalent. They are not even causally equivalent, since if the machine malfunctions their correct usage will diverge.

7 It is crucial to this example that neither of the parties should know the position the other is in. For it is designed to be a case in which speakers know nothing beyond the material equivalence of one another's statements. It is of course a truism that two people can, in general, attach different contents to a given expression and yet still understand one another in its use, in virtue of knowing the content which the other attaches to it.

8 Note that the argument given here suggests that the notion of logical equivalence involved in the account of semantic content should be explicated in terms of analytic, as opposed to metaphysical, necessity. For only so will speakers who attach the same semantic content to an expression possess a shared conception of what is to count as a reason for or against their statements involving it, in advance of exchanging further information. So someone who understands 'water' as a definitional equivalent of 'H_2O' (perhaps a foreign laboratory technician), and someone who understands it in the usual way, ought not to be counted as communicating successfully by means of statements involving the term 'water', despite the fact (if Kripke and others are correct) that water is necessarily H_2O.

9 The alert reader will have noticed that this list is culled from *PI* 23.

10 Wittgenstein can reply similarly to quite another sort of objection, that discourse (including factual discourse) is governed by conventions of conversational implicature which require, for their operation, mutual knowledge of cognitive content. He can, while acknowledging the existence of such conventions, claim with some plausibility that they do not belong to the essence of factual communication. But in any case it is by no means obvious that such conventions really do require mutual knowledge of cognitive content. For example, one convention seems to be that less information should not be provided on a given topic than can easily be done. Thus if my mother asks me about my love-life and I reply that I have a girl-friend when in reality I have several, then I may be said to have spoken misleadingly, despite the fact that what I said was literally true. But the notion of 'information'

here is not especially cognitive, being characterizable rather in truth-conditional terms.

11 This may be taken as a criticism of the simple one-word imperative language-games of the early sections of *PI* if, as seems plausible, Wittgenstein's intention is that these are the only uses of signs in which the players engage.

12 See the account of opacity which Frege provides in 'On Sense and Reference'. (See for example Frege, 1984.)

13 In fact there are yet other perspectives on descriptions of propositional attitudes not relevant to the present issue, such as the one I characterize in my (1987b) as 'The Practical Reasoner's Perspective'.

14 I intend to take no particular stance here on the semantics (or lack of semantics) for live metaphors, since this metaphor would appear to be dead.

15 This is an idea which plays an important part in Wittgenstein's later philosophy of mathematics. See the discussion of surveyability in Wright (1980).

CHAPTER 6 SENSE AND NONSENSE

1 See his 'Function and Concept' in Frege (1984).

2 See for example Frege (1984), p. 193.

3 See Frege (1984), p. 147. Roger White first pointed this remark out to me.

4 Although I originally owe this suggestion to Tim Williamson, I have since found just such a purely-causal account in Favrholdt (1964), p. 142, in the course of which he likens philosophical propositions to bird-song!

5 This suggestion is made by Hacker in his (1986), p. 26.

6 Just such a view is taken by McDonough, who argues that the tautology 'P v −P' does not really contain the symbols for negation or disjunction, nor the proposition P, at all. See his (1986), pp. 81–9. This goes too far, making it difficult to keep track of the distinction between nonsense and senselessness. McDonough is correct in attributing to Wittgenstein the view that the signs in a tautology are in one respect not performing their usual role. For that role is to contribute to the semantic content of sentences in which they occur; but since a tautology is lacking in such content, there is nothing for the component expressions to contribute to. This in itself is sufficient to explain Wittgenstein's remarks about the 'disintegration of signs'. Yet it does not follow that the signs in a tautology do not constitute their usual symbols (do not express their usual senses). Nor does it follow that they do not serve to introduce their usual semantic contents (that they are not about anything). Rather, the symbols in a tautology are 'combined' in such a way that their contents fail to be combined into the sort of semantic content that significant sentences have – a Sinn.

7 I here rely upon the general tenor and subject-matter of *TLP* rather than upon specific remarks. But see 3.3421 and 5.641.
8 That Wittgenstein speaks of 'logical form' of both pictures (propositions) and reality, might seem to count against the suggestion canvassed in ch. 4, that the form of a proposition is in effect the predicative element in a sentence (see also in ch.11). But in fact a form is a possibility. The form of reality is the set of possible truths about the world; the form of an object is the set of its possible combinations with other objects; and the form of a sentence is a possible mode of combining proper names, realized in the structure of the sentence (each such mode of combination providing a mode of comparison with reality – i.e. the semantic content of a predicate, as we shall see in chs. 15 and 16). In the exposition which follows I employ a restricted (Fregean) notion of logical form for the sake of simplicity.
9 See Anscombe (1959), p. 164 for further examples of this sort.
10 An argument for such a view is given by Pears (1987), p. 143, in the course of his exposition of the Picture Theory.

CHAPTER 7 UNITY OF CONTENT

1 Since both formal argument and mathematical calculation occur frequently in science, it might be argued that we do after all have sufficient reason for insisting on mutual knowledge of cognitive content as the condition for communication in scientific discourse. Yet it can be replied, with some plausibility, that the matter is merely one of convenience. What is important is that our respective interpretations of scientific theories and of the statements of the evidence which support them should be logically equivalent. How easy it proves to be to get one another to follow the course of our calculations is an inessential matter of psychology.

But what of simplicity-considerations in science? On any adequate account of the scientific enterprise these must surely play an essential role. Yet do not they too presuppose mutual knowledge of cognitive content? I think not. Since appeals to simplicity are introduced into accounts of scientific method in order to explain how we may rationally choose between empirically equivalent but logically non-equivalent theories, the notion at issue is not an especially cognitive one. It will rather involve, for example, such things as the postulation of fewer types of theoretical entity.
2 It is then no accident that Frege proposes to take mutual knowledge of cognitive content as the condition for communication, since his main interest is in logical and mathematical knowledge.
3 The allusion to the ideas of the later Wittgenstein here is intentional. For it is one of the themes of the early sections of *PI* that understanding is a family resemblance (and hence fragmentary) concept. See *PI* 65, 108 and 164.

4 Provided, of course, that they understand the other words in the statement.
5 I am inclined to agree with Davidson that the semantic content of a live metaphor is exhausted by its literal (non-metaphorical) meaning. See essay 17 of his (1984).
6 See *PI* 65–9. This was the only option I thought available in my (1984b).
7 Moreover, even within the area of factual discourse, conditions for understanding might be expected to vary with context. Thus someone who knows only that elms are a kind of tree may be said to understand statements involving the word 'elm' in contexts where the rational grounds for those statements are not in question. In these contexts they can defer to the understanding which other people possess of the term, knowing that they can at any time fill-out their understanding by consulting reference books or competent speakers. This enables them to build up a file of information about elms in advance of knowing what distinguishes elms from other sorts of tree, and enables them to serve as a channel through which information about elms can be passed on. But if the context is such that they themselves need to be in a position to challenge or to appreciate the justification for those statements, then they require an ability to tell elms apart from other sorts of tree. And if they lack such an ability, then they cannot be said to have understood those statements.
8 See Essay 13 of Lewis (1983), 'Scorekeeping in a Language-game'.
9 I intend this vague formulation to be ambiguous between internalist and externalist accounts of knowledge, since this is not an issue on which I need to commit myself for present purposes.
10 Indeed it seems to me on the basis of these considerations that the Wittgenstein of *PI* goes wrong in insisting that understanding is a family resemblance concept. We can provide for unity in diversity by construing the concept as purpose-relative.
11 Can it really be so easy to side-step the philosophy-as-nonsense doctrine? Especially since Wittgenstein himself places so much stress upon it, for example in the preface to *TLP*, and in the 1919 letter to Russell where he says that the main point of the work lies in the showing/saying doctrine (see his 1974, p. 71). One reply is that Wittgenstein's failure to allow for purpose-relative concepts is all-of-a-piece with his lack of attention to the context-dependent aspects of language generally, such as indexicals. But a different sort of reply is that he did not really *want* to avoid the philosophy-as-nonsense doctrine. On the contrary, he needs it in a place to give symmetry with his views on the inexpressibility of the Ethical; providing, as it were, innocence by association.

CHAPTER 8 GEDANKEN

1 This interpretation is a rational reconstruction of Frege's position, since Frege himself makes no use of the notion of a possible world.

2 See in particular Favrholdt (1964), ch. 3, Kenny (1973), pp. 58–60 and (1981), Malcolm (1986), chs. 4–7 and McDonough (1986), ch. 6.
3 Only the text-based part of the argument will be completed in the present chapter. Arguments from Charity will be pursued in chs. 9 and 10.
4 Maslow (1961) rightly stresses that for Wittgenstein thought and language are inseperable (ibid. p. 49 ff), though in many other respects he gets *TLP* wrong.
5 See Wittgenstein (1974), p. 72. Those influenced by the letter include Favrholdt (1964), p. 81, Kenny (1973), pp. 58–9 and Malcolm (1986), pp. 65–6.
6 Malcolm makes heavy weather of this remark, and tries unconvincingly to work it around to support his own psychological interpretation. See his (1986), p. 65.
7 Ogden actually uses 'the thinking' instead of 'the thought', which seems unnecessarily barbaric.
8 For example, at 5 he is careful to say that *the* proposition is *a* truth-function of propositions. For on the use of 'proposition' common to the 5s, which we noted in ch. 4, there exist truth-functions (namely tautologies and contradictions) which do not express genuine propositions.
9 For a vigorous defence of this way of interpreting Frege's notion of sense, see Evans (1982), ch. 1.
10 I am not aware of any significant distinction between 'das Denken' and 'der Gedanke' in the terminology of *TLP*. Indeed, see the preface where they seem to be used interchangeably.
11 I am aware that some have claimed our knowledge of the meaning of a proposition to be a matter of perception, claiming that we literally hear the meaning in the person's utterance. See for example McDowell (1980). For an effective critique see Cooper (1987). But in any case the distinction between sign and symbol will remain.
12 See for example Shwayder (1963), and Griffin (1964), p. 124ff, both of whom apparently conflate the essential directedness of truth-conditions (which we acknowledged in ch. 3) with the idea that propositions are essentially assertoric.
13 This remark of Wittgenstein's then embodies a serious misunderstanding of Frege's mature view of his judgement-stroke, in which he makes a sharp distinction between sense (the content judged) and force (the linguistic act of assertion) – see *BLA* 5. It is not, however, wholly inaccurate as an account of Frege's view in *Begriffsschrift* where he says that the judgement-stroke (like the predicate 'is a fact' in a language where all assertions are made in the form 'Such-and-such is a fact') is the common predicate involved in all judgements – see his (1972), p. 113.

CHAPTER 9 THE EXISTENCE OF THOUGHTS

1 See *MT* ch. 4 for further discussion of this idea.
2 The talk of 'fixing conventions' in this paragraph should not be

understood in terms of conscious selection and explanation. For on the *TLP* account of thinking to be defended in ch. 10, conscious thinking is itself language-like and hence convention-involving. But it is in any case plausible to maintain that there are other ways for norms to arise than by conscious decision.

3 For example Katz (1981) takes such a view, for reasons which appear similar to Frege's reasons for believing in the necessary existence of thoughts.

4 Frege nowhere explicitly says that sentences have temporal existence. But such a view would seem to be implicit in the fact that he continually stresses the necessary existence of thoughts without once mentioning language in this connection. See also *BLA* xvi, where he implies that syntax is dependent upon historically conditioned facts of human psychology, and that languages are in consequence subject to change.

5 On this see Dummett's discussion in his (1981b), ch. 3.

6 As an aid to the reader, whenever designating a particular thought I employ square brackets to indicate its scope.

7 A limited version of this idea has been defended recently by Evans (1982) and others, particularly in connection with demonstrative thoughts. For a critique, see my (1987a).

8 Note that the arguments deployed here count equally against the Russellian model of thinking, which requires us to be in cognitive contact with a necessarily existing universal. This point will prove to be of some importance in ch. 16.

9 These arguments are discussed in greater detail in my (1984c). I also respond there to the suggestion that thoughts might have an existence which is timeless, where this means that it is nonsense (rather than necessarily true) to say of a thought that it exists at particular times. The immediate problem with such a suggestion is that it is then difficult to see how it can be possible for thoughts to be *grasped* at particular times either, given that the grasping-relation is supposed to be a real (as opposed to an intentional) one.

10 See Frege (1984), pp. 361–3 and 369, and Frege (1979), pp. 133–4 and 137.

11 Of course we have also seen that there is a strong case for rejecting the first premiss as well, at least where factual communication is concerned. See ch. 5 for the argument that understanding does not require mutual knowledge of cognitive content.

12 See *FA* vi, Frege (1984), pp. 363, 368 and 370–1, and Frege (1979), pp. 129, 135 and 148.

13 This principle needs to be made marginally more complicated to accommodate thoughts which themselves imply that they are not asserted at the time in question, such as the thought [that there are no intelligent agents prior to 20 million BC]. We need to add the rider: 'So long as the content of the thought does not imply that it is not entertained at the time in question'.

14 I owe this distinction to Dummett's (1973), pp. 368–70.
15 See for example *FA* vii, where Frege argues that if nothing remained fixed for all time then there could be no knowledge and no truth.
16 There is perhaps one possible difference between the two cases, in that I cannot in principle get into the remote past, whereas it is only the laws of nature which prevent me from getting into remote regions of space. But consider thoughts about all places. I cannot, even in principle, get into all places at once.
17 For further development and discussion of this position see *MT* chs. 4 and 5.
18 See *FA* vi–vii, Frege (1984), pp. 363, 367–8 and 370 and Frege (1979), pp. 133, 135 and 148. The argument I give in the text is of course a rational reconstruction, since Frege himself does not make use of the notion of a possible world.

CHAPTER 10 THINKING AND LANGUAGE-USING

1 This use of 'thought' is especially common amongst philosophers. Indeed it is quasi-technical, since someone with a long-term desire to be famous would not normally be described as thinking or entertaining a thought at all.

The distinction is of some importance since many of those who discuss the question whether thinking is linguistic fail to draw it, yet some of their arguments for a negative conclusion only succeed if 'thought' is taken widely. See for example McGinn (1982b), ch. 4.

2 One related issue, which does need to be pursued further, is that one clearly cannot maintain any simple version of the thesis that thinkings (narrow sense) are linguistic. For as Dummett points out in his (1986), p. 144, there are conscious thinkings which are not, on any account of the matter, linguistically formulated. He gives an example of a canoeist seeing two boats closing on one another and deciding that he just has time to slip his canoe between them. This decision is an occurrent event, not a standing state; yet it clearly need not have been formulated in words or anything like words. The distinctive feature of such thinkings is that there need be no events in the thinker's consciousness at the time which may be said to express them. But then just for this reason (and for reasons similar to those which will emerge in the final section of this chapter) I do not see what account can be given of what it is for such a decision to be a conscious one (as opposed to the sort of non-conscious decisions one takes while driving the car with one's conscious mind wholly occupied with something else) except to say that it is an event apt to emerge in an explicitly formulated thinking with the same content. If this is correct, then all conscious thinkings may turn out to be language-involving in the same way that I suggested in the text that conscious beliefs and desires

might – provided, of course, that we can show that all explicitly formulated thinkings are linguistic.

3 I here bypass contemporary debates over whether images are themselves propositional (see for example the essays in Part Two of Ned Block, 1981), and whether thoughts are themselves imagistic (see for example Johnson-Laird, 1988). For I take it that these debates concern the appropriate sub-personal explanations of imagery and thought. What is clear is that at the personal (conscious) level, images and (some) acts of thinking are quite distinct. It is also clear that no image can constitute an act of thinking by itself, but only when embedded within an appropriate propositional context (explicit or implicit). And even here, it is not the image itself, but the image used or taken in a particular way, which contributes to the content of the thought. See the discussion which follows later in the chapter.
4 The idea was first introduced in Putnam's seminal paper 'The Meaning of "Meaning"', which is reproduced as Essay 12 of his (1975).
5 For example, if I think to myself 'I have a girl-friend' when in fact I have three, then I shall not have misled myself in the way that I would have misled my mother if I had asserted that sentence aloud to her. On the other hand, if I think to myself 'Some Australians are too big for their boots' while watching a young man who I know to be an Australian strut by, then I shall take myself to have implied that that man is conceited, just as my audience would have understood from my utterance if I had spoken the sentence aloud. (The example is Blackburn's. See his 1984, p. 308.)
6 Locke is generally credited with having held such a view.
7 As did Russell in his (1940).
8 See *PI* 332. Note that I am claiming that Wittgenstein's views on the nature of thinking remained basically unchanged throughout his career.
9 See Grice (1957) and (1969).
10 The fact that the use of speech in soliloquy is rare need not prevent it from assuming a central theoretical importance. (Compare: reading aloud to oneself is rare amongst adults, yet that is how we all learned to read.) Nor is it really so very rare. Many of us chat to our dogs and cats (and babies) without intending to induce beliefs in them. Many of us first work out our thoughts and calculations on paper, thinking with our fingers as it were. And in philosophy one famous lecturing technique is to think aloud in the presence of an audience.
11 See Grice (1969), pp. 174–7.
12 Let me stress that I do not mean that there are some things which can only be thought aloud. Rather, there are some token-utterances which express thought, but where there is no separable process of thinking them.
13 The issues surrounding names will be discussed in ch. 13. I also abstract from debates as to whether 'hot', in such a use, is a natural-kind term, rigidly designating mean molecular momentum. This

would unnecessarily complicate the discussion without affecting its outcome. For even so the word will designate a natural kind in virtue of expressing a particular rule of classification along the lines of 'heat is whatever fundamentally explains *this* range of phenomena' (with here a gesture at a range of recognizable examples of hot places and things).

14 This idea will be discussed in some detail in *MT* chs. 4 and 15.

15 Dummett argues against equating knowledge of a language with mastery of a technique in his (1986), pp. 146–7. But the contrast he draws between knowing a language and knowing how to swim fails to make his point. It would indeed be peculiar for someone who had never learned Russian to say 'I don't know whether I can speak it; I have never tried', in a way that it would not be so peculiar to say 'I don't know whether I can swim; I have never tried'. This is because swimming is not a normative activity. But it does not follow that knowing a language is a matter of genuine (propositional) knowledge. For it would be equally strange for someone to say 'I don't know whether I can play chess; I have never tried'. Yet knowing how to play chess is surely a mastery of a technique. One could learn it without ever being given, or formulating for oneself, an explicit statement of the rules; just gradually acquiring the ability to distinguish allowable from unallowed moves. In the same way, Dummett's point that someone who has not learned Russian does not know what it is to speak Russian, being incapable of distinguishing genuine Russian speakers from others, holds equally in the case of chess. Someone who has not learned to play does not know – in precisely the same sense – what chess is, being incapable of telling whether or not two people moving pieces around on a board are playing it.

Where Dummett is right, is that to know that I speak Russian (or any other shared language) I have to know that my capacities coincide with those of other speakers. And this will be genuine propositional knowledge. The truth is that knowing an idiolect is mastery of a normative technique, whereas knowing a shared language is this together with the knowledge that one's normative capacities coincide with those of others; it being this propositional knowledge which underpins communication.

16 See for example Smith and Jones (1986), Part III.

17 See Davidson's 'Thought and Talk' in his (1984) or in Guttenplan (1975).

18 This is Loar's strategy in his (1981), following Stalnaker (1976).

19 This account is not unlike that given by Geach in his (1957), ch. 5.

20 Of course I do not mean that subjects must be capable of thinking precisely these thoughts – they may never have heard of Aberdeen.

21 Not that the complete structure must occur in every instance of thinking – for as Wittgenstein remarks at *PI* 319, I can entertain a thought in a flash in the same sense that I can make a note of it in a few pencilled words. What makes the incomplete sign into something expressing a complete thought is that I know how to complete it, and

act exactly as if I had completed it. The point here is related to the one made in note 2 above – it is the aptness of the incomplete thought-token to give rise to complete thinkings with a particular content which constitutes it as a conscious expression of that content.

22 Here I consciously echo Wittgenstein's remarks in his 1919 letter to Russell, to emphasize the point that they do not commit him to any version of the code-breaking conception of language. (See Wittgenstein, 1974, p. 72.)

23 The two are isomorphic not just in that both employ structured arrangements of sign-tokens, but in that anything thinkable will be sayable and vice versa. For someone who entertains privately the thought [that P] need only select some public markers to play the same roles as the ones which exercise the capacities involved in their thinking. And conversely, someone who asserts publicly that P need only find some markers in consciousness to play the roles of their public words, in order to be able to entertain that thought privately.

24 It is worth indicating how the position outlined in this chapter differs from the thoery of mental representation defended by Fodor (1981). There is agreement that thoughts are relations to sentences. But Fodor denies that these sentences will belong to a natural language, whereas I maintain that they very likely will be. Given that public thinking takes place in natural language, parsimony supports the suggestion that private thinkings will similarly employ natural language sentences. Moreover Fodor believes that all propositional attitudes are relational, whether they be conscious or non-conscious, personal or sub-personal; whereas I am inclined to believe that only conscious propositional attitudes are relations to sentences; a conscious attitude being one which is apt to emerge in a conscious thinking (an event employing an arrangement of signs) with the same content. I hope to develop these ideas elsewhere.

CHAPTER 11 NAME AND OBJECT

1 Some have sought to find a distinction between objects (Gegenstanden) and things (Dingen) – see for example Finch (1971). I myself can see no significant difference between the two. Indeed the way in which the terms are introduced at 2.01 strongly suggests that they are to be understood equivalently. There Wittgenstein tells us that a state of affairs is a combination of objects (or things).

2 Those who adopt the wide interpretation include Stenius (1960), Allaire (1963), Mounce (1981) and Hintikka and Hintikka (1986).

3 Those who adopt the narrow interpretation include Copi (1958b), Anscombe (1959), Sellars (1962a), Griffin (1964) and Fogelin (1982).

4 Pears (1987, pp. 137–9) has suggested that Wittgenstein does not

commit himself to either these two doctrines in particular, arguing that what is of value in the Picture Theory is consistent with either of them. I think this suggestion is intrinsically implausible, for reasons which will emerge shortly. But in any case, since he concedes that what he finds important in the Picture Theory is consistent with the narrow reading, a demonstration that there is additional significance to be found in that theory if the narrow reading is adopted will provide a reason for embracing it. This is what I shall argue.

Ishiguro (1969, pp. 48–9) also suggests a third alternative, arguing that the Simples referred to by the names of *TLP* are instantiations of simple properties (immanent universals). Although this reading does have some advantages, it is hard to see how, in that case, Simples could have necessary existence. (See *MT* ch. 8.) For there is no reason to think that the set of universals which are immanent in a world should be the same across all possible worlds. Moreover, on this account it is hard to see what the Picture Theory, as it applies at the level of elementary propositions (which would consist only of 'names' of immanent universals), could usefully show us about the semantics of ordinary sentences: though Ishiguro herself defends an interpretation of the Picture Theory similar to my own (see ch. 15 of this work) in her (1979).

5 See Allaire (1963), who argues that objects and properties (and names and predicates) are much more nearly alike, in Wittgenstein's view, than Frege thinks. On the interpretation to be defended in ch. 15, on the other hand, Wittgenstein not only accepts Frege's distinction between names and predicates but widens it still further, claiming that predicates and relational expressions do not have reference. His view is that their Bedeutungen are not items in reality, as are the Bedeutungen of names.

Note that the central importance of the concept/object distinction in Frege counts also against Pears' suggestion, mentioned in note 4 above, that Wittgenstein leaves the categorial status of objects unresolved.

6 Though strictly speaking, whether they are metaphors at all is a matter of interpretation. I think they clearly have to be, since if states of affairs were literally spatial configurations of physical particles then there could be no question of them being logically independent of one another. See the discussion which follows.

7 See Long (1982) for an account of the distinction.

8 See for example Stenius (1960), p. 132.

9 See Stenius (1960), p. 62.

10 I am aware that it is to a degree controversial to take the objects of *TLP* to have necessary existence. I shall return to the matter in *MT* ch. 8.

11 Notice that on the wide reading the claims in 2.0231–2.0232 become utterly banal. They would merely deny that any individual, or property, or relation can constitute a state of affairs by itself. Rather it is only 'combinations' of objects with properties, or objects with re-

lations, which can constitute a state of affairs. And the corresponding semantic claim would merely be that no proper name or predicative expression can constitute a sentence by itself.

12 Indeed it has been claimed that since all the links in the chain serve equally to hold it together, Wittgenstein is here expressing the view that Simples are neither individuals nor universals, but some unique category of entity containing elements of both. (Peter Long put this view to me in correspondence.) The trouble with this suggestion is that it is impossible to see what would motivate the resulting doctrine.

13 It had been briefly mentioned at 1.21.

14 This is why Wittgenstein's talk of states of affairs being configurations of objects must be metaphorical – see note 6 above.

15 Yet it still leaves us with entailment-relations between elementary propositions. Thus 'abc' will imply 'cba', and 'abc & cde' will entail 'bcd'. I owe this point to Tim Williamson.

16 See Stenius (1975).

17 See Wittgenstein (1973), p. 23.

18 Anscombe in her (1959), ch. 7, combines a narrow reading of 'name' with the thesis that the forms of elementary propositions are logical ones. She can do this because she thinks that amongst the names within an elementary proposition will be names of property and relation tokens. But such an interpretation faces overwhelming difficulties, most notably over the supposed necessary existence of Simples (see *MT* ch.8) and the possibility of falsehood (see ch. 15 of this work).

19 Griffin endorses such an interpretation. See his (1964), p. 13ff. and p. 89ff.

A plausible account of the genesis of the terminology would be as follows. In the 'Notes on Logic' Wittgenstein speaks of predicates and relational expressions as 'forms' because there is a sense in which they carry with them the form of a sentence, in a way that proper names do not. (This had been one of the strands in Frege's metaphor of the 'incompleteness' of predicates – see my 1983b.) He also thinks that properties and relations are all 'copulae' – i.e. that there are no logical forms of the sort Russell believed in (see *NB* 120–1). Then in *TLP*, when he moves to the view that elementary propositions consist only of proper names, the 'form' of a sentence has become the possibility of combining names in a given way, with different such modes of combination signifying different relations between objects.

20 C.f. *NB* 70: 'The watch is sitting on the table is nonsense!' (The German says 'sinnlos', usually translated as 'senseless'. But Wittgenstein obviously does not mean that 'The watch is sitting on the table' is either a tautology or a contradiction!) Frege had notoriously believed that in a properly constructed language predicates and relational expressions would be defined over all objects, so that truth-conditions would have to be fixed for 'Seven is heavier than five' – see his (1984), p. 148 and *BLA* 56. Wittgenstein on the other hand feels that

these examples show that the idea of a Begriffsschrift has not been carried far enough. He thinks that in a properly constructed, fully analysed, language its very syntactic structures would prevent us from formulating sentences such as these.

21 See Stenius (1960), p. 126.

22 For example, the inference: $\forall x(abx \rightarrow edx)$, abc $\vdash$ edc, treats the sentence 'abc' as having the form 'Fc'.

Notice that we can respond as we have done in this paragraph to an argument based upon 4.1211, which says that the proposition 'fb' shows that the object b occurs in its Sinn. It does not follow from this that there are any elementary propositions consisting only of a name and a predicate.

23 This argument is made much of by Hintikka and Hintikka. See their (1986), pp. 35–7.

24 Notice that this qualifying remark was added late to *TLP*, not occurring after the otherwise similar passage in *PTLP* (4.1022331).

25 Note that Wittgenstein's preparedness to talk here about internal relations between properties need not commit him to the existence of universals, but only to the existence of concepts (senses) and property-tokens. See ch. 15 for my account of the *TLP* semantic ontology as including only individuals and property- and relation-tokens.

26 Note that even if 'Bedeutung' in this passage means 'reference' it still does not commit Wittgenstein to the view that predicates have reference. Rather, it could be read as saying that to attempt to characterize the difference between proper names and predicates by saying that they have different kinds of referent (as Frege does) is to make the distinction between them too slight.

27 See Sainsbury (1979), pp. 305–7.

28 Again this passage is strongly emphasized by Hintikka and Hintikka (1986), pp. 32–3.

29 Virtually every commentator who adopts the wide reading mentions this passage.

30 See for example the evidence assembled by Hintikka and Hintikka in their (1986), ch. 2.

CHAPTER 12 NAMES, KNOWLEDGE AND IDENTITY

1 This is the view to which Baker and Hacker are committed, since they see *TLP* as endorsing what they call 'The Augustinian Picture of Language'. See their (1980), pp. 36–41 and 57–9, and my critique in my (1984a).

2 Note that this combination of views enables us to rebut the criticisms made by the later Wittgenstein at *PI* 40, which many have taken to be directed against the *TLP* view of names. To say that the distinctive semantic content of any given name is exhausted by its reference is not

at all to confuse its meaning with its bearer. On the contrary, understanding a name will also mean knowing its logical grammar. And where a name refers to a temporally existing thing, part of understanding it will mean knowing that the name can still be used to refer to that thing even after the latter has ceased to exist.

3 Indexicals receive no special mention in *TLP*. It seems to be assumed either that they are dispensable, or that they do not differ significantly from proper names. Neither thesis might seem very plausible in the light of the work which has been done on indexicals over the last decade. (See in particular Perry, 1977 and 1979, and Evans, 1982.) But recall that Wittgenstein's primary concern is with semantic content, whereas both the indispensability and many of the distinctive features of indexicals relate to their role in human cognition. Abstracting from the undoubted differences in logical grammar, Wittgenstein is in fact correct that names and indexicals do not differ in semantic content. For in both cases knowledge of reference suffices for understanding.

On this issue I disagree with Evans, who argues that in order to understand a statement involving an indexical you have to have, yourself, a suitable indexical thought about the referent (see his, 1982, ch. 9). This seems to me to be both intuitively implausible and unmotivated. Consider the following example. Imagine a security guard in a museum sitting outside a room in which a recently acquired piece of sculpture is the only work on show. She herself has not seen the sculpture, and cannot see it from where she sits, but she knows quite a lot about it: she knows what it depicts, who the artist was, and how much it cost the museum. Now suppose she overhears a visitor say as he enters the room, 'That sculpture ought never to have been purchased'. Does she not understand this remark? Surely she does: she knows which thing the visitor is talking about, and what he is saying about it. I can see no motive for denying understanding in a case such as this.

4 This is the way in which Anscombe takes it. See her (1959), p. 26.

5 Ishiguro goes wrong in claiming that the simple objects of *TLP* cannot be referred to by description. (See her, 1969, p. 44.) It is true that 3.221 tells us that objects can only be named, and that 3.261 says that names cannot be anatomized by means of definitions. But these remarks should be understood as relating to the semantic content of simple names, not to their idiolectic senses. Since objects are simple, there is no contentful description which can convey what they are. For not being made up out of parts, one cannot analyse the semantic content of their names by means of a description of the mode of their construction out of parts, as one can in the case of ordinary names (see the next section). And of course an analysis which tried to specify the object by means of an essential attribute of it would fail to have semantic content, whereas one which employed some contingent feature of it would for that very reason fail as an analysis, since

correctness of analysis requires logical equivalence. But it does not follow that people cannot think of simple objects by means of descriptions of one or other of these kinds.

What is true, is that not all simple names can have senses expressible as definite descriptions, because of Wittgenstein's view that there must be some genuinely singular (non-descriptive) propositions. On this see *MT* chs. 10 and 12. Rather, the senses of at least some simple names will have to consist in a recognitional capacity or memory-based demonstrative.

6 This interpretation will be substantiated in *MT* ch. 8.

7 In more detail: we can here set a dilemma parallel to the one we set Frege. Either the acquaintance-relation obtains in virtue of the thinker's conscious states, which derive their causal powers from the object of acquaintance – in which case our knowledge of the essential features of an object would have to be caused by non-necessary properties of it. Or the acquaintance-relation is a bare one – in which case the thinker will have no immediate knowledge of its obtaining, and like anyone else will have to infer that it does from their own behaviour.

8 It is clear that the names in question at 4.243 are genuine (logically proper) ones. For the remark occurs within a sequence of passages concerned with elementary propositions (4.21–4.25).

9 It is worth noting that *TLP* employs another epistemic term besides 'know' in a non-belief-involving sense. Thus at 4.464 and 5.525 the word 'certain' is used in an account of objective probability, to contrast with 'possible' and 'impossible'. On this usage all tautologies are certain, irrespective of whether or not anyone believes in their tautological status.

10 Griffin argues convincingly that analysis, on the *TLP* conception, involves defining terms for complexes (the latter being ordinary physical objects) into arrangements of component physical parts. See his (1964), pp. 42–50.

11 This is one possibility for what Wittgenstein has in mind at 3.24, when he says that propositions containing a sign for a complex will have a degree of indeterminacy. Perhaps he is thinking that their analysis will take the form 'The thing which contains most of the following parts arranged in something like the following manner. . .'. Other possibilities will be considered in *MT*.

12 In this I follow Kripke. See his (1980), pp. 112–15.

13 We owe it to Kripke that we are now able to see this distinction so clearly. See his (1980).

14 For a full exposition and discussion of Wittgenstein's views on identity, see White (1978).

Note that Wittgenstein's insistence that identity is *not* a relation between objects need not be taken to suggest that other relational expressions *do* serve to refer to relations. Rather, what is distinctive about the identity-sign is that not even a relation-token figures in the truth-conditions of sentences containing it. (What makes an identity-statement true is an object, not a state of affairs.) See note 15 below, as well as chs. 15 and 16 where a non-referential semantics for predicative expressions is outlined.

15 This way of handling identity-statements is similar to that suggested by Salmon (1986) pp. 78–9, as well as having much in common with Morris (1984). But Morris thinks that what I call the pragmatic function of identity-statements should be used to elucidate their content. I am unconvinced by his arguments against what he calls the 'objectual analysis', which holds that the content of an identity-statement concerns the referents of the names involved. To endorse this is not necessarily to claim that identity is a genuine relation, nor that what makes an identity-statement true is a special sort of fact, namely an object being self-identical. For as will we shall see in ch. 16, I deny that *any* relational expressions serve to refer to relations. Rather they express rules for mapping the objects referred to onto truth-values. In the case of the identity-sign, the rule is that an atomic sentence containing it is true if and only if the objects referred to on either side of it are one and the same. What is distinctive about the identity-sign, as against genuine relational expressions, is that there is no relation-token involved in its truth-condition, but simply an object.

16 Note that even if we were wrong in arguing in the last chapter that 'name' in *TLP* means 'proper name', this interpretation would remain unaffected. It would merely follow that the doctrine should be extended more widely, to cover predicates and relational expressions as well.

CHAPTER 13 PROPER NAME SEMANTICS

1 Versions of this theory have been defended by Searle (1958) and by Dummett (1973), pp. 95–102. See also *PI* 79.

2 Russell certainly held a shifting-sense theory, though it is doubtful whether he requires mutual knowledge of sense for successful communication. See his (1917), p. 158.

3 I first developed an example of this kind in my (1983a).

4 See 'On Sense and Reference' (for example in Frege, 1984), where the bulk of the paper is taken up with this issue.

5 Of course Mary's belief is not *about* the mode of thinking α, but is expressed by means of it.

This way of handling belief-sentences is very similar to that given by Salmon (1986), pp. 111ff., though arrived at independently. However, Salmon does not notice the distinction between the belief-acquisitive and explanatory perspectives on belief-description. And although it is clear from the context of his discussion that he is concerned with descriptions of belief from the explanatory standpoint, he makes no real attempt to show how a name can be used to convey something about the believer's mode of thinking, as manifestly it can. In fact his proposal is adequate only to express the content of belief-ascriptions made from the belief-acquisitive perspective, where we have no interest in the believer's mode of thinking. It is clear, moreover, that Salmon would want to deny (what I have asserted) that it is the mode of thinking which a believer associates with a name which determines the reference which it has for them.

6 Hence the difficulties Kripke notices in his (1979). In my view the correct solution to his puzzle is that the principle of Disquotation (if A is prepared to assert 'P' then A believes that P) is only fully adequate for descriptions of belief from the belief-acquisitive standpoint. Where our interest is explanatory we may have to do more to characterize A's understanding of any names involved.

7 So when Kripke presses the question 'Does Pierre, or does he not, believe that London is pretty?' (Margalit, 1979, p. 259), the correct response is that both of these reports can serve as adequate characterizations of (non-contradictory) beliefs, when set against the background of the story Kripke has told us.

8 I focus here on the use of bearerless names in factual discourse, leaving to one side the problem of names in fiction. On this see Evans (1982), ch. 10.

9 For present purposes it matters little whether or not 'exists' is ever a predicate.

10 Compare *PI* 79: 'If we are told "N did not exist" we do ask: "What do you mean? Do you want to say . . . or . . . etc.?"'

11 In this much, at least, I agree with Donnellan (1974).

12 Perhaps Noonan (1979) holds such a combination of views, as does Searle (1983). However Searle seems prepared to allow that speakers' modes of determining the reference of a name can form part of the semantic (communicated) content of sentences containing that name (ibid. pp. 256 and 260). Moreover he is sloppy about what does and what does not belong to the cognitive content of thoughts employing names, making no real attempt to distinguish between what belongs to that content and what is implied by it (on which see the discussion in the final section of this chapter).

13 See Donnellan (1972) and (1974), Kripke (1980), and many others.

14 This is Evans' view. See his (1982), ch. 11.

15 At this point causal theorists might attempt to deploy the distinction between what a speaker literally says and what they mean, claiming that the external causal chain is part of a theory of literal saying. But this is not a plausible move for them to make. It would, for example, be plainly crazy to base a semantics for words like 'carburettor' on what it is about a speaker's use of that word which makes it true that they have said that there is a fault in the carburettor, when what they meant is that there is a fault in the exhaust system.

16 See Kripke (1980). In the preface Kripke tries to distance his views on names from the question of their behaviour in modal discourse, claiming that the issue of rigidity arises in connection with simple

sentences, such as 'Aristotle was fond of dogs', which contain no modal terms (ibid. p. 11). He says that the issue concerns the truth-conditions of such sentences with respect to counter-factual situations (ibid. p. 12). But I agree with Dummett that there is no way for someone to manifest grasp of such truth-conditions except in judgements where the simple sentence occurs within the scope of a modal operator. See his (1981b), pp. 571 and 582.

17 This defense of description-theories has been employed, in rather different ways, by Dummett (1981b), pp. 557–600, and Noonan (1979).

18 Burge gives a similar explanation of rigidity to that given here. See his (1979), p. 413. See also Noonan (1979).

19 This point is also sufficient to undermine A. D. Smith's argument in his (1984), pp. 186–7, which attempts to attack description-theories by showing that names refer to the very same individuals with respect to all counter-factual situations, even in a language containing no modal operators. He claims very plausibly that when speakers of such a language are first introduced to modal operators it would not need to be explained to them that such operators always take narrow scope with respect to a name. But this does not show that reference is not determined by *fit* with the descriptions which speakers associate with names. For if they know that it is not a requirement for them to understand one another that they should all associate with those names the same modes of thinking, then they will automatically take names as having wide scope with respect to modal operators. For they will see that they would otherwise be constantly at risk of misunderstanding one another.

However I agree with what is in fact the main thesis of Smith's paper, that the important thing about names is not their behaviour in modal contexts but rather that they are what he calls 'purely referential' (ibid. p. 190) – if this just means that their semantic content is exhausted by their bearers. But it does not follow from this that reference is not determined by *fit*.

20 See Kripke (1980), pp. 83–92.

21 It also is sufficient to counter one of the main arguments of his (1979), involving the premiss that speakers will often have only an indefinite description to associate with a name, for example 'Tully was a famous Roman orator'. (See Margalit, 1979, p. 246.) For there is in fact a further (definite) description here, namely 'The person referred to as "Tully" by those from whom I acquired this use of the name'.

A similar suggestion can solve the problem of Pierre who learns 'Platon' in France as the name of a Greek philosopher and learns 'Plato' in English with the same (indefinite) identification, subsequently asserting both 'Platon était chauvre' (Plato was bald) and 'Plato was not bald' (ibid. p. 260). There need be no contradiction in Pierre's beliefs if in the first case he believes that the man called 'Platon' by those from whom he acquired this use of the name was bald, whereas in the second case he believes that the man called 'Plato' by those from whom he acquired this use of that name was not bald.

22 See Evans (1982), ch. 11.

23 For further development and defence of a view of this sort in connection with demonstratives, see my (1987a).

24 As before, such a description is implied by the producer-sense of a name, rather than being identical with it.

25 The proposal made here is sufficient to handle Donnellan's example (Davidson and Harman, 1972, p. 368) of the man who introduces the names 'Alpha' and 'Beta' to refer to each of two similar squares visible before him on a screen, when unknown to himself he is wearing spectacles which invert his visual field. For then even if he believes Alpha to be the upper square he is in fact referring to the lower, since it is the lower square through acquaintance with which he acquired this use of the name 'Alpha'.

CHAPTER 14 ISOMORPHIC REPRESENTATION

1 This does not mean that the concern with sentential significance has been dropped, however. On the contrary, in the 'Notes dictated to Moore' of April 1914 Wittgenstein explicitly deploys a fact-analysis of propositions to explain the impossibility of wrong substitutions (*NB* 115).

2 Thus Stenius, who has been foremost in interpreting the Picture Theory as expressing the thesis of isomorphism, says that there are two aspects to the understanding of a sentence: there is knowledge of the 'key of interpretation' (which elements in the sentence stand for which elements in reality), and there is the general knowledge that the sentence, like any other, is intended to represent isomorphically. See his (1960), pp. 91–9.

3 This would then be isomorphism, not in the sense of 1–1 correspondence of parts, but rather in the sense that states of affairs of a given type (e.g. relational ones) would be symbolized by sentences belonging to the same type.

4 There could be a similar convention governing spoken discourse, perhaps relating to the tones of voice with which predicates and relational expressions are spoken. Of course either form of language would suffer from severe practical limitations, since there may be many more things that we want to refer to than there are distinguishable styles of script or tones of voice. But all this shows is that such languages would have to use one and the same name for a variety of different individuals (as natural language in fact does), leaving it to the context to disambiguate the different uses.

5 Many, of course, regard this as the defining characteristic of genuine language. The later Wittgenstein apparently disagrees – see *PI* 2.

6 This is the line taken by Stenius in his (1960).

7 Only if the wide interpretation is adopted can 'in the same way' be read as literal identity. Otherwise a spatial picture, for example, would be incapable of depicting anything other than spatial states of affairs. If we adopt the narrow interpretation, then 2.15 has to be read as saying that the elements in a picture and the individuals in the state of affairs depicted are related to one another in an analogous way (by means of a relation allowing the same 'degrees of freedom'). The original German literally says 'represents that things are so combined with one another', which is ambiguous between identity and likeness.

8 This is not strictly accurate. There are also the suggestions made by Pears, that Wittgenstein found the analogy with pictures illuminating in bringing out why a sentence cannot represent its own mode of representation (see his 1987, p. 143), and by Anscombe, that the analogy helps us to understand propositional negation (see her 1959, ch. 4). No doubt these ideas are present in the Picture Theory – like any fruitful metaphor, one would expect this one to be many-faceted. But each of the above suggestions is consistent with either the wide or the narrow reading of the *TLP* terminology of 'name' and 'object', and so cannot help us in choosing between them.

9 Note that if Sellars is right, then 'relations between names' would include, as a limiting case, a proper name signifying by means of some significant property of itself that a Simple possesses a non-relational attribute. See the discussion in ch.11, and Sellars (1962a).

10 This is the interpretation offered by Long in his (1969).

11 This gives us the sense in which predicative expressions carry with them the form of the sentences in which they can occur, which makes it natural for Wittgenstein to speak of such expressions as 'forms'. See the discussion and notes in ch. 11.

12 I am told that something like this possibility is realized in Latin.

CHAPTER 15 THE PICTURE THEORY

1 It is here that he mentions the use of models in the Paris law-courts to represent accidents.

2 Let me stress the very close proximity to one another of these two strands in the text of *NB*. This is in marked contrast to the passage which Pears selects as setting the problem which the Picture Theory is designed to solve, which does not occur until a full month after the introduction of the comparison with pictures (see Pears, 1987, pp. 117 and 130). This is at *NB* 21 where Wittgenstein writes thus:

> This is the difficulty: How can there be such a thing as the form of P if there is no situation of this form? And in that case, what does this form really consist in?

Pears sees the difficulty in question, as arising for the theory of judgement developed by Russell in his 1913 manuscript 'Theory of

Knowledge' (now published in his 1984), which Wittgenstein had seen. There Russell had claimed that judgement requires acquaintance not just with the things for which the individual words in a sentence stand (namely individuals and universals), but also with logical forms. So the judgement [that aRb] would require acquaintance with a, b, the relation R and the logical form Øαβ. Pears claims that the Picture Theory is designed to refute such a view.

There are a number of points to be made about this. The first is that when Wittgenstein speaks of 'form' in the above passage it is by no means obvious that he has in mind something of the same sort as Øαβ. For there is the evidence of the 'Notes on Logic', where he speaks of 'xRy' (i.e. a relational expression) as being the form of the sentence 'aRb' (*NB* 98). And as we saw in ch. 11, there is some reason to think that this use continues into *TLP* itself. So the difficulty raised in the passage above might not be a difficulty for Russell, but rather the problem of what the relation (the form) in 'aRb' is to stand for in a case where that sentence is false. On this see the discussion in the next section of this chapter.

No doubt Pears is correct that Wittgenstein rejects the existence of forms such as Øαβ. For this is the same as saying that he denies the existence of copulae (see the next section of this chapter). But it is quite another matter to characterize the point of the Picture Theory in such terms. Indeed it is hardly very likely that Wittgenstein would have given such prominence to the theory, if its point had been to refute a doctrine whose falsity he was able to see at a glance. (See Blackwell, 1981, p. 16ff, for an account of Wittgenstein's reaction to 'Theory of Knowledge'.)

3 But it seems that he himself did not immediately appreciate their significance. For in the very last remark relating to the Picture Theory which occurs in *NB*, dated April 1915, he laments that he cannot even bring out the sense in which a proposition is a picture, and says that he is almost inclined to give up all his efforts (*NB* 41).

4 This would be the relation which holds between two names and a relational expression when one of the names is followed by the relational expression which is followed by the other name.

5 This regress is, of course, just another version of the regress generated by any version of Platonism about universals which construes participation in a universal as being yet another universal.

6 Much of the reasoning in this paragraph is implicit in Wittgenstein's January 1913 letter to Russell (*NB* 121).

7 To get around this problem we might try equating the reference of a significant relation with a *set* of relation-tokens. But this would run into trouble over the principle of Semantic Ordering. (This is the principle that sense determines reference which determines truth-value – see ch. 2). The argument to show this is essentially the same as that developed in the next chapter against the view that the reference of a predicate is a set of objects.

8 This example is similar to one of Wittgenstein's own – see *NB* 20–1.

9 This suggestion is natural for two distinct reasons. Firstly, because if the coordinate system is to be an analogy for a proposition, it is clear that the signs 'a' and 'b' must be the analogue of proper names, leaving the background rule of projection as the only candidate to play the role of a predicate. And secondly, because of Frege's famous identification of functions (such as that expressed by 'the point xy') with concepts, which Wittgenstein would of course have been aware of. See for example 'Function and Concept' in Frege (1984).

10 Note that 4.0141 does not occur in *PTLP*, only being added to the final draft of *TLP*. This may be an indication of the difficulty Wittgenstein had in seeing his way clear of the strong isomorphism thesis.

11 Similar interpretations of the Picture Theory are provided by Ishiguro (1979) and Bell (1979), pp. 131–3.

12 Strictly speaking, in the terminology of *TLP*, an existing state of affairs.

13 Anscombe, too, sees *TLP* states of affairs as involving only individuals and property- or relation-tokens (i.e. as not involving universals – see her 1959, ch. 7). But she thinks that a fully analysed sentence would employ names of these tokens. I can see no reason for this interpretation. Indeed it faces severe problems if Simples (referents of simple names) have necessary existence, as I argue in *MT* ch. 8 that they do.

14 I here disagree strongly with Baker and Hacker, who see the semantics of *TLP* as dominated by the Augustinian thesis that all words are names (see their 1980, pp. 57–9). This leads them entirely to misrepresent the nature of the contrast between Wittgenstein's earlier and later philosophies, as I argued at length in my (1984a).

CHAPTER 16 PREDICATE SEMANTICS

1 Hintikka and Hintikka use this as one of their main arguments for claiming that *TLP* is committed to the existence of universals, and hence for their wide reading of the *TLP* use of 'name' and 'object'. See their (1986), pp. 35–7.

2 See for example Mates (1972).

3 In practice the range of the quantification will often be restricted by the context; for example to 'Susan and Mary share some obvious feature of their appearance'.

4 For Frege's unequivocal commitment to this view, see his posthumously published paper 'Comments on Sense and Meaning' in his (1979).

5 It is noteworthy that Frege's argument for extensional reference for predicates (in 'Comments on Sense and Meaning') occurs as part of an argument supporting extensional against intensional *logic*.

6 In fact we can here deploy the arguments we used against Frege's theory of thinking in ch. 9.

7 On the non-referential account we are causally related to objects-having-property-tokens, it being the fact that there is a token of freckledness present in Susan which causally underlies my classification of her as being freckled. But there is no problem about this (in the way that it *is* problematic how we could be causally related to objects participating in transcendent necessarily existing universals); for property-tokens, remember, form part of the ordinary physical realm.

8 I am not aware of any philosopher who actually endorses such a view (though no doubt some do); I mention it only as a possibility. Armstrong has been prominent in defending immanent universals, but he is at some pains to distinguish his doctrine from any form of semantic theory for predicates. See his (1978).

The only place I know of where immanent universals are used as objects of reference is Ishiguro (1969), pp. 48–9, where instantiations of simple properties are said to be the Simples referred to by the names of *TLP* . See note 4 to ch. 11.

9 See Armstrong (1983).

10 What acceptance of Armstrong's view would mean, however, is that we could not allow our ontology to be driven purely by semantic considerations (unless that view could somehow be interpreted as a proposal for the semantics of 'cause'). There is then a criticism of *TLP* latent here, since as I shall show in *MT*, for Wittgenstein semantics is the beginning and end of ontology. For he is surely mistaken in thinking that there can be no reason for believing in the existence of a certain class of entities except where this is required of us by the demands of an adequate semantics.

11 This was persuasively argued by Putnam (following Kripke) in 'The Meaning of "Meaning"', reprinted in his (1975). The idea is that besides having a nominal essence which guides their ordinary application (e.g. for 'water', being colourless, tasteless etc.), natural kind terms are used with the intention of designating whatever property fundamentally explains the features which go to make up that nominal essence in most (at least) of the cases of the kind with which we are acquainted.

12 It is then a further criticism of *TLP* that it assumes that the semantics for all types of predicative expression will take essentially the same form. However, it is another question to what extent terms such as 'water' are actually used *as* natural kind terms – that is, in such a way as to refer to an inner constitution, whatever it may be. It is arguable that in many contexts such terms are used as ordinary (non-referential) predicates. For suppose it had turned out that the stuff we had been calling 'water' was in fact composed, in differing circumstances, of a heterogeneous range of chemical substances sharing only their superficial characteristics. Would it then have been *false* that there is water in the Thames (as it would have been were 'water' attempting, but failing, to refer to a natural kind)? This is implausible. See my (1987b) for some further discussion.

Bibliography

Albritton, R. (1959): 'On Wittgenstein's use of the term "Criterion"' *Journal of Philosophy*, 56, 845–57.
Allaire, Edwin (1959): 'Tractatus 6.3751' *Analysis*, 19, 100–5.
____(1963): 'The Tractatus: nominalistic or realistic?' in Copi and Beard (1966), 325–42.
Ambrose, Alice (1979) ed.: *Wittgenstein's lectures, Cambridge 1932–35*. Oxford: Blackwell.
Anscombe, G. E. M. (1959): *An introduction to Wittgenstein's Tractatus*. London: Hutchinson.
Anscombe, G. E. M. and Geach, P. T. (1961): *Three philosophers*. Oxford: Blackwell.
Armstrong, D. M. (1978): *Universals and scientific realism*. Cambridge: CUP.
____ (1983): *What is a law of nature?* Cambridge: CUP.
Ayer, A. J. (1936): *Language, truth and logic*. London: Gollancz.
____ (1985): *Wittgenstein*. Harmondsworth: Penguin.

Baker, G. P. (1981): 'Following Wittgenstein' *Wittgenstein: to follow a rule*. S. Holtzman and C. Leich eds. London: RKP.
Baker, G. P. and Hacker, P. M. S. (1980): *Wittgenstein: understanding and meaning*. Oxford: Blackwell.
____ (1984): *Frege: logical excavations*. Oxford: Blackwell.
____ (1985): *Wittgenstein: rules, grammar and necessity*. Oxford: Blackwell.
Bell, David (1979): *Frege's theory of judgement*. Oxford: OUP.
Benacerraf, Paul (1965): 'What numbers could not be'. *Philosophical Review*, 74, 47–73.
____ (1973): 'Mathematical truth'. *Journal of Philosophy*, 70, 661–80.
Bennett, J. (1974): *Kant's dialectic*. Cambridge: CUP.
Black, Max (1964): *A companion to Wittgenstein's Tractatus*. New York: Cornell UP.
Blackburn, Simon (1984): *Spreading the word*. Oxford: OUP.
Blackwell, Kenneth (1981): 'The early Wittgenstein and the middle Russell'. In Irving Block (1981), 1–30
Block, Irving (1981) ed.: *Perspectives on the philosophy of Wittgenstein*. Oxford: Blackwell.
Block, Ned (1981) ed.: *Readings in philosophy of psychology*, vol. II. London: Methuen.

Bogen, James (1972): *Wittgenstein's philosophy of language*. London: RKP.
Bolton, Derek (1979): *An approach to Wittgenstein's philosophy*. London: Macmillan.
Bradley, Raymond (1987): 'Tractatus 2.022–2.023'. *Canadian Journal of Philosophy*, 17, 349–60.
Butterfield, Jeremy (1986) ed.: *Language, mind and logic*. Cambridge: CUP.
Burge, Tyler (1979): 'Sinning against Frege'. *Philosophical Review*, 88, 389–432.

Carruthers, Peter (1981): 'Frege's regress'. *Aristotelian Society Proceedings*, 82, 17–32.
—— (1983a): 'Understanding names'. *Philosophical Quarterly*, 33, 19–36.
—— (1983b): 'On concept and object'. *Theoria*, 49, 48–86.
—— (1984a): 'Baker and Hacker's Wittgenstein'. *Synthese*, 58, 451–79.
—— (1984b): 'Fragmentary sense'. *Mind*, 93, 351–69.
—— (1984c): 'Eternal thoughts'. *Philosophical Quarterly*, 34, 186–204; also in Wright (1984b), 1–19.
—— (1985): 'Ruling-out realism'. *Philosophia*, 15, 61–78.
—— (1986): *Introducing persons: theories and arguments in the philosophy of mind*. London: Croom Helm, New York: SUNY.
—— (1987a): 'Russellian thoughts'. *Mind*, 96, 18–35.
—— (1987b): 'Conceptual pragmatism'. *Synthese*, 73, 205–24.
—— (1990): *The metaphysics of the Tractatus*. Forthcoming.
Coope, C., Geach, P., Potts, T. and White, R. (1971): *A Wittgenstein workbook*. Oxford: Blackwell.
Cooper, David (1987): 'The epistemology of testimony'. *Aristotelian Society Proceedings*, supp. vol. 61, 85–106.
Copi, Irving (1958a): 'Tractatus 5.542'. *Analysis*, 18, 102–4
—— (1958b): 'Objects, properties and relations in the Tractatus'. *Mind*, 67, 145–65.
Copi, Irving and Beard, Robert (1966) eds.: *Essays on Wittgenstein's Tractatus*. London: RKP.
Currie, Gregory (1982a): *Frege: an introduction to his philosophy*. Brighton: Harvester.
—— (1982b): 'Frege, sense and mathematical knowledge'. *Australasian Journal of Philosophy*, 60, 5–19.
—— (1984): 'Frege's metaphysical argument'. In Wright (1984b), 144–57.

Davidson, Donald (1980): *Essays on actions and events*. Oxford: OUP.
—— (1984): *Inquiries into truth and interpretation*. Oxford: OUP.
Davidson, Donald and Harman, Gilbert (1972) eds.: *The semantics of natural language*. Dordrecht: Reidel.
Diamond, Cora (1976) ed.: *Wittgenstein's lectures on the foundations of mathematics*. Brighton: Harvester.
Donnellan, Keith (1966): Reference and definite descriptions. *Philosophical Review*, 75, 281–304.
—— (1972): 'Proper names and identifying descriptions'. In Davidson and Harman (1972), 356–79.

—— (1974): 'Speaking of nothing'. *Philosophical Review*, 83, 3–31.
Dummett, Michael (1973): *Frege: philosophy of language*. London: Duckworth.
—— (1975): 'What is a theory of meaning? (I)'. In Guttenplan (1975), 97–138.
—— (1976): 'What is a theory of meaning? (II)'. In Evans and McDowell (1976), 67–137.
—— (1978): *Truth and other enigmas*. London: Duckworth.
—— (1981a): 'Frege and Wittgenstein'. In Irving Block (1981), 31–42.
—— (1981b): *The interpretation of Frege's philosophy*. London: Duckworth.
—— (1982): 'Realism'. *Synthese*, 52, 55–112.
—— (1984): 'An unsuccessful dig'. In Wright (1984b), 194–226.
—— (1986): 'The philosophy of thought and philosophy of language'. In J. Vuillemin ed. *Merites et limites des methodes logiques en philosophie*. Paris: Singer Polinac, 141–55.

Engelmann, Paul (1967): *Letters from Ludwig Wittgenstein with a memoir*. Oxford: Blackwell.
Evans, Gareth (1973): 'The causal theory of names'. *Aristotelian Society Proceedings*, supp. vol. 47, 187–208.
—— (1982): *The varieties of reference*. Oxford: OUP.
Evans, Gareth and McDowell, John (1976) eds.: *Truth and meaning*. Oxford: OUP.

Favrholdt, David (1964): *An interpretation and critique of Wittgenstein's Tractatus*. Copenhagen: Munksgaard.
Field, Hartry (1978): 'Mental representation'. In Ned Block (1981), 78–114.
Finch, Henry (1971): *Wittgenstein: the early philosophy*. New Jersey: Humanities.
Fodor, Jerry (1981): *Representations*. Brighton: Harvester.
Fogelin, Robert (1976): *Wittgenstein*. London: RKP.
—— (1982): 'Wittgenstein's operator N'. *Analysis*, 42, 124–7.
Frege, Gottlob (1952): *Philosophical writings*. Trans. P. Geach and M. Black. Oxford: Blackwell.
—— (1964): *The basic laws of arithmetic*. Trans. M. Furth. California: California UP.
—— (1968): *The foundations of arithmetic*. Trans. J. Austin. Oxford: Blackwell.
—— (1972): *Conceptual notation and related articles*. Trans. T. Bynum. Oxford: OUP.
—— (1979): *Posthumous Writings*. Trans. P. Long and R. White. Oxford: Blackwell.
—— (1980): *Philosophical and Mathematical Correspondence*. Trans. B. McGuinness and H. Kaal. Oxford: Blackwell.
—— (1984): *Collected Papers*. Trans. various. Oxford: Blackwell.

Geach, Peter (1951): 'Frege's Grundlagen'. *Philosophical Review*, 60, 535–44.
—— (1955): 'Class and concept'. *Philosophical Review*, 64, 561–70.
—— (1957): *Mental acts*. London: RKP.
—— (1961): 'Frege'. In G. Anscombe and P. Geach (1961), 127–162.
—— (1962): *Reference and generality*. Ithica: Cornell UP.
—— (1974): 'Six lectures on Wittgenstein's Tractatus'. Unpublished typescript.
—— (1981): 'Wittgenstein's operator N'. *Analysis*, 41, 168–70.
—— (1982): 'More on Wittgenstein's Operator N'. *Analysis*, 42, 127–8.
Goddard, Leonard and Judge, Brenda (1982): *The metaphysics of Wittgenstein's Tractatus*. Australasian Journal of Philosophy Monograph.
Goldstein, L. (1983): 'Scientific Scotism'. *Australasian Journal of Philosophy*, 61, 40–57.
—— (1986): 'The development of Wittgenstein's views on contradiction'. *History and Philosophy of Logic*, 7, 43–56.
Grice, H. P. (1957): 'Meaning'. *Philosophical Review*, 66, 377–88.
—— (1969): 'Utterer's meaning and intention'. *Philosophical Review*, 78, 147–77.
Griffin, James (1964): *Wittgenstein's logical atomism*. Oxford: OUP.
Guttenplan, Samuel (1975) ed.: *Mind and language*. Oxford: OUP.

Hacker, P. M. S. (1972): *Insight and illusion*. Oxford: OUP.
—— (1986): *Insight and illusion*. Revised edition. Oxford: OUP.
Harrison, Bernard (1979): *An introduction to the philosophy of language*. London: Macmillan.
Hertz, H. (1899): *Principles of mechanics*. London: Macmillan.
Hintikka, Jaakko (1958): 'On Wittgenstein's "Solipsism"'. *Mind*, 67, 88–91.
Hintikka, Merrill and Hintikka, Jaakko (1986): *Investigating Wittgenstein*. Oxford: Blackwell.
Hughes, G. and Cresswell, M. (1968): *An introduction to modal logic*. London: Methuen.

Ishiguro, Hide (1969): 'Use and reference of Names'. In Winch (1969), 20–50.
—— (1979): 'Subjects, predicates, isomorphic representation and language-games'. *Essays in honour of Jaakko Hintikka*. E. Saarinen, R. Hilpinen, I. Niiniluoto and M. Hintikka eds. Dordrecht: Reidel, 351–64.
—— (1981): 'Wittgenstein and the theory of types'. In Irving Block (1981), 43–59.

Janaway, Cristopher (1988): 'History of philosophy: the analytical ideal'. *Aristotelean Society Proceedings*, supp. vol. 62, 169–89.
Johnson-Laird, P. N. (1988): *The computer and the mind*. London: Fontana.

Kant, I. (1929): *Critique of pure reason.* Trans. N. Kemp Smith. London: Macmillan.
Katz, Jerold (1981): *Language and other abstract objects.* Oxford: Blackwell.
Kenny, Anthony (1973): *Wittgenstein.* London: Penguin.
—— (1974): 'The ghost of the Tractatus'. *Royal Institute of Philosophy Lectures*, vol. 7. London: Macmillan, 1–13.
—— (1981): 'Wittgenstein's early philosophy of mind'. In Irving Block (1981), 140–8.
Keyt, David (1963): 'Wittgenstein's notion of an object'. *Philosophical Quarterly*, 13, 3–15.
Kilminster, C. W. (1984): *Russell.* Brighton: Harvester.
Klemke, E. D. (1968) ed.: *Essays on Frege.* Chicago: Illinois UP.
Kripke, Saul (1979): 'A puzzle about belief'. In Margalit (1979), 239–83.
—— (1980): *Naming and Necessity.* Oxford: Blackwell.
—— (1982): *Wittgenstein on rules and private language.* Oxford: Blackwell.

Lee, Desmond (1980) ed.: *Wittgenstein's lectures, Cambridge 1930–32.* Oxford: Blackwell.
Lewis, David (1983): *Philosophical papers*, vol. 1. Oxford: OUP.
Loar, Brian (1981): *Mind and meaning.* Cambridge: CUP.
Long, Peter (1969): 'Are predicates and relational expressions incomplete?' *Philosophical Review*, 78, 90–8.
—— (1982): 'Formal relations'. *Philosophical Quarterly*, 32, 151–61.

Mackie, J. L. (1976): 'The riddle of existence'. *Aristotelian Society Proceedings*, supp. vol. 50, 247–67.
Malcolm, Norman (1958): *Wittgenstein: a memoir.* Oxford: OUP.
—— (1986): *Nothing is hidden.* Oxford: Blackwell.
Margalit, A. (1979) ed.: *Meaning and use.* Dordrecht: Reidel.
Maslow, Alexander (1961): *A study in Wittgenstein's Tractatus.* Los Angeles: California UP.
Mates, Benson (1972): *Elementary logic.* Oxford: OUP.
McDonough, Richard (1986): *The argument of the Tractatus.* New York: SUNY.
McDowell, John (1977): 'On the sense and reference of a proper name'. *Mind*, 86, 159–85.
—— (1980): 'Meaning, communication and knowledge'. In van Straaten (1980), 117–139.
—— (1984): 'De re senses'. In Wright. (1984b), 98–109.
—— (1986): 'Singular thought and the extent of inner space'. In Pettit and McDowell (1976), 137–68.
McGinn, Colin (1982a): 'The structure of content'. In Woodfield (1982), 207–58.
—— (1982b): *The character of mind.* Oxford: OUP.
—— (1984): *Wittgenstein on meaning.* Oxford: Blackwell.
McGuinness, Brian (1974): 'The Grundgedenke of the Tractatus'. *Royal Institute of Philosophy Lectures*, vol. 7. London: Macmillan, 49–61.

—— (1981): 'The so-called realism of Wittgenstein's Tractatus'. In Irving Block (1981), 60–73.
—— (1982) ed.: *Wittgenstein and his times*. Oxford: Blackwell.
—— (1988): *Wittgenstein: a life*, vol. 1. London: Duckworth.
Moore, G. E. (1903): *Principia Ethica*. Cambridge: CUP.
Morris, Thomas (1984): *Understanding identity statements*. Aberdeen: Aberdeen UP.
Mounce, H. O. (1981): *Wittgenstein's Tractatus: an introduction*. Oxford: Blackwell.

Nagel, Thomas (1986): *The view from nowhere*. Oxford: OUP.
Noonan, Harold (1979): 'Rigid designation'. *Analysis*, 39, 174–82.
—— (1980): 'Names and belief'. *Aristotelian Society Proceedings*, 81, 93–108.
—— (1984): 'Fregean thoughts'. *Philosophical Quarterly*, 34, 205–25.
—— (1986): 'Russellian thoughts and methodological solipsism'. In Butterfield (1986), 67–90.

Ogden, C. K. and Richards, I. A. (1923): *The meaning of meaning*. London: RKP.

Pears, David (1971): *Wittgenstein*. London: Fontana.
—— (1981): 'The logical independence of elementary propositions'. In Irving Block (1981), 74–84.
—— (1987): *The false prison*, vol. 1. Oxford: OUP.
Perry, John (1977): 'Frege on demonstratives'. *Philosophical Review*, 86, 474–97.
—— (1979): 'The problem of the essential indexical'. *Nous*, 13, 3–21.
Pettit, Philip and McDowell, John (1986) eds.: *Subject, thought and context*. Oxford: OUP.
Putnam, Hilary (1973): *Mind, language and reality*. Cambridge: CUP.

Quine, W. V. O. (1953): *From a logical point of view*. Harvard: Harvard UP.
—— (1960): *Word and object*. Massachusetts: MIT Press.

Ramsey, F. P. (1923): 'Review of the Tractatus'. *Mind*, 32, 465–78.
—— (1978): *Foundations*. London: RKP.
Russell, Bertrand (1903): *The principles of mathematics*. London: Allen & Unwin.
—— (1910a): *Philosophical essays*. London: Allen & Unwin.
—— (1910b) with A. N. Whitehead: *Principia mathematica*. Cambridge: CUP.
—— (1912): *The problems of philosophy*. Oxford: OUP.
—— (1914): *Our knowledge of the external world*. London: Allen & Unwin.
—— (1917): *Mysticism and logic*. London: Allen & Unwin.
—— (1921): *The analysis of mind*. London: Allen & Unwin.
—— (1940): *An inquiry into meaning and truth*. London: Allen & Unwin.
—— (1956): *Logic and knowledge*, ed. R. Marsh. London: Allen & Unwin.

—— (1984): *The collected papers of Bertrand Russell*, vol. 7, E. Eames and K. Blackwell eds. London: Allen & Unwin.

Sainsbury, Mark (1979): *Russell*. London: RKP.
Salmon, Nathan (1982): *Reference and essence*. Oxford: Blackwell.
—— (1986) *Frege's puzzle*. Massachusetts: MIT Press.
Searle, John (1957): 'Russell's objections to Frege's theory of sense and reference'. *Analysis*, 18, 137–43.
—— (1958): 'Proper names'. *Mind*, 67, 166–73.
—— (1983): *Intentionality*. Cambridge: CUP.
Sellars, W. (1962a): 'Naming and saying'. In Copi and Beard (1966), 249–69.
—— 'Truth and "Correspondence"'. *Journal of Philosophy*, 59, 29–56.
Shwayder, David (1963): 'On the picture theory of language'. *Mind*, 72, 275–88.
Sluga, Hans (1980): *Gottlob Frege*. London: RKP.
Smith, A. D. (1984): 'Rigidity and scope'. *Mind*, 93, 177–93.
Smith, Peter and Jones O.R. (1986): *The philosophy of mind*. Cambridge: CUP.
Stalnaker, Robert (1976): 'Propositions'. In *Issues in the philosophy of language*, A. Mackay and D. Merrill eds. New Haven: Yale UP, 79–91.
Stenius, Erik (1960): *Wittgenstein's Tractatus*. Oxford: Blackwell.
—— (1975): 'Wittgenstein and Ogden'. *Philosophical Quarterly*, 25, 62–8.
Stock, Guy (1974): 'Wittgenstein on Russell's theory of judgement'. *Royal Institute of Philosophy Lectures*, vol. 7. London: Macmillan, 62–75.
Straaten, Zak van (1980) ed.: *Philosophical subjects*. Oxford: OUP.
Strawson, P. F. (1959): *Individuals*. London: Methuen.
—— (1971): *Logico-linguistic papers*. London: Mathuen.

Tugendhat, E. (1970): 'The meaning of "Bedeutung" in Frege'. *Analysis*, 30, 177–89.

Waismann, F. (1965): *Principles of linguistic philosophy*. R. Harre ed. London: Macmillan.
—— (1979): *Wittgenstein and the Vienna Circle*. Trans. J. Schulte and B. McGuinness. Oxford: Blackwell.
White, R. M. (1973): 'Wittgenstein and the general propositional form'. Unpublished manuscript.
—— (1974): 'Can whether one proposition makes sense depend on the truth of another?' *Royal Institute of Philosophy Lectures*, vol. 7. London: Macmillan, 14–29.
—— (1978): 'Wittgenstein on identity'. *Aristotelian Society Proceedings*, 78,
Winch, Peter (1969) ed.: *Studies in the philosophy of Wittgenstein*. London: RKP.
Wittgenstein, Ludwig (1922): *Tractatus Logico-Philosophicus*. Trans. C. Ogden. London: RKP.
—— (1929): 'Some remarks on logical form'. *Aristotelian Society Proceedings*, supp. vol. 9, 162–71.

—— (1953): *Philosophical investigations*. Trans. G. Anscombe. Oxford: Blackwell.

—— (1961a): *Tractatus Logico-Philosophicus*. Trans D. Pears and B. McGuinness. London: RKP.

—— (1961b): *Notebooks 1914–16*. Trans. G. Anscombe. Oxford: Blackwell.

—— (1971): *Prototractatus*. Trans. D. Pears and B. McGuinness. London: RKP.

—— (1973): *Letters to C. K. Ogden*. G. von Wright ed. Oxford Blackwell.

—— (1974): *Letters to Russell, Keynes and Moore*. G. von Wright ed. Oxford: Blackwell.

—— (1975): *Philosophical remarks*. Trans. R. Hargreaves and R. White. Oxford: Blackwell.

—— (1978): *Remarks on the foundation of mathematics*, 3rd edn. Trans. G. Anscombe. Oxford: Blackwell.

Woodfield, Andrew (1982) ed.: *Thought and object*. Oxford: OUP.

Wright, Crispin (1975): 'On the coherence of vague predicates'. *Synthese*, 30, 325–65.

—— (1980): *Wittgenstein on the foundations of mathematics*. London: Duckworth.

—— (1983): *Frege's conception of numbers as objects*. Aberdeen: Aberdeen UP.

—— (1984a): 'Kripke's account of the argument against private language'. *Journal of Philosophy*, 81, 759–77.

—— (1984b) ed.: *Frege: tradition and influence*. Oxford: Blackwell.

—— (1986a): 'Inventing logical necessity'. In Butterfield (1986), 187–209.

—— (1986b): *Realism, meaning and truth*. Oxford: Blackwell.

Wright, G. H. von (1982): *Wittgenstein*. Oxford: Blackwell.

Young, Julian (1984): 'Wittgenstein, Kant, Schopenhauer and critical philosophy'. *Theoria*, 50, 73–105.

Index of References to the Tractatus

Index of Names and Subjects

KING ALFRED'S COLLEGE
LIBRARY